THE GREAT ROMANTIC

Other Cricket Books By Duncan Hamilton

Harold Larwood: The Biography
A Last English Summer
The Kings of Summer
A Clear Blue Sky (with Jonny Bairstow)
Wisden on Yorkshire (ed)
Sweet Summers: The Cricket Writing of J. M. Kilburn

THE GREAT ROMANTIC:
Cricket and the Golden Age of
NEVILLE CARDUS

DUNCAN HAMILTON

HODDER

Firs n

1

A CIP catalogue record for this title is available from the British Library

Paperback ISBN 9781473661851

Typeset in Adobe Caslon by Hewer Text UK Ltd, Edinburgh
Printed and bound in Great Britain by Clays Ltd, Elcograf S.p.A.

Hodder & Stoughton policy is to use papers that are natural, renewable
and recyclable products and made from wood grown in sustainable
forests. The logging and manufacturing processes are expected to
conform to the environmental regulations of the country of origin.

Hodder & Stoughton Ltd
Carmelite House
50 Victoria Embankment
London EC4Y 0DZ

www.hodder.co.uk

*To all those who live or have lived
in press boxes*

CONTENTS

DID WE REALLY KNOW HIM?

JOHN ARLOTT INTRODUCED me to Neville Cardus; he did so twice. The first time was on television. In the early autumn of 1973 Arlott interviewed Cardus – who was Sir Neville by then – for three 25-minute programmes on the BBC. Each was a journey around his life and career. Cardus was in his mid-eighties, but looked much older. He looked so old, in fact, that I wondered whether the Queen would shortly be sending him a centenary telegram to complement his knighthood. He sank convivially into a high-backed leather chair, the sort you would find in the library of some distinguished London club. The chair was a shade of dark green not dissimilar to the outfield at Old Trafford after a downpour. Cardus's pale face was terribly gaunt. His skin was a spidery web of broken capillaries and heavily creased too, the deep cross-hatching of lines caused by both age and a lifelong smoking habit. At one point he ran a hand over his cheeks, as though these wrinkles might miraculously be smoothed away. There was also a small indentation, beneath the left cheekbone, where overnight bristle had defeated the razor's attempt to remove it that morning. Cardus's lips were slit-thin. His silver-streaked hair was swept back with Brylcreem and parted on the left, exposing a high forehead. A pair of black-rimmed spectacles were looped over his large-lobed ears, which stuck out prominently.

Photographs of Cardus, even from as late as the 1950s, showed someone who at first sight could have passed for an anonymous civil servant or the assistant cashier of a bank. He always wore a light-coloured, double-breasted suit, a dark tie, tightly knotted, and a snow-white shirt. Hanging off his spindle-slender frame, the jacket could sometimes seem too broad across the shoulders and too loose around the midriff. The pleated trousers looked more ill-fitting still; indeed, it was as if he'd filched them from the wardrobe of someone a little fuller around the waist and at least an inch and a half taller than him. But, thinking these set-piece interviews with Arlott could be his last in front of a camera, Cardus had greatly fussed over his appearance for them. He wanted to make an impression, rather than appear as cricket's scruffy equivalent of the Ancient Mariner.

For one thing, the *Radio Times* was taking him on a nostalgic tour of Manchester, stopping off and snapping photographs at places pivotal to him. Among them was the modest house where he'd grown up and also the site of the Cross Street offices of the *Manchester*

Beneath the studio lights, John Arlott and Neville Cardus chat informally before recording the BBC programmes filmed in Manchester and broadcast in 1973.

Guardian, which a wrecking ball and a bulldozer had recently reduced to dust and rubble. For another, more homes were finding the monthly rent on a colour television affordable at last. Cardus thought it sensible to get dry-cleaned one of the three identical grey suits he owned. He matched it with a blue shirt, a shiny, bright-blue silk tie and blue socks. A white linen handkerchief was folded neatly and slipped into his breast pocket, adding a sartorial flourish. He also wore, slightly incongruously, dark brown suede shoes, chiefly as a balm for aching feet.

In his later years Cardus complained that weight loss was making him slowly disappear. 'I can scarcely find myself in bed when I wake in the dead of night,' he said. His shirt collar certainly seemed to be at least one size too big for his scrawny neck. On occasion, as Cardus nodded at Arlott or leant forward to make a point, he reminded me of a wizened tortoise, inquisitively poking its head out of its shell.

The TV critic of *The Times* neither appreciated nor understood the programmes. He dismissed them sourly as nothing much more than 'two old men sat in deckchairs'. He was wrong. The conversation – one master talking to another – was a prime example of what John Reith, the BBC's first director-general, had originally demanded of the corporation: to inform, educate and entertain. After a while I almost completely forgot Cardus's physical frailty because his voice, which seemed a generation younger than his body, performed that wonderful trick of conjuring the past.

He had witnessed the march of cricket's history from a front-row seat. He'd once glimpsed the semi-retired W. G. Grace in the bulbous flesh – grey-bearded and so big-bellied and arthritic that he couldn't bend down to pick up a ball. He'd sat in a state of constantly recurring astonishment as Victor Trumper played extravagant strokes, each attacking shot going off the bat with a bang. He'd followed Donald Bradman during his four tours of England, a pageant of scoring that made respectable his lust for hundreds and double hundreds.

Some of the names that swam out of Cardus's memory, such as A. C. 'Archie' MacLaren, Johnny Tyldesley and Harry Makepeace, were then complete strangers to me, as remote as figures from medieval England. But Cardus brought sharply back something of them he'd known long ago and so made the dead live again. This occurred especially when describing the man he called 'my idol, my hero', the imperious R. H. 'Reggie' Spooner. He spoke in bursts of love about Spooner, compelling you to love him too.

He did so in a genteel, slightly cracked accent, more redolent of the mellow Home Counties than the industrial Manchester of rain and factory smokestacks, the landscape in which he'd lived. Elocution lessons can make someone sound awkwardly stilted, as if English has been learnt as a foreign language. Cardus cultivated his voice gradually and without the need for a coach, making it seem natural rather than manufactured. Even in the mid-1920s, when radio broadcasters on the nascent BBC were required to speak as though slowly masticating crystal, his pronunciation was considered plummy enough not to frighten the nation with a dropped or crooked H. Cardus had nonetheless never forgotten what he'd consciously shed. To dramatise a story, the showman would slip effortlessly into broad 'Lenkysheer' and mimic equally broad 'York-sheer' or cockney barrow boy, replete with rhyming slang. He'd gurn and contort his facial expressions with an actorly magnificence and gesticulate with his hands, the veins enlarged and the fingers bony. This was a theatrical performance as well as an interview.

Arlott and Cardus were born a generation apart. Cardus on the lip of cricket's Golden Age; Arlott in the very year when it ended to the boom of guns from the Great War. But, as if the two of them were somehow in perfect synchronisation, the discrepancy in their ages meant that Arlott grew up and fell headlong for the game at the precise moment Cardus was in his roaring heyday, emerging serendipitously from provincial obscurity to become 'Cricketer', surely one of the most unoriginal noms de plume ever set in hot metal. He established himself in a wondrous rush. It was as though he'd been born in a cricket press box and had glided towards fame. Precisely the opposite was true; for Cardus was the accidental cricket writer. He'd had no plan and no ambition to fill one summer after another with the sport.

In that convulsing pocket of time between the wars, during the Jazz Age of the 1920s and throughout the Devil's Decade that followed it, Cardus was venerated even among the London literati as no sports writer had ever been; but then no sports writer had possessed his felicity for phrase-making, daily writing prose that passed for poetry. Anthologies of his newspaper work became that rarest thing: the instant classic. Any respectable cricket library was naked without them. Arlott was smitten. He bought every one of Cardus's books, sending them to him to be signed and dedicated. He was still smitten half a century later. That much was apparent from the way he gazed so solicitously towards his ageing friend and from the respect he paid him. He looked proud to be sitting opposite Cardus, and prouder still to be his confidant. Something complicit and conspiratorial between them sparked from the screen.

Similarities made Arlott and Cardus compatible in so many ways. They were autodidact boys who took unlikely paths, rose unexpectedly to be cricket correspondent of the same newspaper and so became in different eras the game's unrivalled voice. Nor did either of them ever allow cricket to slavishly dominate their lives to the exclusion of everything else. Everyone can recite C. L. R. James's philosophical musing 'What do they know of cricket who only cricket know?', his clever adaptation of a question Rudyard Kipling originally asked about an entirely different matter. Long before James realised it, Cardus and Arlott – who both came late to cricket reporting – appreciated that to write well and distinctively about the magnificent triviality of sport meant being aware of character and the human condition. For the best sports writing is never just about sport.

Each was immersed in the game, but objective about how much it really mattered. Arlott said that he'd 'enjoyed cricket more and served it better for realising it was never the be-all and end-all'. He was able to say so truthfully because he had a hinterland: politics, poetry, art, ceramics, book-collecting and especially the world of the licensed victualler. Cardus's hinterland was classical music, allowing him to put into perspective the joys and travails of cricket and also to dot his columns with musical allusions.

Arlott had known Cardus longer than any cricket writer then travelling peripatetically from ground to ground. He'd co-authored a coffee-table book with him called *The Noblest Game*. No one was more qualified to shepherd Cardus through each biographical landmark. His illegitimate birth in near slum conditions and the tangled lineage of his family. The fact both his mother and his aunt were prostitutes. The additional fact that he had never met his father. The way in which he underwent the grandest of reinventions, changing everything about himself. His speech. His appearance. His clothes. His class. His baptismal name.

Arlott covered the lot. Cardus's curious assortment of ragtag jobs before his improbable appointment as assistant cricket coach at Shrewsbury School. His compulsion to write for the *Manchester Guardian* and the peculiarly favourable turns and twists that took him there. His breakdown, physical and mental, that changed the shape and purpose of his life. His fondness for telling a great story . . . and for slightly stretching it into an even better one. And, finally, the way in which he showed that writing with élan about cricket didn't prevent you from writing with erudition on classical music.

As Cardus saw it, there was no difference between filing one thousand words on a Hallé concert and another one thousand words on an Ashes Test. The skill was simply to have something new and knowledgeable to say about each of them. That seems perfectly logical to us now only because Cardus established it as such then, few thinking the feat possible until he did it. Arlott knew that. He also knew that Cardus had profoundly changed British sports writing and the sniffy, lowbrow attitudes towards it. He made it a job for artists as well as artisans. Not bad for someone born as a bastard in a backstreet.

Before Cardus, there were cricket writers who still called the ball 'the crimson rambler', referred to the wicketkeeper as the 'custodian of the gauntlets' and saw the ball speed 'across the greensward', as though the vocabulary of Merrie Olde England had never gone away. What in cold ritual the copy-boy carried to the telegraph office could be starkly factual – paragraphs of piled-up statistics as dry as kindling. Most match reports were written chronologically, beginning with the toss, and read for information rather than pleasure. The reader hardly ever got to find out the way the ground looked, the hue of either the pitch or the sky, or whether the clouds were wispy cirrus or moody nimbostratus. There was little sense either of how a batsman, bowler or fielder went about his work. Or how his physical appearance and mannerisms, quirky or otherwise, influenced it. Cardus painted all this on the page impressionistically and in primary colours. He was the first to share not only what he saw but also what he felt. With him, you got every blade of freshly mown grass and the way in which the light fell across it. He became the first newspaperman to look at a cricket match as a reviewer, wonderfully expressive, rather than a reporter, sent to mechanically tell you how the scoreboard ticked over. The game's aesthetics, rather than its statistics, motivated him.

After him – and strictly because of his influence – came R. C. Robertson-Glasgow, J. M. Kilburn, Dudley Carew and, much later, Alan Ross, who said that 'thanks to Neville Cardus' there was an expectation that newspapers would print 'fine writing about cricket'. In Australia, Ray Robinson and Jack Fingleton fell under Cardus's influence too. He created a new journalism for sport and established cricket as the poet's game. The *Manchester Guardian* basked in the cachet his byline brought them and relished even more the extra copies it sold. He was the patron saint of the newspaper's circulation department. Arlott spoke of hundreds of *Manchester Guardian*s being bought as soon as sellers untied the string on bundles thrown from the back of delivery vans and then stood beside advertising boards that declared in black capitals:

NEVILLE CARDUS REPORTS ON THIS MATCH

I was dumb-ignorant about this as Arlott, the friendly interrogator, gently nudged Cardus through his reminiscences. In fact, I barely knew of Cardus then. I'd switched on the TV specifically to see Arlott.

Everyone tends to think of him first and foremost as a commentator on radio – *Test Match Special*, naturally – and on TV, particularly the John Player League, which arrived in the late 1960s to enliven Sunday afternoons that had previously been as dreary as a meeting of Victorian Sabbatarians. To mention Arlott is to instantly hear that ravishingly warm, slightly breathless Hampshire lilt, which he marinated in vats of fine claret. Where Arlott is concerned, his use of the spoken word nearly always eclipses his use of the written one. There is a tendency to overlook him in the trade that his friend Dylan Thomas described as the 'sullen art'. I had read whatever Arlott wrote – books and booklets, newspaper articles, columns in copious magazines. I had admired in them his lyricism and his authority. No one else seemed to know more or appreciate as much as him. Absorbed in his conversation with Cardus, and aware now of his worship of him, a thought hit me like the descending apple which once struck Newton. If Arlott regarded Cardus as incomparable, then no other reference to support the claim was required.

I *had* to read Cardus. There were none of his cricket titles in the village library. He'd published his last collection of articles over a decade earlier, and it had drifted out of print. I had to go into the dark and musty stacks of the county library, where hardbacks were stored along a mile of metal shelves. The stacks were then just a meaty hit away from Trent Bridge. I found *Cardus on Cricket* sitting on a neglected row. The paper was lightly foxed, the brown smudges like the liver spots on the back of an elderly man's hand. I blew the dust off the book and took it home. I am ashamed to say that I 'forgot' to take it back. I own up now only because I am guessing there is a statute of limitations over late return and loss, protecting me from a hefty fine. At the foot of page 48, I found the sentence of Cardus's that is quoted more often than most.

Trent Bridge, a 'Lotus-land' for batsmen, a place where it was always afternoon and 360 for two wickets.

Every summer someone drops it into their own copy. Not only because it saves them from the burden of original thought, but also because it's convenient shorthand, conveying something that requires no further explanation. The line, already half a century old when I came across it, appeared new and shiny to me, as if the ink was still wet.

I like to think I saw in the very moment I read it the exact image Cardus intended to fix in the mind's eye: a ball as it's just about to be bowled; the biscuit colour of the pitch; the field well spread and the batsman's clean white bat raised a little. Just 18 words; but what Cardus manages to evoke in them is all that we imagine – and hope – a cricket match will look like in the dry heat of high summer. We see what we long for – a perfect pellucid day, the sky as an unblemished curve of polished glass, iridescently blue, and the sun so strong and big that every shadow it casts is pit-black. Trent Bridge was my home ground. So I saw also, as if staring at a broad canvas, the sweep of the stately pavilion, the low roofless stands, the rise of George Parr's elm, the crowd clustered around the loop of boundary rope and a huge spread of parched outfield.

I didn't know then that Cardus had been too timid to step into Trent Bridge before writing it. He'd been sent to Nottingham to cover a Test match for the first time. The day before, he'd got as far as the high gates, beyond them spying 'one or two men with cameras' who looked so 'alarmingly efficient and possessive' that his courage failed him. He bought a copy of the *Nottingham Evening Post* and read the grounds-man's boast about the beauty of his pitch. It made Cardus think of Reggie Spooner, and of watching him cut and drive 247 runs there almost two decades before. He composed his most famous sentence while standing at a counter in the city's main post office.

I chased down everything I could find of Cardus's. When I could eventually afford them, I bought the books in their original bindings.

An infatuation had begun.

Only in retrospect did I realise that those BBC programmes resonated with me for a particular reason. They were shown in the month my grandfather fell ill and died. He looked a little like John Arlott and sounded a little like Neville Cardus; not in his accent – he came from a different and further-flung part of the north – but definitely in his enthusiasm for the cricket he'd seen before the Great War and espe-cially after he came home from it. Before that war, which was supposed to end every other, cricket brought fresh air and dazzling light, a reward for labouring for a week in a coal mine without either of them. After it, the grounds on which the games were played became sanctu-aries – places of convalescence for men like him who nightly saw again in their sleep, but were unable to talk about next morning, those faraway fields on the map that held brothers, friends, fellow soldiers.

The quality of the match was immaterial. What mattered was the solace just being there brought them. There was no whiff of cordite. No stink of churned mud. No commotion in those still hours other than the crack of a boundary, the fall of a wicket, the sound of clapping. Cricket was a consolation to those who came back with His Majesty's service medals. The sight of figures immaculately clad in white was proof of home. The game's stable, peaceful order also reassured those who hadn't fought. Arlott credits Cardus as being the first cricket writer to put 'the feelings of ordinary cricket watchers into words', which tells us how sensitively he reacted to what he saw and also why his appeal was immediate. His descriptions of cricket gave it a pulse but, more significantly, chimed with the post-war mood for something romantic, something dreamy, something purely for fun. He spoke to a generation which already felt old, and his tender approach to cricket, as well as his empathy for it, gave whoever read him a feeling for matches they'd never seen, players they barely knew and even places – backwater towns and major cities alike – they couldn't visit.

My grandfather's hero was the lean, languorous Frank Woolley, but the geography of the County Championship dictated that his team were the ruthless, 'give nowt away' Yorkshire of Wilfred Rhodes and Herbert Sutcliffe. He watched them whenever a 'charabanc outing' took him to the Scarborough Festival for ale, fish and chips and a ticket in the cheap seats. Reading Cardus comprehensively – even at a glacial pace, since ordering his books and waiting for them to arrive from libraries took for ever – had a secondary purpose for me. Cardus once said that 'the Present is usually impatient when the glories of the Past are dinned in its ears.' That is true. Whenever the old talk about the world of yesterday, the young are inclined to yawn. In that respect each generation is alike. But Cardus made me wish I'd listened more attentively to my grandfather. Whenever I read him, I saw my grandfather again. He was sitting in his brown leather chair, hands gripping the worn armrests, and dressed in his favourite ribbed cardigan and a collarless, sparkling-white shirt. Cardus brought him back to me. He assuaged my grief a little.

I began to type a fan letter to tell him all this, stopping midway only because I didn't know where I would send it. I had no idea that his address, 112 Bickenhall Mansions, a brisk walk across Marylebone to Lord's, and even his number – 01 935 5234 – were in the London telephone directory, as if he wanted someone to ring or call on him there.

I tucked what I'd written into a folder, forgetting about it until February 1975, when news of his death broke. Next morning I cut out and pasted the numerous tributes to him in a scrapbook, and also stared uselessly at my unfinished letter. With ambitions to become a sports reporter, I resolved there and then to write to Arlott instead. I spent a few weeks composing it, asking him straightforwardly 'how to write?' A few months later – for goodness knows how many bulging sacks of mail Arlott received – back came a neatly typed reply above an equally neat signature, steeply underlined in black ink. No doubt what Arlott said to me he'd also said to all those who'd bothered him before with the same damned fool question. The letter comprised 105 words and the kernel of his advice was: 'Almost any good book would be a help because it would help you to write. But then any good book on English literature or essay writing would do that. As I was once told – the only way to write is to write.'

Two summers later I found myself sitting alongside Arlott at Trent Bridge. Here I got my second introduction to Cardus.

To catch his breath, John Arlott stood momentarily beneath the lintel of the press-box door, which framed him like a tall National Gallery portrait. In one hand he carried a brown leather briefcase, bulging like a magician's bag of tricks. His initials were stamped on to it in faded gold leaf. In the other hung a portable typewriter. He was dressed in a dark suit, a dark wool tie and a striped shirt. With a statesman-like slowness, he found a seat at the end of the second row and wiped beady sweat from his brow with a handkerchief. He unclipped the lid of the type-writer and opened his briefcase. Out came a wedge of copy-paper, the latest edition of *Wisden*, a bottle of red wine, a French goblet made from thick glass and a corkscrew with a smooth wooden handle. He swivelled towards me and asked to borrow a telephone. It was May 1978, a damp, drizzly day with barely a blink of sunlight. Nottinghamshire were play-ing the tourists, Pakistan.

For hours Arlott had been like Godot, spoken of but never seen. He'd spent the morning and most of the afternoon taking advantage of the hospitality that Notts' committee had willingly laid on for him. Most of it came in liquid form, and the measures can't have been miserly. This much was clear from Arlott's demeanour. He hunched over his type-writer, punching the keys singularly and ponderously, as if locating them was a struggle of eyesight and coordination. Wanting another drink, he reached for the bottle and the corkscrew. There was a loud plopping sound, like a stone dropping into water, before the gurgle of pouring began. His hand was unsteady. Thin dribbles of wine ran down the side of the glass and he soaked them up with a fist of the copy paper.

I was 19 years old then. My journalism jobs were menial. I was steward of the telephones. I provided the score updates for the two national news agencies. I looked after the teapot when it arrived in late afternoon, a huge metal thing with a black handle. I was callow, nervy and desperately unsure about whether I belonged there. I toted a thick Reporter's Notebook, bought from W. H. Smith, which I hoped gave the impression that I knew what I was doing.

Arlott looked bone-weary, so I volunteered to phone over his report, concerned how smoothly it might read given the difficult circum-stances of its creation. 'Couldn't bear to put you to the inconvenience,' he said, softly. As the evening wore on, I reluctantly left him alone in the semi-darkness of the press box. I said goodnight and he promised to lock his phone away after using it.

Often it is said that the cure for admiring someone is to meet them. Not in this case. The following day, Arlott went out of his way to be kindly towards me. Indeed, I felt as if I'd been adopted. He drew me into his yarning conversations about topics that, as a know-nothing novice, I lacked any qualifications to discuss. But – and I can't stress this enough – he never once made me feel patronised, embarrassed or inadequate about that. On the contrary. He paid rapt attention to whatever I contributed, however inconsequential, and replied studiously, always augmenting my remark with one of his own, as though I had initiated some bright notion that otherwise would never have occurred to him. He spoke of many things. *Wisden* seemed boringly staid to me then. 'As you get older,' he said, like a teacher instructing a pupil, 'you'll be able to look at a scoreboard in it and imagine an entire match again.' He recalled the eccentrically stubborn George Gunn – 'bowlers winced at the sight of him and he gave them nothing except a wink' – and the sweet soul that was Jack Hobbs. 'No man I have ever met was so self-effacing about his own talent. You'd think someone else had scored the runs for him.' Hobbs blushed to his fingertips if anyone gave him excessive praise, he added. In the pavilion, Arlott had been looking at a cream-coloured etching of William Clarke, the father of Trent Bridge. Clarke's woolly sideburns and the sheen of his top hat, which was extravagantly high, impressed him as much as the zeal and swagger of this 19th-century entrepreneur of cricket. Arlott spoke to me about the origins of Trent Bridge, and Clarke's part in it, the dates and the matches whizzing by.

Arlott was familiar with the village team to which I belonged; or – more precisely – he was very familiar with the beery warmth of the popular inn on the apron of the ground, where years before the local constabulary not only turned the blindest of eyes to lock-ins for writers and players alike, but had actually joined them at the bar to sup and chat until the wee small hours. There were also eclectic asides from him on the comfort of listening to the radio late at night and the wide-eyed surprise of serendipitously coming across a second-hand bookshop, the windows 'pockmarked grey' and the shelves within constituting 'three hundred years of print and thought'. I didn't know then that he was reciting a few lines from one of his own poems.

I had plenty of chances to thank Arlott for the letter he had sent in reply to mine. I was too shy and too timidly self-conscious to take them. Instead I asked him about Neville Cardus and the filming of those BBC programmes. 'Oh,' he said, breathing deeply, the words coming out in a wheeze, 'there was enough material for a dozen of those.'

Cardus had been very keen to be interviewed and had prepared scrupulously for it. Arlott thought he'd seen them as a chance to leave something of himself behind; something that supplemented the stack of newspaper cuttings and books and the transcripts of radio broadcasts. Fretting about the glare of the studio lights, imagining every crack and fissure in his face illuminated harshly, Cardus had charmed the make-up woman: 'Make me look 40 years younger,' he'd pleaded, mischievously. And Arlott explained that even though Cardus spoke fast and furiously, as if afraid his tongue would suddenly glue up and leave a story dangling there, limp and only half-told, he rarely fluffed a line. In fact, the difficulty had been to get him to stop talking.

Cardus needed no advocate other than Arlott. He didn't only adore his writing. He said he owed a debt to it too. Cardus had shown him it was possible to write about cricket in a way that Arlott hadn't contemplated before. There was a minor pause, like a semi-colon scribbled in the air, before Arlott went on: 'He taught me to *see* rather than just *look*.'

Often Arlott picked up one of Cardus's books at home and turned the pages at random, taking in a passage wherever his eyes fell. He especially liked doing so in the gloom of midwinter, the summer to come impossibly far away. Cardus pulled him towards another season. Arlott could quote lines of Cardus the way he could quote Thomas Hardy. He spoke, too, about the lovely experience of reading Cardus's *The Summer Game*, so slim and light that you barely knew you were holding it. The book was 'a revelation' to him.

Arlott had been talking for a while when another journalist, an interested eavesdropper, grabbed his attention with a short blizzard of questions about Cardus the man rather than Cardus the writer. He wanted to know why Cardus had been such a private fellow, easy to approach but infernally hard to fathom. There was a sudden swivelling of heads, the match momentarily forgotten. The conversation that followed, during which I was spectator rather than participant, roamed around the long, dusty press box. What emerged from it counted as breaking news to me. I learnt Cardus was someone impossible to understand through his work alone.

The novelist Nathaniel Hawthorne once wrote: 'No man, for any considerable period, can wear one face to himself, and another to the multitude, without finally getting bewildered as to which may be the true.' Cardus, it seemed, was the exception to Hawthorne's rule. He was not only quixotic, but also infinitely complicated, a puzzle unsolvable no matter how long you tried to unpick it. He had worn a mask over a mask, leaving only the bright wicks of his eyes visible beneath it. He had written three autobiographical works, totalling almost 800 pages, but the private Cardus still remained in hiding somewhere, out of reach.

He was made up of striking contradictions too. He began his career mistrusting and even loathing the Establishment before – much to his untrammelled joy – becoming a card-carrying member of it. Ostensibly an extrovert, he was at heart an introvert, diffident and a bit shy. His breezily confident front obscured from view the vulnerability he felt, his ego bruising easily. He was a loner – and sometimes a very lonely one at that. He pretended not to care about his reputation when, actually, he cared about it a great deal, afraid he'd become too popular to be taken seriously. For the sake of self-protection, he often dismissed his own writing as frivolously unimportant, but applied himself to it with the dedication of the workaholic scholar, worried constantly about what the critics would say. He made an ostentatious show of adoring Manchester, but could barely wait to abandon the place and eventually disliked returning there at all unless obligation demanded it. He was prodigiously intelligent and ferociously well read, but so crassly naive and unworldly – a pure innocent sometimes – that he mucked up, muddled or miscalculated decisions that made his life and career more difficult than they ought to have been.

Cardus earned a lot of money, often spending it in a gush of generosity, but could never comprehend exactly where – or why – it had gone. He was seldom in the best of health, suffering perpetually the painful upheavals of gastric and digestive complaints, but tried to pass himself off as someone hale and fairly hearty. He was prone to bouts of maudlin introspection, often tilting into black depressions.

Cardus had changed the way I saw the cricket world before I was born. That day, Arlott changed the way I saw Cardus.

He was 'a maze', said Arlott, pursing his lips. There were 'several Neville Carduses'. The one you knew depended on who you were; he made it sound as though Cardus slipped into and out of character as easily as changing clothes. In a plain but memorable phrase, he explained that Cardus had 'his music friends, his cricket friends and his girlfriends'. He 'stored them in different rooms,' he said. Arlott pondered, however, whether a lot of 'friends' were only casual acquaintances in disguise. He didn't have bosom pals; he chose his companions to match the occasion. Each group was rigidly compartmentalised, usually quite separate from every other; Cardus made certain that tittle-tattle about him could seldom be swapped between them. Arlott surmised that each set of 'friends' knew some small something about him – a mere fragment – which another didn't. This was like being given only the corners of a jigsaw.

Arlott thought that Cardus was defending himself against exclusion or abandonment, a consequence of his scarred childhood. If music let him down, he could turn to cricket. If cricket let him down, he could turn to music. A vital piece of supporting evidence was a birthday party for Cardus, which revealed divisions between his music life and his cricket life that were conspicuously deep. Arlott flashed back to it, starting to elaborate, before stopping abruptly and changing tack, as though the picture that slid into his mind troubled him a little. Cardus's romantic 'dalliances', more complicated still, produced another theory. He was married for almost 50 years, but seldom lived with his wife. He flaunted several relationships that were essentially platonic, but had once become a hopeless casualty of Cupid's bow and arrow, sending him into despair. Arlott was convinced that only the women in his life made an indelible mark on him. They got to know him better than any man.

Arlott had been a policeman for a dozen years, rising to the rank of sergeant. He'd been trained to notice the infinitesimal, giveaway 'tells' in personality, and also schooled through hard experience to interpret behaviour. His perspective on Cardus was neither flippantly compiled nor casually expressed, but based on hour upon hour of close-up observation and a lot of weighty thinking about what his eyes had seen and his mind had filed away.

Arlott began to list Cardus's virtues, giving each of them a fat tick. He was genial, benevolent towards others and self-effacing. He passed on advice to aspiring writers, often inviting them to lunch, because he remembered his own difficulty in gaining a foothold in newspapers.

He even tolerated a lot of fools, apparently gladly, so as not to upset them; for he didn't have it in him to be spectacularly rude. He was intensely hard-working, frequently to the detriment of his well-being. He seemed not to envy anyone either. And, of course, his writing would survive the generations because it was 'too good' to be neglected or perish.

Only after all that was said, assembled rather like a case for the defence, did Arlott admit: 'Did any of us *really* know him? . . . Perhaps not.'

Then he shook his head.

Though decades have passed, I can still see that shake of the head and hear the two brief sentences preceding it. John Arlott spoke them quite slowly, and my memory preserves a small wave of sadness in that 'perhaps not'. I think now what I thought then. He regretted not asking the questions that might have made Neville Cardus less enig-matic even to him, a friend. The chance was gone and irrecoverable, and Arlott mourned its passing.

I like to think something else too: that Arlott talked at such length about Cardus purely for my benefit. He indulged me – pleased to entertain, pleased to explain and pleased to do both on my behalf and no one else's. In retrospect, I realise the scale of that privilege: it was rather like having Coleridge talk to you about Wordsworth. Possibly my offer to be his messenger the night before had impressed him. Possibly he wanted to put at ease someone whom he saw, quite correctly, as being utterly in awe of him and his reputation. Possibly the wine was a contributory factor. Only after telling the story to his son Tim did an alternative scenario arise. He reminded me that his stepmother had died only shortly before and, though his father had recently remarried, he could still feel 'a particular loneliness'.

Later that summer, when England faced New Zealand at Trent Bridge, Arlott spent most of the game camped in or near the *Test Match Special* box in the pavilion. When he finally appeared at the 'print end' of the ground, and needed a telephone, I turned around and found him at my shoulder. 'I hope your reading is going well,' he said, by which he meant my reading of Cardus. He had recommended four books. The first two were *The Summer Game*, which had so enchanted him, and also the 1948 edition of *Days in the Sun*. The other two were *Australian Summer*, an account of the MCC's 1936–37 tour, and a slim softcover called *The Playfair Cardus*, a collection of articles from *Playfair Cricket Monthly*. I read and reread them with an attention to detail, as though Arlott might one day quiz me about them.

That Cardus was more of a tormented genius than I'd ever judged possible has never detracted from the pleasure of reading him.

I follow Arlott's example, choosing a title from the shelf and flicking to wherever Fate takes me. Also as Arlott did, I find him an antidote to the worst of winter. For in Cardus-land it seldom rains. And the grass is greener than you can ever visualise. And around the boundary there are white picket fences, unsullied by advertising or sponsorship boards. And the County Championship has a cut and mean thrust about it, fought for as though nothing – *absolutely nothing* – is more important than any of life's other great schemes. And the crowds watching these matches are jammed together tightly, applauding rather than chanting, drinking tea rather than swilling beer. And during a festival week somewhere, but especially on a spot beside the sea, there are streaming flags and pitched tents and the brine and the salt-taste of gusty air. And what's long lost is found again – grounds such as Hastings, quaintly handsome, and Bramall Lane, industrially smoky. And a bygone age – as well as the Gentleman and the Players who shaped it – is alive once more, as though each summer is unfolding just as you begin reading about it.

Arlott described Cardus as 'the father of literate sports writing'. He justified the statement with an argument so solidly logical that only a pedant can protest against it. 'Just as there can never be a greater cricketer than W. G. Grace – because he created the whole technique of modern cricket, and no one can ever do that again – so there can never be a greater cricket writer than Neville Cardus.' He 'created' the very art of it, added Arlott, and 'others performed what he showed'.

That's high praise, but all those years ago at Trent Bridge I heard Arlott say something I believe matches it. Whatever anyone thought of Cardus, and however idiosyncratic or mysterious he seemed to them, Arlott clearly didn't care; and he clearly didn't believe Cardus's contribution to cricket should suffer devaluation for it either. He searched for and found a simple line to encapsulate his impact on the game and particularly – as if this reminder was pressingly urgent – on the craft of writing about it. Adamant that he had influenced everyone, whether they acknowledged it or not, Arlott said that he was picturing his own bookshelves at home, full of Cardus and full of his imitators too. He let the image settle; and then he asked: 'Can you imagine how the literature of cricket would look without him?'

In reply came only respectful silence.

ALSO, I WRITE ON CRICKET

O LD TRAFFORD WAS hardly dressed finely for the first matches since the end of the Great War. At the season's start, in 1919, the ground, like every other, was dowdy-looking, a tad sombre and sorely in need of renovation. The pavilion had been used as a Red Cross hospital, and no amount of paint, slapped about in likely places, could adequately camouflage five years of neglect, incremental decay and patchwork repairs. Still clinging to it was the dust of the last Edwardian summer before the world had been wrenched askew.

Gloomy about the game's ability to grasp public affection, the MCC had debated whether to increase an over from six balls to seven, enlarge the stumps and shrink the size of a bat. Even the possibility of banning left-handed batsmen was mooted and then dismissed. It plunged into a different experiment entirely. Matches would last two rather than three days. The first day would span 11.30 a.m. to 7.30 p.m. The second would start half an hour earlier.

The *Manchester Guardian* plunged into an experiment too. It sent someone obscure and inexperienced to cover Lancashire. This was an act of compassion, salted by a little guilt.

The writer chosen had worked for the newspaper for only two years and two months. The spot he had on it was so serendipitously secured – and came after he'd travelled such a labyrinthine path – that you can only agree with his own assessment of what occurred. Aware of how blessed in retrospect his career looked to others, shaped as it occasionally was by chance, coincidence and sheer bloody luck, he referred to it as 'My Destiny', offering no alternative explanation.

It unfolded like this:

Often Neville Cardus had stood on the corner of Cross Street and Market Street, opposite the *Manchester Guardian*'s offices, to gaze into the large, lighted windows of the newspaper. He imagined the creative labour and the intellectual debate going on behind them in oak-panelled rooms, each the domain of C. P. Scott.

Charles Prestwich Scott *was* the *Manchester Guardian*. He owned it, edited it and ran it as a reasonably kind dictator. When, in January 1917, Cardus gathered up his courage and wrote speculatively to Scott, he was already pushing 30 years old – practically broke, desperate and in all sorts of anguish. Nor did he have much to offer.

Cardus had left school at 13, never believing 'in formal education'. His schooling had been grimly hostile – the bleakness of rote learning, chalk blackboards and unheated rooms. There was the swish of the cane for anyone who 'showed the faintest sign of free will', he remembered. He had never sat an academic examination. He had seen the inside of a university only to attend free lectures, benevolently thrown open to the public.

As both adolescent and very young man, he had found eclectic employment. As a pavement artist, painting scenes such as a storm at sea, a churchyard, a salmon cut in two, a robin perched in a tree. As a carpenter's dogsbody, pushing a handcart. As a messenger running errands. As an assistant boiling type in a printer's shop, the stench of which never left him. As a confectionery salesman in a theatre, which at least brought the perk of free tickets there and elsewhere.

Cardus considered himself to be 'an extremely well-educated uneducated man', courtesy of Manchester's municipal libraries. He roamed through them, soaking up what interested him. He read ravenously:

newspapers and penny dreadfuls as well as the grandee novelists, among them the two Henrys, Fielding and James, the two Thomases, Hardy and De Quincey, and also Thackeray and Conrad. Later, when able to grasp the plays properly, came Shakespeare too. When the Everyman classics were published in 1906, priced at a shilling, he built his own library and assembled rickety shelves on which to display it. He read the books by the light of a tallow candle, conscientiously drawing up – and sticking rigidly to – a timetable of learning both austere and aesthetic. As well as literature, it covered philosophy, politics, economics and comparative religion. Manchester was culturally resplendent, crowded with theatres and music and concert halls. He filled his weeks with the Hallé Orchestra, a light opera, a variety show, or the arrival of a play before or after its London run. Cardus was convinced that self-improvement would lead eventually to self-sufficiency.

It didn't seem so early on. He peddled insurance policies 'on the knocker', a profession for which he lacked the prerequisite – the ability to fake sincerity. He became an office-bound clerk for marine insurers, a company run by two brothers. He'd sit on a high-legged stool and write in copperplate from nine-thirty to five. This was another position to which Cardus was temperamentally unsuited. He survived only because the brothers tolerated for seven years – and to an unbelievably saintly degree – his 'absent-mindedness' and his scratchy timekeeping. He called his position there 'tragi-comic' and 'an embarrassment'. He would pin a note on to his door that promised 'Back in Ten Minutes' and then hide in the reference library for an hour or more.

Using the firm's stationery to practise poetry and prose, Cardus strongly identified with the Preston-born poet Francis Thompson, who in 1907 wrote the acclaimed, if slightly baroque, 'At Lord's', in which 'a ghostly batsman plays to the bowling of a ghost'. He saw himself as a man of letters in the Thompson mould. He envisaged composing thunderous editorials for the *Manchester Guardian*, which would make or change the political weather. He would write elegant musical criticism, the reviews so evocative that you would hear every note as you read them. And he planned to submit poems or short stories to respectable journals and small literary magazines, establishing his reputation as a polymath.

The *Daily Citizen*, a fledgling newspaper supporting a relatively fledgling Labour Party, had briefly hired him as the northern, penny-per-line music critic obliged to pay his own expenses. 'The first time in print is like the first time in love,' said Cardus, nonetheless. A solitary article appeared in *Musical Opinion*, a publication that today counts as the oldest classical music magazine in Britain.

Wanting to get a foothold on the *Manchester Guardian* – but never daring to think about a place in the newsroom – he asked Scott about vacancies in the proofreading department or the 'general office', telling him in his letter: 'I am a young student, intent upon devoting his life to politics and art.' Some begging followed. 'I am finding it hard to keep alive,' he added.

Deaths and casualties from the war were still multiplying at a shocking rate then, the conflict's end unforeseeable. Cardus had been turned down for military service because of myopia. His first pair of spectacles, required in boyhood, had been a glorious marvel, lifting him out of one world, indistinct and misty, and dropping him into another where 'the delicate tracery of a tree in the spring-time' became sharply defined at last. But there was now the possibility that even someone as unsuitable as Cardus could be called up to replenish the army's depleted ranks. Few reputable organisations would hire a man who, at only 48 hours' notice, could be given a khaki uniform and a rifle, leaving them a worker down.

Scott still invited Cardus to The Firs, his imposing eight-bedroomed home in Fallowfield. The house had a clean white façade, tall windows

427

154, Moseley Road,
Fallowfield,
Manchester.

Jan 18, 1917.

Dear Sir,

I am writing to ask if you would
be so very kind as to let me know whether
there are at present any vacancies on the
staff of the 'Manchester Guardian', amongst
the proof-readers, or in the general offices.

I am a young student intent upon
devoting his life to politics and art. In these
times, however, I am finding it hard to keep
alive. My particular fear is that necessity
will drive me to at least suspending my
studies, which happen to be at a critical and
fascinating stage. I have had to educate
myself, and my culture, such as it is, has
been got by scorning delights and living
laborious days for some eight years. Immediate employment would enable me to
find the means whereby to continue my
education, and I would gladly accept any
position, however modest, that you might
possibly be able to offer me.

I enclose some specimens of

*The letter Neville Cardus wrote C. P. Scott pleading
for a position on his newspaper.*

and a scattering of trees that stood as nobly as sentries across spreading lawns. He found himself in a cold drawing room, austerely furnished and decorated in the style of William Morris, whose credo was: 'Have nothing in your houses which you do not know to be useful or believe to be beautiful.' Scott, then a few months past 70, wore a tweed suit and his white whiskers had a scimitar curve to them.

What came next put Cardus through the emotional wringer. In one act of remarkable generosity, Scott, as if adopting an orphan, made him a sort of personal assistant. In another of astonishing heartlessness, he didn't pay him and then, after less than a month, dispatched a short letter of dismissal without prior warning, blaming himself for being 'congenitally incapable' of using a secretary. In a third, suggesting some remorse for the insensitivity of the second, he asked Cardus to present himself at the reporters' room, promising him a role 'if you can make yourself useful'.

Cardus would always ponder, without ever resolving the matter satisfactorily, why Scott had let him go and then hired him again. 'I came to know Scott more or less intimately. He was a man who once he had made a decision, or cast an event or person from his mind, never or seldom returned to it or him . . . Yet one day he looked back, and reviewed a decision – and by doing so settled the shape of my career.'

The *Manchester Guardian* was 'a paper of ideas'. Neville Cardus said you would be asked many things to get on to the staff, but that only one of them counted: 'Can you write?'

C. P. Scott would quixotically throw out advertising if he thought too much of it encroached, like bindweed, into the space allowed for the bright flowers of his writers' prose. 'This is not a circular we push through the door,' was his peeved response to the ad department's attempts to stop him.

Entering Cross Street was 'like being baptised into a new life', explained Cardus. That new life, bringing about a sensation of unreality at first, demanded a new name and a new image. He had been born John Frederick Cardus. In adulthood, passing over John, he preferred to call himself 'Fred' until literary pretension got the better of him. He adopted 'Neville' – though he never explained why. His early, meagre work had been published under an assortment of initials, among them 'J. F. N.', 'J. F. N. Cardus' and 'J. F. Neville Cardus'. It was as if he was trying on names like new suits before deciding which one fitted him properly. On the *Manchester Guardian* his first pieces were signed 'N.C.'. 'Fred' was cast aside; he was almost immediately known as Neville on the editorial floor.

He put on other airs and affected graces. He swapped his spectacles for a pince-nez, made popular by Chekhov and then Theodore Roosevelt; he wanted to look more sophisticated than someone earning 30 shillings a week. The editorial staff 'all carried a book and a cane', said Cardus, each a prop to differentiate themselves from the 'riff-raff' of more popular newspapers. He did the same.

Like other broadsheets, the nonconformist *Manchester Guardian* was a clutter of type, multi-deck headlines and a font tiny enough to look from a distance like marching rows of ants. It comprised 12 pages. The front page, below the splendid gothic masthead, contained nothing but line advertising, promoting boarding houses and hotels, haberdashery and hardware, miracle health cures such as lung tonics, chest embrocation and pills that guaranteed to turn someone fat into someone slim.

Cardus was put into the reporters' room. He soon revealed sufficient promise to be billeted in a 'little' office at the end of what was called 'The Corridor', home of the editorial aristocracy.

Scott's ablest lieutenant was W. P. Crozier, who devoured work with fabulous efficiency. His head looked like a boiled egg and rimless glasses made him appear formidably dour. It was said of Crozier that 'declarations of affection were alien to his temper'. But it was also said, softening the verdict, that his 'cold exterior' hid 'fires of passion'. He was interested in the classics, military strategy and sport.

Cardus was drawn to two of Crozier's more celebrated colleagues. The first was C. E. Montague, drama critic and chief leader writer. Cardus said he liked to watch him 'carefully choosing his adjectives'. Montague was Scott's son-in-law, and a 'fiery particle' of a man. When the Great War began, he was 47 – too old to enlist. Still patriotically and morally compelled to do his King and Country bit, he dyed his white hair black to get into the Royal Fusiliers, prompting a friend to remark: 'Montague is the only man I know whose white hair in a single night turned black through courage.' He became a grenadier sergeant, then a lieutenant and finally a captain in the intelligence corps. Sick of the fighting, appalled by the huge losses of life, he damned the war as 'a shabby epidemic of spite' in his bestselling book *Disenchantment*.

The second – and Cardus's mentor – was Samuel Langford, the music critic whose successor he someday planned to be. He called him 'the greatest man I have ever known'. Langford looked like a cross between Karl Marx and a Christmas-card Santa. Starlings could have nested undisturbed in the bushy drop of his beard. He was moon-faced and portly. His forehead resembled the dome of St Paul's Cathedral. He walked flat-footed, always carrying a brass magnifier in his pocket, and wore his clothes with 'an elephant's looseness of fold'. His lumbering gait and rumpled appearance didn't discourage Cardus from wanting to be exactly like him. He saw something of himself in Langford, who had once been an outsider too, a self-educated man from 'the common, everyday world' about whom there was 'the smack of earth and dust'. Much more poignantly, what Cardus said of Langford – suggesting an unknowable remoteness in his personality – others would say about him in decades to come: 'Many of his casual acquaintances who thought they knew his main characteristics pretty well did not understand him by half,' said Cardus. He thought it was a 'loss to literature' that James Boswell was born too early to have met Langford. Had he done so, he'd have written a Dr Johnson-like biography of him.

Cardus covered the courts, town hall meetings and lectures. He wrote the odd leader, diary items and also short, observational features. He commissioned pieces and became a theatre critic. Scott, quickly and miraculously overcoming his aversion to secretaries, made Cardus fetch and scuttle around after him too. He handled the owner-editor's heap of correspondence, especially the most awkward and whining of complaints. Cardus was a loyal acolyte and an acquiescent slave, who said he forged his 'own shackles'. He clocked on at 10 a.m. and was supposed to clock off to catch the last tram shortly before midnight. Often he missed it and was forced to walk home.

As a former Liberal MP, and still a substantial figure in the party, Scott was politically up to date. But, born in 1846, the nuts and bolts of contemporary cultural and social life had a tendency to float past him. Anyone asking for a rise – and Scott seemed to have a sixth sense about when such a request was coming – would be met with a half-rebuke: 'I don't know what you youngsters spend your money on. Now in my day . . .' He was a tough and indomitable old bird. Irrespective of the seasons, and ignoring inclement weather, he cycled the three miles from The Firs to the office and back again. Very late one wintry evening he tumbled off his bike and was rescued by a concerned policeman, who didn't recognise him. The short exchange between them began with the constable asking Scott why he wasn't at home in front of the fire or tucked up in bed.

The legendary Manchester Guardian *editor C. P. Scott, who would cycle around the city – irrespective of his age and whatever the weather.*

SCOTT: I have been working.

POLICEMAN: Who do you work for?

SCOTT: The *Manchester Guardian.*

POLICEMAN: Gawd, well, the *Manchester Guardian* ought to be bloody well ashamed of itself for keeping an old man like you out at such an hour like this.

Seldom prone to sickness himself, Scott seemed to think those who were had some deficiency of spirit. He relished 15-hour working days, thinking everyone else should accept them uncomplainingly too. You coveted his praise. You recoiled, trembling, from his wrath. Cardus called Scott the All-Father, a pun on the Lord's Prayer, and said of him: 'He simply could not believe in making life easy for anybody.' Only occasionally did he send a congratulatory note to Cardus and become 'almost fatherly', such patronage guaranteeing gratitude and further dependency.

Scott still took advantage with 'indirect coercion' and proved 'unsparing in his demands'. Cardus put it like this: 'I was taken possession of, body and soul ... There was scarcely a moment from waking to sleep when something was not on my mind ... I walked the Manchester streets by pure instinct.' He constantly worried about receiving another letter from Scott, thanking him for his services and asking him to close the door on his way out.

This led to two attempts to leave the newspaper in case Scott pushed him out again.

Cardus had dismissed the *Manchester Guardian*'s cultural pretensions with the barb 'There is as much sense of the arts [here] as in an Urban district council.' He saw the glow of London and strove to get there. He almost signed a contract to work for a new 'literary journal', his pen hovering over the paper before changing his mind. He pleaded with *The Observer* for 'a chance' too. He was 'young and intensely keen', he told them. Cardus highlighted his book reviews and his theatre and music criticism. Lastly, as an afterthought, he added: 'Also, I write on cricket,' a statement true then only in the very loosest sense.

The workload Scott heaped on him gradually began to wear Cardus down, inducing a 'nervous strain'. In 1919, as spring approached, he broke down physically and also mentally, absolutely exhausted. If Scott ever noticed his weariness and distress, he chose to ignore it.

Upheavals of the digestive system had affected Cardus almost as soon as he began at the *Manchester Guardian*. Unable to eat properly, he shed considerable weight. He diagnosed himself as suffering from 'severe gastritis and nervous exhaustion'. His symptoms indicate ulcerative colitis. 'Terrific pains' in the stomach afflicted him a few hours after meals. He would press his stomach into the edge of a table and bend over 'to ease one sort of ache by provoking another'. He ate 'vast amounts of charcoal biscuits and bismuth', drank barley water and took spoonfuls of castor oil, which offered only a palliative cure.

Cardus once complained of a sensation that he likened to 'a garden rake ... being clumsily and impatiently drawn through my bowels'. He thought he would die. 'I realised that this was a crisis ... Here was no ordinary agony.' In the silence of one early morning he was conscious of the sound of his own dreadful and 'blood-curdling' moaning. Panic overwhelmed him. He fainted, falling on to the wooden floor of his lodgings. His landlady, hearing first his cries and then the hard crash of his body, summoned a doctor, who advised him to undergo an intestinal operation.

Cardus refused even as the flesh melted from his bones. 'When I saw myself naked in a mirror, I wept,' he said.

He convalesced in April, just when the trees were budding, and returned to the newspaper in early May, just when Lancashire were about to begin the County Championship season.

Crozier, knowing nothing of Cardus's attempts to move on, thankfully saw what Scott didn't: Cardus needed nursing. To resume his previous, punishing schedule would have wrecked him irrevocably. Crozier, looking at the pitifully thin Cardus, thought he ought to be breathing lungfuls of fresh, spring air rather than office tobacco smoke. He sent him to Old Trafford for medical reasons. Perhaps, said Crozier, he could report on 'one or two matches'. Cardus, determined to pursue music, regarded it as a holiday, a small excursion into sport.

The illness and his recuperation from it was the axis on which his whole future turned. 'It made me,' he said.

The *Manchester Guardian* had assigned no one to follow Lancashire, continuing its somewhat ad hoc approach towards coverage of cricket. It had previously been a duty done by anyone who volunteered, anyone who wasn't otherwise engaged or anyone who loosely counted as a regular freelance. This included the barrister (he later became a judge)

E. H. Longson, who also contributed reports on golf and the arts. Longson's copy was formulaic and seldom took flight. It was as if back then cricket reporting – and sports reporting in general – had to be boring to comply with some ancient, unbreakable law of journalism. The structure of a report and the stock list of permissible phrases was hidebound too. A batsman 'compiled an innings'. A bowler 'bowled steadily'. In the press box it was customary to scribble down ball-by-ball data. Some accumulated more of it than the official scorers, making them statistical stenographers rather than writers. These figures dominated rather than complemented pieces that, shorn of verse, read like an accountant's ledger of profit and loss. Neville Cardus called it 'clerical conscientiousness'.

Goodness, it was dull.

Dispatching a writer such as Cardus to Old Trafford seemed logical to W. P. Crozier. He had every qualification. As a boy, Cardus had played truant to go there. He remembered the huge acreage of countryside around the ground, the landscape barely scarred then by either housing or industry. He remembered the low, badly bruised cloud, promising rain, and the forbidding sign that hung beside the main gates, warning of the consquences of bad weather: 'YOU ENTER AT YOUR OWN RISK. NO MONEY REFUNDED'. He remembered the weight of the turnstile as he pushed through it. Inside, the scene was thick with life and talk. Cardus liked the anonymity that disappearing into the crowd afforded him. He spoke about the benches where he sat and also the sight of the 'greenest grass' in England, the field the colour of a cooking apple. There was a deluge, ending play after he'd seen barely a pinch of it. Cardus said he sheltered in a niche near the pavilion long after the game had been abandoned. A smallish man in a blue serge suit appeared, saw him close to tears and took pity on his misery, pressing a sixpence into his palm as compensation for the lost day. The man was Lancashire's J. T. 'Johnny' Tyldesley, scorer of nearly 40,000

*The stylist J. T. Tyldesley, who once gave Cardus a sixpence
and became instantly and for ever one of his heroes.*

first-class runs. Cardus showed off the shiny coin to his friends next
morning. None of them believed where it had come from. He'd spend
a tower of other sixpences at Old Trafford, watching his benefactor
Tyldesley square-cut innumerable crash-wallop fours, the shots
thumping so powerfully against the railings that white paint flaked off

them and scattered on to the outfield like snow. He'd seen 'The Croucher', the stocky Gilbert Jessop, smash a window with a typically muscular six, shards of glass spraying everywhere. He'd also seen Johnny Briggs, Lancashire's left-arm spinner, take all ten wickets in an innings against Worcestershire.

He'd learnt to play cricket on a patch of blasted wasteland, mostly shorn of grass. The ball was made of cork and stained with ruby dye. In the rain the ball shrank and the dye came off, leaving your hands stained red, as though you'd been handling raw meat in a butcher's. There were four stumps and the bat, yellow with age, gradually got covered with as much binding as an Egyptian mummy. In Manchester's hottest months the makeshift pitch became a dust bowl, enabling an off-spinner to turn a delivery as wide as the Ship Canal. Like everyone else who could get hold of a library copy, Cardus's rudimentary skills were cribbed from K. S. Ranjitsinhji's 475-page *The Jubilee Book of Cricket*, lavishly illustrated with portraits of W. G. Grace, A. E. Stoddart and the prince himself. Each held a pose as still and decorous as an artist's model. Cardus always tried to bowl like Briggs, practising 'for hours' against a bucket and a broad piece of board. And he always tried to bat like Jessop, adopting a low hunch at the crease.

His off-breaks – or so he said – would 'whip upwards viciously straight at the most important and tender part of a man's anatomy'. He insisted wickedly and with a distinctly non-Corinthian attitude: 'I am not ashamed to confess that I seldom hesitated, as soon as a bats-man came to the crease, to let him have a quick one bang in the penis.' He made three other boasts about his talent – none of which can be satisfactorily substantiated: that he'd claimed a hat-trick; that he'd taken nine wickets in a match; that he'd won a game, Jessop-like, with two blows after a mid-order collapse. In photographs, he doesn't conform to the manly stereotype of a cricketer. He resembles the weedy, bespectacled actor Charles Hawtrey, who half a century on would haplessly stumble across the cinema screen in the *Carry On* films.

Crozier also knew that during the two summers before the Great War began, Cardus had been assistant professional at Shrewsbury School, founded in the mid-16th century and the alma mater of Charles Darwin and the Elizabethan courtier-poet Sir Philip Sidney. The acquisition of that position was even more improbable than his arrival on the *Manchester Guardian*. It was like sticking a spade randomly into the ground and turning up gold coins. Out of desperation rather than expectation, he had answered an advertisement in the *Athletic News and Cyclists' Journal*. For weeks no reply came. 'I forgot all about it,' admitted Cardus, who returned to his room one evening to discover an envelope emblazoned with the school's crest. He was hired – for two pounds ten shillings per week – without the rigmarole and chore of an interview. It was as though everyone else's response to the vacancy had got lost in the post. Or Cardus was confused with someone immensely more qualified, his new employers too embarrassed to say so. As he confessed: 'A miracle happened' that 'I cannot explain.'

In Crozier's opinion, the miracle bestowed 'cricket cachet' on Cardus. He had reviewed that year's *Wisden*, an edition that stood as a monument in print for those cricketers who had died during the Great War. He had already previewed the summer to come too. He consequently took his place in the cramped wooden press box, perched at the Stretford End of Old Trafford.

Neville Cardus, tentatively and self-consciously, began by aping his predecessors. His first report, in May 1919 – Lancashire against Derbyshire – comprised five long paragraphs of 700 words. The only flourish was his description of leaving behind the 'dusty town' and looking again on the 'soft green' field splashed with the spring sun and

Frank Woolley, one of the most ravishing stroke-makers in the English game.

of the 'county flag streaming in the wind'. This was not the writer who would say of the imperious Frank Woolley that he 'made music' and 'spread beauty' with his bat. Or the one who would describe Ted McDonald as a fast bowler capable of making batsmen 'not merely his victims but his prey'. Or the man who'd compare the expression of first slip dropping a catch to the torment seen 'in a painting by El Greco' and liken the sight of the fielding side descending from the pavilion steps to 'a white waterfall'.

'I made notes of the number of fours a batsman hit, the time he stayed at the wicket, the amount of overs bowled in a given period,' he admitted. He stopped doing so during the Roses match, which took place in June, only because Samuel Langford, sitting beside him, became irritated. He thought Cardus was wasting paper, jotting down things he would never use, and also wasting his chance to look properly at what was in front of him. 'Throw your notebook away. Watch the players and get the hang of their characters,' he ordered.

This was Cardus's eureka moment.

From then on he decided to treat the cricketers of Lancashire and Yorkshire as if each was an actor in a play or a figure from a novel. And he decided to treat the match itself as a spotlighted drama. The plot was the flow of the game. The lead characters sprang from whoever was dominant in it. The scoreboard, though not superfluous, was just another piece of scenery, not always important to him.

Cardus was fortunate. He found a jester, a player so outlandishly unconventional and idiosyncratic that he seems too large and quirky to possibly be true. If you didn't know otherwise, you'd suppose someone had invented him purely for the purposes of comic fiction.

'Nobody who saw him could forget him in a lifetime,' said Cardus.

*　　*　　*

Rarely still or silent, possessing the spark of perpetual motion, Lancashire's Cecil Parkin had an intrinsic need to entertain, sometimes clownishly, and badly wanted to please. 'Cricket,' he said, 'should be as bright as the players can make it.'

Cecil Parkin, who Cardus called 'the first jazz cricketer', 'the Card' and also 'the Artful Dodger'.

Everything he did was designed as a show.

He could slide a watch off a wrist or out of a waistcoat pocket without the wearer knowing a thing about it. He'd produce a coin from behind someone's ear and then make it vanish. Playing cards appeared too – as easily as though he'd plucked them out of the mysterious ether. But what he could do with a penny, or the ace of spades, were trivial party pieces compared with the gift of his bowling.

Parkin had a lean figure then, becoming bulkier only much later, and his run to the crease was peculiarly jerky – spine straight, head back, hands clasped together and elbows sharply jutting like small swords of bone. At the point of delivery his arms cartwheeled, the quick whirl of them disguising the trick his supple fingers were about to perform. For, as an accomplished amateur magician, he knew that every conjuring success is nine-tenths deception; he knew, too, that the practised hand moves faster than the eye.

With the ball, sent down at a pace somewhere between medium and quick, he could do everything and even a bit more besides: deceive in flight; beat with rasping turn; flim-flam a batsman into a misjudgement. Ask him to bowl anything – fast, slow, googly, swing, 'backbreak' – and he'd do so apparently without conscious thought or much effort. Ask him to bowl each of them in the same over, and he could do that too, the task rudimentary.

He'd regularly hone his bowling in the nets against his tolerant wife, a task unmentioned in her marriage vows. A homely woman with dark, bobbed hair, she was a complete novice, who had only ever glimpsed a cricket match before the two of them met. When the ball popped and fizzed, she was struck repeatedly on the hands, splitting her nails, and on the legs and on the lower torso, leaving her with livid bruising. He even blacked her eye once, albeit inadvertently, after a ball rose off a length. 'Scores of times I have seen her crying with pain,' he said, failing to understand what outsiders would think of it.

Eccentric wasn't the half of it with Parkin.

There were pros who preferred the ball to be returned along the ground, roughing the leather up a little and taking off the shine. With the ridge of his left boot, Parkin learnt how to flick it from grass to hand and into his palm like a scampering mouse. Every dancing appeal – long and loud, like a ship's foghorn – was slapstick comedy too. He once walked off the field in a premeditated strop after three of them (all plumb, he insisted) received in return nothing but a solemn shake of the umpire's head.

He could pretend to bowl normally, bringing down his right arm when the ball was actually in his left; he'd then lob it underarm at the unsuspecting batsman. Sometimes, instead of a ball, he'd take an orange out of his pocket and hurl it towards the wicketkeeper from the boundary. Especially when the sun shone, he'd go back to his mark singing the popular numbers of the period or of an earlier one: 'Lily of Laguna' and 'Tea for Two', 'She's My Lady Love' and 'You're a Sweetheart'. He encouraged the umpires to ask for requests; he knew verbatim the lyrics to whichever piece of sheet music had sold well. When batting, once caught at the same end as his partner after a hopeless misunderstanding at Lord's, he celebrated extravagantly after the straightforward throw to run him out hopped a mile wide of the stumps. He shouldered his bat like a soldier's rifle and marched to safety, crooning two verses of 'The British Grenadiers'.

In photographs, for which he willingly posed, Parkin always seems to be juggling with the ball, flicking it off his knee or upper arm. Otherwise he'd turn an umbrella inside out, lean back or into the camera, or arrange his face into a mocking expression. It's as though, unable to portray himself conventionally, he had to put on a song-and-dance performance – even if the photographer was his only audience.

Parkin never passed up the chance to be the centre of attention. So a cardinal match demanded a cardinal performance from him.

This Roses game had a pendulum swing about it.

On the first day almost 12,000 spectators went through the gates. The *Manchester Guardian* photographed those in the pavilion wearing natty straw boaters, waistcoats and wing collars. Lancashire piled up what Neville Cardus said was a 'respectable' 319. The backbone was a century from Harry Makepeace, an opener of oaken sturdiness who could late-cut 'beautifully'.

When Cecil Parkin got at Yorkshire, Cardus reckoned he was 'at his most resourceful' – 'varying his length and pace skilfully, seeking out the weak points in a batsman's defence audaciously'. He complimented him on his 'gigantic labours', the 'zest' of which 'set the crowd simmering'. He watched a sumptuous slow ball clean-bowl George Hirst, conned into attempting a 'prodigious drive' against a delivery he supposed was the loosest of donkey drops. At the close, Yorkshire were floundering a little at 195 for six; Parkin had taken three of the wickets.

But the real suspense lay ahead.

Those who cannot live without cricket are attracted not only by the rhythms of the game, the variety of the landscapes in which it is played and the intriguing individual contests within the rival teams. What pulls them towards it is also the soaring unpredictability of every new day, the astonishment of watching a team either win or save a game that only an hour before looked lost to them. This is what Cardus saw. The way he wrote about it was so distinctive that it set him apart from everyone else. No one then had a voice like his.

On day two Yorkshire were bowled out for 232. Parkin finished with six for 88. With Makepeace again dominant – he made 78

– Lancashire were able to declare on 206 for nine, leaving Yorkshire to get 294 to beat them. The wicket was wearing. The time, however, was four o'clock. Irrespective of which side of the Pennines you came from, you expected nothing but a final session of exemplary stonewalling, the honours amicably shared. Pessimistic Lancastrians, absolutely certain of that, shuffled off to catch the tram home, underestimating Parkin, who then played for them only in midweek matches because of his Saturday commitment to Rochdale in the Central Lancashire League.

Crafty and determined, he had something to prove. As far back as 1906, he had appeared in one match for Yorkshire before a suspicious busybody at the MCC dug into his background and discovered he'd been born in Durham, making him ineligible. He didn't debut for Lancashire until 1914. Yorkshire hadn't floated into his orbit since. Parkin, fired with indignation, 'turned the scale', said Cardus.

Within an hour and a half, Yorkshire were 63 for five. Gone was the guts of the batting: Wilfred Rhodes and Percy Holmes, Roy Kilner and Hirst. Only Herbert Sutcliffe remained. Cardus said Parkin was 'almost unplayable' until a thin drizzle made finger-spin difficult. When it stopped, and the sun broke through to rapidly dry the pitch, he became rampant. At 6.40 p.m., with 50 minutes left, he claimed Sutcliffe. 'After that,' wrote Cardus, 'the batsmen could hardly look at him.' The seventh wicket fell at 7.05 p.m. The eighth at 7.12 p.m. The ninth at 7.16 p.m. In came David Denton, who had retired hurt in the first innings, his right thumb crushed fending off a bouncer. He trudged out, almost with a one-step-forward-and-two-steps-back slowness. Cardus thought the clock hands would get to 7.30 p.m. before he reached the crease. Parkin bowled him – 'neck and crop' – with the second ball of the penultimate over. There were barely five minutes to spare. Yorkshire had fallen for 153 – 140 adrift. Parkin had taken eight for 35, giving him match figures of 14 for 123.

In celebration, Cardus ennobled Parkin in words. He wrote about the 'consummate alternating' of his deliveries, tailoring them to 'the special needs of the moment' through 'watchful study'. Parkin, he said, tossed the ball up, inviting the off-drive but pitching the thing just short and 'gradually' slackening its pace. He'd then drift one marginally wider than normal to induce the batsman into the shot. To someone who played back, Parkin fed it to him 'until the batsman was on his toes'. He'd then send up a delivery 'that hangs as though he had pulled it back with a string', forcing the fatal mistake. Cardus concluded: 'Not since Albert Trott played has one seen the "hanging" slow ball managed so skilfully . . . on present form Parkin is probably the finest bowler in the game.'

Like every writer, Cardus had his battles with sub-editors who thought less about his copy than he did. His piece on the climax to the Roses match was more than double the length of his earlier ones. The subs, alarmed at the unprecedented indulgence 'for a cricket match', wanted to slash rather than trim. C. P. Scott knew so little about cricket that he thought Frank Woolley was a right-handed bat. He had been unable to detect Cardus's nervous breakdown while it took place in front of him. But at least he had an antenna for quality writing. Scott intervened, decreeing Cardus must be published 'uncut'.

Cardus would later say of Parkin, who became his friend, that he'd been constantly engaged in 'the great cause of cheering us all up', which meant always taking decorum by the ears. He thought of the bowler as 'a genius' and christened him 'the first jazz cricketer', 'the *enfant terrible*', 'the Card' and also 'the Artful Dodger', the consequence of a remark Parkin made to him: 'On a good pitch, you've got to dodge them out.'

In his career, Parkin claimed more than 1,000 first-class wickets; 32 of these came in ten Tests. His legacy nonetheless goes well beyond these sober figures. He was responsible – however unwittingly his seminal role was accomplished – for changing the way that cricket was reported on and written about.

It can still be difficult to grasp the significance of something in the absolute hour it occurs. Cardus left Old Trafford still thinking of cricket as a 'spare-time affair' for him. He had 'no intention' of pursuing it 'for any length of time'.

Seldom can someone have been so unaware of the start of his own Golden Age, a period spanning two decades that was filled with approximately three million words.

2

THE MEANING OF
EPIC ROMANCE

NEVILLE CARDUS BEGAN to chase the sun, going wherever Lancashire's fixture list or the Test matches sent him. The *Manchester Guardian* gave him more than a pay increase, the dizzy sum of five pounds weekly when the average worker took home a pound and a few shillings. It also handed him a free passport to 'see England for the first time', he said.

The cricket season followed a fairly regimented template, allowing one County Championship campaign to melt into another almost indistinguishably. Cardus remembered: 'For years ahead it was possible for me to know in what place I would be and what I would be doing almost at any given moment, noon and night, during the months of summer.' You could have deprived Cardus of a calendar, and he would have unfailingly recognised each month from the horticulture and agriculture of the landscape. He always saw the daffodils sway in blustery Oxfordshire, where it was impossible to put down a foot on the outfield without stepping on a daisy, the flowers spread like foam. He saw the 'winsome meadowland' of Essex, the fields stained with crimson poppies, and the slow-moving sails of a windmill against the wide sky. He saw orchards blossom in Gloucestershire and the whiteness of summer's longest days in Kent, where the mornings were as bright as shiny paper and he'd sit under delicious shade to shelter his eyes from the glare. And he saw the first turn and drop of the leaves in Sussex, where the harvest was reaped and the fields became brown again, the soil furrowed like bolts of soft corduroy.

Cardus liked some of the showery weather of May, of which he said: 'Unspeakable is the bliss of those few moments of shelter in the darkened dressing room,' where 'everyone sits ... and enjoys the pleasure of a quick cigarette.' He called June and July 'a pageant with many hues', the bowlers who worked tirelessly on 'scorched' pitches reminding him of 'labourers in the field'. In August he registered the 'brilliance' of the days swiftly departing and heard also the ambient 'sounds' of 'melancholy' in them as the Championship gently got 'ready to go'. And in September he watched 'the yellow glow of an afternoon beginning to fade and mists coming over the grass'.

He went annually to the grandest grounds – Trent Bridge and Edgbaston, The Oval and Lord's – and trekked to those tucked-away and pastorally quainter corners, where there were deckchairs instead of wooden slatted seats, clumps of trees instead of banked stands, a church spire instead of a textile chimney. There was Dover and Kidderminster, Ashby-de-la-Zouch and Weston-super-Mare, Hastings and Southend-on-Sea. He packed only a single suitcase, taking a proliferation of pens and pencils, his pads and notebooks, his pipe and cigarette case, a pair of Zeiss binoculars, a rolled-up umbrella, a belted coat and a large, floppy felt hat which could be folded up and stuffed beside his clothes and his washbag. He left his copy of *Wisden* on the bookshelf, never wanting to be a slave to statistics that bored him. 'The true lover of the game often forgets the existence of the scoreboard,' he said. If you judge cricket merely from numbers, he added, 'you see the body and miss the delectable spirit'. The important 'big' book Cardus carried was *Bradshaw's Railway Guide*.

Some seasons 'passed like a dream', he explained. Cardus recalled preparing for one journey, staring from his bedroom window at passersby who, 'poor souls', were 'going to work, going to the city, there to live stuffily in one dingy spot'. He thought of his fortunate self, always travelling hopefully through a 'drowsy landscape'. Everything was new to him then and he experienced the acme of human happiness. Cardus defined satisfying work as 'something you would never give up – even if tomorrow you came into money'. Writing about cricket definitely wasn't work ... or at least not in the beginning.

It was the age of the steam locomotive. The railway snaked every-where, no town without a track and a station. Cardus, travelling first class courtesy of the *Manchester Guardian*, liked the 'sumptuous cush-ioned privacy' of the restaurant car and the coffee and liqueurs served in it. After a long hard day, he would look through the window of his compartment, catching a glimpse of lives mysterious to him – 'a white house on a hill top ... paths winding into woods ... an old woman walking along a lane ... a man knocking at a cottage door'. He felt the tilt of the train as it swung around a bend, taking him away from these strangers. 'I never knew what happened to them next,' he lamented.

Cardus's time and also his country seem so distant and so different from our own. This was the England J. B. Priestley later saw in *English Journey*: the 'three Englands' of 'the Old, the Nineteenth Century and the New ... most fascinatingly mingled'. It was George Orwell's England too: the clatter of clogs in the Lancashire mill towns ... the rattle of pin-tables in pubs where the beer was bitter on the tongue ... the queues outside the Labour Exchange ... the dirty copper coins, heavy in the pocket. You were considered to be improperly dressed without a hat. You relied as much on weird elixirs and empirical, cure-all remedies – Dr Williams' Pink Pills and Elliman's Embrocation – as on prescription medicines. You were lured by posters that advertised Wills's Gold Flake cigarettes and Fry's Chocolate, Dandy Shandy and Charrington's Pale Ale. You went to the music hall and the picture house, where all the films were in black and white, and the talkies had still to make the silent screen obsolete. You bought the 'late finals' or the 'extras' to read the telegraph brevity of the Stop Press. And, if you were a boy of summer, you begged smokers to give you the cigarette cards that depicted star cricketers, some in brilliant colour rather than the smudgy monochrome of every newspaper.

Those newspapers were slow boats of information, but remained the dominant method of conveying it because radio had yet to reach most living rooms, either through crystal sets or wirelesses encased in oak cabinets. Some nooks and crannies of England waited impatiently to be wired up. In 1927 the journalist H. V. Morton wrote about a remote farm cottage in Cornwall, where a 'wireless' had just been connected and the sonorous introduction to the programmes – 'This is London calling the British Isles' – was greeted miraculously, like the voice of God. With the elderly farmer and his wife, Morton listened to the crackle of music transmitted from the Savoy ballroom. Neither of his hosts knew what London, let alone the Savoy, actually looked like. Morton had to describe to them the city, the ballroom and also Broadcasting House. John Betjeman even told how a West Country worker, arriving at Paddington Station for the first time, wandered about, unable to tear his eyes away from the soaring glass roof which Isambard Kingdom Brunel had designed. He thought the whole of London must be encased beneath glass too.

There is an alien strangeness about this England. You can barely conceive that it once constituted the modern world.

Like the country itself, the Championship when Cardus reported on it was a class-conscious, upstairs-downstairs affair. The world of the unpaid gentleman amateur, who was always the captain, met the world of the flinty professional, relying on cricket to scrape a living. Some of the amateurs possessed enough initials to make you wonder whether there was an anagram hidden within. Etiquette and obligation demanded that the pros called the amateur captain 'sir' to his face. Behind his back, he was frequently chastised as a bloody idiot – or far worse – because status didn't necessarily equate to talent. The wise

The amateur captain of Yorkshire, Major Lupton, seems so different from the sons-of-toil senior pros George Hirst (centre) and Wilfred Rhodes, hands casually thrust into pockets.

amateur captain deferred to the senior pro. For Yorkshire, Major Arthur Lupton, a Boer War veteran, made only 668 runs and took no wickets in 104 matches, a record so pathetically meagre that he wasn't worthy of his place except as a stabilising presence in a volatile team. The county won the title under Lupton only because his tactical influence was minimal. He once marched out to bat only to discover that Wilfred Rhodes had declared the innings closed without telling him. Sensibly, he decided not to make an issue of it.

Not only did these separate tribes mostly use different dressing rooms and different gates on to the field, but the amateurs went first class and checked into high-end hotels. The pros travelled third class and bunked in guest houses. The business of travelling from one ground to another could be torturous. It took four and a half hours to get from Manchester to London; a further two hours to journey from there to Brighton. And from Cardus's Manchester the cider-land of Taunton took five hours. Even a trip to Trent Bridge was three hours.

In the beginning Cardus kept himself a little aloof from the players. Knowing them only by reputation, and lacking the self-confidence to assert himself, he drifted around the periphery of their card schools and their cliques. He suspected anyway that some would 'bore' him or 'burst the bubble of my literary fancies and conceits about them'.

Percy Holmes, the Yorkshire opener, used to get to a hotel reception before the rest of the team and briskly ring the bell on the desk before telling the uniformed clerk: 'Book us in as Percy Holmes and his Circus.' Eventually Cardus thought of all cricket teams in much the same way – a performing troupe of entertainers or a travelling theatre group. He settled in, finding acceptance and companionship. Lancashire's leg-break bowler Dick Tyldesley, chubby-faced and red-cheeked, always bellowed to the railway guard: 'Has't got beer on board?' Tyldesley would then make the same offer to Cardus that he made to the amateurs: 'Coom and 'ave a drink with us.' Cardus did so, also frequenting sawdust-on-the-floor saloons with the pros when the amateurs retreated to the hotel bar for a nightcap. He gradually became a part of the party – rather than apart from it – and cocked an attentive ear towards its conversations. 'We were a seasonal community,' he said. 'We knew one another. We would indulge in the candour reserved for friends.'

Cardus revelled in the camaraderie, the leg-pulling and the late-night stories made for the ages. There was the Lancashire wicket-keeper he found wearily traipsing the Regency crescents of

Cheltenham, who asked Cardus with a cheery optimism: 'Tell me. Wheer's t'seafront?' There was the fast bowler Walter Brearley, who would always tell of hitting George Hirst on the kneecap, his appeal for lbw unsuccessful. Every time Hirst subsequently drove a four, the crowd would yell 'Ow's that?', until Brearley, his complexion the colour of a boiled lobster, broke his middle stump and brandished the broken pieces in front of them. And there was another Lancashire bowler, Harry Dean, who was told he'd be toiling all day on a flag-stone-hard, batsman's paradise of a pitch. He borrowed 'two of the thickest pairs of socks' he could find to absorb the blood from his bleeding feet.

Blake discovered Heaven in a wild flower; Cardus discovered it in cricket and in cricketers.

In later life he would insist that he'd become the *Manchester Guardian*'s cricket correspondent to his 'disgust and frustration'. When it occurred, Cardus clung to the thought that his true destiny – writing exclusively on music – had still to declare itself. He would also blithely claim that he had never been 'ambitious' and 'seldom, if ever' worked 'for advancement'. All these were fibs of Olympian proportions, a striving to appear absurdly humble. Self-deprecation didn't suit him. Once asked how someone became successful, Cardus merely replied: 'Work, work, work.' He was the absolute embodiment of the self-made man, brimming with will and purpose and forever on the trail of success. He was always convinced the destination would make the difficulty of the journey worthwhile. At first, Cardus simply didn't want to acknowledge the magnitude of his efforts.

He managed to transform himself so successfully into the figure he had wanted to be all along – a gentleman writer – that the figure he had once been all but vanished. Eventually, no one meeting him cold could have guessed the difference between the new Cardus and the old – or how such a profound separation between them had been

The grey double-breasted suit. The regulation white shirt and tie. This was the uniform Cardus, seen walking through London, wore throughout his life.

achieved after an upbringing as convoluted as the narrative in one of those epic Victorian novels.

Throughout his early life, Neville Cardus purposefully dusted over the tracks of his upbringing even when pretending to come clean about it. On different occasions, he gave the date of his birth as both 2 April and 3 April. He gave the year of it as 1889, 1890 and 1891. None of these was correct.

The sailor who would not go to sea until the 1930s.
Cardus is dressed up in his Sunday best.

As a boy he was told three things about his father. He had been 'first violin' in an orchestra. He had been 'tall' and 'saturnine of countenance'. He had gone 'on business' to the coast of West Africa and had 'died there', distance making his grave conveniently impossible to visit.

These were fairy tales fed to him. This was the truth: in 1888, aged 17, his mother, Ada, wed John Frederick Newsham, a 21-year-old blacksmith.

On the evidence of the two names that Ada gave to her only son immediately after his birth, plus exhibit A – the marriage certificate – Sherlock Holmes would never describe the deduction of Cardus's paternity as a 'two-pipe problem'. His baptism record, as well as the 1891 census, even registered his surname as Newsham – even though his mother and her husband had already long parted, the relationship never conforming to the romantic code of a happy ending. The couple were divorced a little over a decade later when Newsham petitioned on grounds of adultery.

He travelled to America – one of Ada's relatives was living there – almost before the confetti had been swept from the church. His wife waved him off from Liverpool quayside. He went to find work and a home before sending for her. He wrote, dutifully dispatched money and asked her to pack up and sail the Atlantic. She consistently refused. In the only photograph that survives of her, Ada looks mousy and demure: a pile of fair curls, small eyes and a slightly long, somewhat flat jaw. She is dressed in a dark, high-necked dress. In correspondence or anecdote she is nonetheless not the sort of woman Jane Austen would have chosen as a frilly heroine. Ada is appalling: schemingly deceitful and chillingly calculating. In the years between the altar and the courtroom, Mr and Mrs Newsham seldom saw one another. With an ocean separating them, absence did not make Ada's heart grow fonder for her faraway spouse. She instead began an affair

Cardus's mother, Ada, who was such a vaporous presence in his life.

with a foreign-born merchant, moving in with him. In one letter she told her husband, who was ill, that she wished he was 'dead'. Divorce was difficult in the 19th century, which also made it juicily rare for newspapers. The process was laborious and expensive too. The stigma of it clung to the couple afterwards like a noxious smell. In 1898, when the Newshams' grubby linen was pegged out in front of a judge, there were only 507 other divorces in England and Wales. Even *The Times* covered the hearing, a short stick of a column that reported how Newsham had twice returned from America to find his wife cosily tucked up with her fancy man.

With much politeness and a lot of decorum, Cardus said that his mother withdrew 'to the wings' during his childhood. The portrait he left of her as a consequence is brief and unflattering. Ada described herself as a 'laundress', planting a discreet full stop there to avoid further elaboration.

The household smelt of soap and steam and sweat. Cardus remembered his mother taking in bundles of dirty clothes and bedsheets, washing them and then wringing them dry. She would spit on the hot iron to make certain it was sizzling. When the laundry was aired and ready, she would pack it into a pram. Cardus pushed it through the streets, resenting the ignominy of being her delivery boy. He remembered – more vividly – his mother powdering her cheeks for evening adventures along Manchester's Oxford Road. She wore a corset that was a 'girder of steel' around a 'buxom' body, he said. She draped a feather boa around her neck and regarded herself as a 'courtesan' rather than a 'common prostitute'. Cardus likened her to Marie Lloyd, the Queen of the Music Hall, known for her cheeky innuendo and double-entendre songs, such as 'A Little of What You Fancy' and 'She Sits Among the Cabbages and Peas'. Cardus called Lloyd 'the benign mother of vulgarity' and thought his own counted as one of her 'daughters'. It was not a compliment.

Providentially for the future cricket correspondent, Cardus's home was on a road called Summer Place in Rusholme. The red-brick, bay-windowed house with an outside toilet belonged to his maternal grandparents, Robert and Ann. Cardus called it 'a semi-slum'. It was hardly the blacking factory, but it wasn't bejewelled either, and the music-hall comedians were right to joke that in areas such as the one

'Where I was born' – Summer Place, Rusholme.

from which Cardus came 'you usually worked yourself up from nothing to a state of extreme poverty'. It was an age when electricity was still a 'wonder', said Cardus. When a man with a red flag walked in front of a motor car as a warning to unwary pedestrians. When the balloon, rather than the aeroplane, passed in the sky, with every head below tilted upward to see it. And when the flickering bioscope was the forerunner of cinema. Working lives were lived in loud desperation, the chances of a release from it infinitesimal.

His grandfather was a former police constable who read only the Bible, the *Manchester Guardian* and the *Sporting Chronicle Handicap Book*. He had left the force after a pockmarked career – it had tipped into drunkenness and assault – and turned to greengrocery and gardening. He claimed the three noticeable dents on his skull had been inflicted by Charles Peace, one of the most notorious cat burglars and masters of disguise. He said Peace, so ugly that he could have frightened a Cathedral gargoyle, had belted him with a crowbar. That fireside story was entertaining but fabricated. The wounds, shown off whenever the chance arose, were the brutal handiwork of a much obscurer criminal.

Cardus grew up surrounded by women. There were initially six in Summer Place – his mother, grandmother, two aunts and two cousins, each of whom contributed to the laundry business. The most important was his brashly flamboyant aunt Beatrice, whom he described as 'one of the most wonderful creatures of my life' and also as 'one of the first naughty girls'.

Whereas his mother is all but a blank in his writing – she passes into and out of Summer Place like a draught – Beatrice strides incandescently about the page. Only a decade older than Cardus, she raised him while his mother was 'otherwise engaged'. She bought him his first cricket bat. She called him 'darling'. She let him fall asleep in her arms. She doted on him, and vice versa. Beatrice was red-haired and blue-eyed and husky-voiced. Her lips, even without make-up, were as 'red as a rose'. She 'walked like one of the well-born of the earth', said Cardus. Beatrice modelled herself on the actress Mrs Patrick Campbell, the lady companion of George Bernard Shaw, her infatuated friend during a long and platonic relationship. The best-known quote attributed to 'Mrs Pat' is her response after hearing the details of a homosexual couple's sex life. 'My dear,' she said, 'I don't care what they do, so long as they don't do it in the street and frighten the horses.' Cardus, a good mimic, used that line whenever he impersonated Beatrice impersonating Mrs Campbell.

Like his mother, Beatrice was a laundress every morning and afternoon and followed the oldest profession every night, dressing in a Zouave jacket, a spotted veil, gold braid and a great outspreading skirt. She was more alluring than Cardus's mother – and clearly more expert at hooking a catch too. She was very profitably at the centre of a cause célèbre, featured in newspapers throughout Britain, after suing the Turkish Consul in Manchester for breach of promise in 1902. The liaison and its aftermath seem like a soap opera until you read the dense coverage about her and the man called 'The Lustful Turk', a case saucy enough to attract the attention of a court artist. He captured Beatrice looking sweetly innocent. The flourish of a hat with an enormous, curved feather seduced the judge as much as her gentle manner. She was awarded £200, a sum worth the equivalent of £12,000 today. Beatrice was a fool with her loot. She lost a good portion of it on a horse. Cardus said she was brought home from the racetrack 'stiff and insensible' from champagne. She took him to Blackpool for a month, throwing away most of what remained of her windfall in a ticker-tape parade of banknotes. He didn't care. Beatrice alone made his childhood tolerable.

To read between the lines of his reminiscences is to realise that Cardus, the boy, considered himself cruelly displaced, as though the midwife had handed him immediately after birth to the wrong family. You know that Cardus, the young man, had a plan to shake them off and grow apart and the certain belief that he would do so – however long the process took. When he began properly making headway in the world, Summer Place had long since splintered apart. His grandparents were dead. Beatrice had married and moved away. His mother had found a man who was fleetingly interested in her but not him. He once lived briefly, but precariously, in lodgings, using newspapers to

THE "LUSTFUL TURK."

MANCHESTER CONSUL'S BREACH OF PROMISE.

THE PLAINTIFF
(BEATRICE CARDUS

TYPES IN COURT

THE DEFENDANT
(MUSTAPHA KARSA)

THE MOTHER
OF THE
PLAINTIFF

THE SISTER
OF
PLAINTIFF

*The court artist at the Trial of the Lustful Turk makes
Cardus's aunt Beatrice look a very alluring figure.*

pad his thin bedding. He only wanted to write – and he wanted to write only for the *Manchester Guardian*.

He could tell C. P. Scott about his commitment to the newspaper. What Cardus couldn't reveal to him was his mother's and his aunt's prostitution. In his youth, Scott had considered becoming a Unitarian minister. He was puritanical and morally highly principled. He refused, despite pleading, to publish a horse-racing column, believing that gambling was a heinous activity. He was also horrified at any remark, however mild and inoffensive, that he considered smutty or ribald. The word 'sex', said Cardus, was 'not allowed in *his* paper'. The strait-laced Scott even banned an advertisement for 'ladies corsetry', believing the line drawing of an attractive brunette with an hourglass figure was far too risqué for the readership. He once managed to lock himself in the lavatory. No one wanted to go to Scott's assistance, because his plight robbed him of his usual power and dignity, and also because 'bodily functions', and why and where these occurred, were not something to be discussed within earshot of him. Decorum had to be maintained; Scott couldn't be reduced to mere flesh and blood.

When discussing his background, Cardus was discreet and selective about what he shared with the staff of the *Manchester Guardian*. In most respects, Scott was liberal in his attitudes and actions. Nor did his newspaper's editorials damn or demonise prostitutes. Telling Scott about his mother and aunt remained nonetheless the risk that Cardus was unprepared to take.

He soon saw cricket as a golden key, capable of opening many doors. He was determined to keep hold of it.

To look at hand-cranked film of the cricket and cricketers of the 1920s and early 1930s is to watch something ethereal. Some of these fleeting, patched-up images are a wispy grey and jerk disconnectedly from one frame to another. You scarcely see the ball – only the bowler's run and delivery stride and then the swing or stone-drop of the bat. What strikes you most are the fielders, so statuesque and laggardly that some of them might be embalmed. There's not much scamper or pounce about chasing down a shot to the boundary; theirs is a dignified, wide turn and then a shuffling pursuit.

It was the time of Blanco, cream flannels as pale as butter and cotton-padded leg guards. There were Gradidge bats and rubber-spiked gloves. There was not much difference either between a pair of miner's boots and a pair of bowler's boots, the metal toecaps hard enough to kick down a door. Helmets were for the far-off future – though the innovative Patsy Hendren briefly stuffed his cap with foam to protect his ears and temples against the bouncer, never caring how unstylish he looked. Showing themselves off more fashionably, Herbert Sutcliffe batted occasionally in a natty black trilby, and George Gunn put on a Panama hat whenever the sun was at its hottest, accentuating the panache of his performance.

In the early 1920s, as Cardus established himself, there were batsmen capable of scoring 2,500 to 3,000 runs per season and bowlers who took 150 to 200 wickets, sending down in excess of 1,000 overs; every September was for them like a release from breaking rocks.

The players who most influenced the way he saw and wrote about the game nevertheless came from sun-struck pre-war years, when all he had to do was sit and watch a game without the burden of trying to think it into poetry.

All of us have heroes on whom we project hope as well as adoration. Most are transitory, for usually someone new comes along, claiming the pedestal we have built in our mind. Cardus was different. For him first love was also last love. He had two boyhood heroes, each impervious to other challengers for his affection.

As a besotted boy, he looked on A. C. MacLaren and Reggie Spooner 'with emotions terribly mixed.' Cardus believed MacLaren and Spooner were 'gods'. He also held the contradictory thought in his mind that both were 'going to get out nearly every ball'. Afraid in particular that Spooner could perish, Cardus averted his eyes whenever a bowler let go of a delivery to him. 'I loved Spooner so much that I dare not watch him make stroke. It is a curious thought – I probably *never* saw him at the moment which he actually played a ball.'

He even went to extremes, developing illogical behaviour so as not to jinx him and MacLaren. He adopted an odd stride to avoid cracks in the pavements and, like Dr Johnson, he would touch each lamp post as he passed it, going back 'if I feared I had missed one or not touched it with enough thought'. It was as though Cardus, the waif, was convinced that he alone was responsible for whether or not Lancashire won, and responsible also for whether MacLaren and Spooner were successful.

He worried unnecessarily. Spooner had charismatic self-command and took his runs with an expected, easy entitlement. He was classically elegant, the connoisseur's cricketer. In a *Vanity Fair* print he is whip-thin and boyishly handsome, every inch of him spick and span. His right hand is leaning on his brown bat. His left is casually resting on his hip. His shirt sleeves are folded to the wrists. Only the thinnest tuft of hair is out of place, the wind catching those few strands that the brilliantine failed to flatten. Otherwise Spooner is suavely immaculate. There is an air of unruffled assurance and supreme equipoise about him. He's a batsman who knows his superiority. J. T. Hearne, the fast-medium bowler who took more than 3,000 wickets for Middlesex and England, told Cardus: 'To bowl at Mr Spooner was a pleasure, a privilege and an honour.' Cardus immediately spotted the grace in him, thinking of a Pre-Raphaelite: 'There was nothing ferocious or brutal in Spooner's batsmanship. It was all courtesy and breeding ...

He was incapable of awkwardness ... He was all easy curves and thrusts.' Cardus added that he couldn't 'remember a crude stroke' from Spooner. 'When he glanced to leg that straight fast ball dead on middle stump, you gasped amazedly.'

Spooner, almost 39 when cricket resumed after the Great War, played just six more matches in two seasons. He gave only cameo performances. There were no more hundreds, and only two half-centuries. No longer could he turn cover-point's fingers blue from bruising. Cardus, not unexpectedly, saw what he wanted to see – the flicker of the old Spooner in these brief innings. 'There was no mistaking the artistry of his batting ... We were back in the Augustan period again,' he wrote of his comeback in the late summer of 1919. He noted the 'easeful stance', compared his wristy turns to the 'daintiness of a man using a feather duster decoratively' and, ignoring the evidence of the scoreboard, concluded that 'Spooner is obviously still a master.' When he became an irritation to Yorkshire, making 62 and then 63 against them, Cardus further declared that 'Spooner is Spooner still' and damned the bowler and the catcher who dismissed him, likening his departure to the sad putting-out of the sun.

The extravagantly wealthy Sir Julien Cahn had the best collection of bats in England. Cahn bankrolled Nottinghamshire and expensively ran his own country-house matches purely to play alongside the cricketers he liked for their personality or envied for their talent. His association with them brought Cahn a little starry celebrity. The bats, labelled and numbered, sat on a long black shelf beneath framed portraits of those who had owned them. There was a bat Fuller Pilch had used, accumulating runs before W. G. Grace outranked him. There was a 'weighty piece of wood' that Gilbert Jessop wielded, often like a willow club. There was a lighter, whippier thing stamped with Victor Trumper's name. The bat that nonetheless always commanded Cardus's attention was number 118. This was Spooner's – 'the most musical of all', he said, seeing on the face of it the shots Spooner had once played in front of him.

A. C. MacLaren didn't figure in another Championship match after the war. To Cardus, however, he remained 'the noblest Roman of them all', a man 'robed in glory' and who 'walked the grass as though he lorded it' with aristocratic entitlement.

From root to tip MacLaren, his heavy black moustache suffocating his top lip, certainly looked as patrician as Cardus suggests. In one staged image, he's audaciously advancing down the pitch – left leg thrust forward, bat above the shoulder, hooded eyes fixed on a distant spot. If there'd been a ball to clout, it would have soared into the next county. On a visit to Old Trafford, Cardus watched him off-drive to the Stretford End boundary in a similar way, the ball zipping over the damp grass. 'His bat swept down and, after his stroke, it remained on high,' recalled Cardus. 'MacLaren stood still, as though fixed by the magnificence of his own stroke.' He was a sharp fielder too. Walter Brearley used to mock the speed of his inferiors with the put-down 'Ah could throw mi hat down the pitch quicker.' When Brearley found the edge to slips, MacLaren was there to pouch it low and Cardus saw him 'throw up the ball with a great sweep of the arm . . . a gesture of majestic finality'. He didn't so much strike the ball as 'dismiss it from his presence', in the way other men would swat a midge or a moth.

MacLaren scored 22,000 first-class runs to Spooner's 14,000 – though he amassed them from nearly 200 more appearances. He captained Lancashire – though he led them to the Championship just once in a dozen years. He captained England too – though he lost four Ashes series.

But everything for Cardus was governed by the emotion it stirred. And it was MacLaren, rather than Spooner, who embodied 'the meaning of epic romance' for him.

His last, unlikely hurrah in England was confirmation of it.

3

A LONG WEEKEND
BY THE SEA

HE POSSESSED NO instinct for exclusive stories, which is why he never pursued them. Nor would he have recognised one even if, like a performing dog, it had danced on its hind legs and then turned a somersault in front of him.

Only by responding to a short letter, which implored him to buy a train ticket to Eastbourne, did Neville Cardus claim what he regarded as the 'only scoop' of his career.

The letter came, in late August 1921, from A. C. MacLaren, who was about to captain an amateur team against Warwick Armstrong's touring Australians. In four months MacLaren would be 50, his hair and moustache already losing colour and his waist slightly thicker than it had been during his pomp. This was 'the old boy's' swansong against the old foe. In a scribbled PS, MacLaren dangled a tantalising prospect in front of Cardus: 'I think I know how to beat the Australians – come and write about it.'

MacLaren, who had played his last Test in 1909, had been making the same brave boast consistently in columns for the *Daily Express*. No one believed him. He harped on like an eccentric inventor, convinced of the merit of his own contraption when it seemed slightly mad to everyone else. The summer had been fantastically dry, and drought was commonplace; so much so that the House of Commons debated whether the government ought to fund 'rain-inducing experiments'. The pitches cracked and flaked and suited the Australians, who were rampant. Having whitewashed Johnny Douglas's MCC in Australia only months before, giving them a huge psychological advantage for the return, Armstrong and his team pitilessly took them apart again. The Ashes were not so much a contest as a coronation. With the pace of Ted McDonald and Jack Gregory, who took 46 wickets between them, England were blasted away, reduced to scraps. The first Test at Trent Bridge lasted only two days. The second at Lord's, done and dusted in the early afternoon of the third, cost Douglas the captaincy. The third Test was at Headingley. The paying customer got a little more value for his shilling there; the Australians didn't close it out until after tea on the third day. In this wretched series England, unluckily robbed of Jack Hobbs, first through injury and then appendicitis, called up a total of 30 players in a forlorn attempt to pinch a win somewhere and anyhow. It was as if the dressing room had a revolving door. The final Tests, at Old Trafford and The Oval, were drawn, bringing respite and relief, but only a modicum of satisfaction to the selectors, who MacLaren believed were buffoons.

Cardus thought 'Mother Nature by herself' had 'fashioned' Armstrong. If so, She hadn't stinted on the portions. He was 6 ft 3 in tall and weighed 21 stone, a stomach on legs. You look at photographs of Armstrong and see a balloon of a man that no blast of warm air could have sent to the ceiling. You wonder who would have forced whom into submission if he and W. G. Grace had worn the mawashi and stepped on to the sumo mat, meeting there in one another's prime. He'd recently been christened the Big Ship. He got that way because of a titanic thirst for booze – particularly whisky – and an iron constitution that allowed him to soak it up. Armstrong seemed immune to hangovers – even after the sort of bender that would have sent a mere mortal to the infirmary. He scorned the teetotallers in his team as 'the lemonade crowd', supping enough for all of them and consequently bulging in all the wrong places. 'The bat in his hands,' wrote Cardus, 'is like a hammer in the grip of Vulcan.' The team in his hands had to tolerate uncompromising brusqueness. Armstrong was no angel; sometimes, like Grace, he regarded the laws as elastic and frequently tested how far he could stretch them. He was the hard master of whichever parcel of English soil he surveyed. No one had beaten the Australians in 34 matches on the tour. The thought that MacLaren, leading a cobbled-together England XI, could even give them a decent game seemed absurd. He and it were considered a tame sacrifice. A windfall of £1,000 for each man awaited the tourists – if Armstrong led them through the tour unbeaten. Only three games remained after Eastbourne; Armstrong, so close to the cash prize, chose nine of the side that had drawn with England at The Oval eleven days earlier.

W. P. Crozier fought against Cardus covering the match. He told him: 'It'll be all over in a day and nobody's interested.' Cardus stubbornly nagged away at him, insisting he'd experienced 'a premonition' that 'something' memorable would occur. More grumbling and haggling between them followed before permission was granted for what still appeared to Crozier, the most practical of men, to be an unfruitfully long and fairly expensive idiot's errand.

Had anyone but MacLaren summoned him – as a cricketer he 'lighted a fire in me never to be put out', said Cardus – he wouldn't have been so intransigent in his struggle with Crozier. Cardus, aged 14, had been sitting on a train when MacLaren got into the same compartment. He sat 'trembling', regarding him as a god who had 'come down for a while to walk the earth'.

So Cardus remembered finding himself at the Saffrons on the last Saturday of the month 'amongst the deck-chairs and the white tents', and 'under a sky of sapphire'. A crowd of 9,000, mostly holidaymakers, were there with him, filling the wooden benches that skirted the boundary. The press box, however, was empty apart from a gaggle of local reporters. No cricket correspondent from any national daily considered it worthwhile to leave London.

Described by Cardus as 'MacLaren's innocents', the England XI comprised five Cambridge University players, each part of a team the Australians had thumped into a pulp at Fenner's in June. There were the three Ashton brothers – Gilbert, Hubert and Claude – as well as Clement Gibson and Percy Chapman, the future captain of England. Their average age was 22. The old lags of the side, apart from MacLaren himself, were the South African all-rounder Aubrey Faulkner, then 39; MacLaren's former Lancashire chum Walter Brearley, 45; and the fast-medium bowler Michael Falcon, who, at 33, was almost a slip of a lad compared with the other seniors. The betting suggested Armstrong would polish off this motley lot faster than he could finish a bottle of his beloved Scotch.

The first hour was a calamity for MacLaren, who won the toss and batted. Cardus admitted: 'I felt like a fool to witness it; I soon knew I was going to become a weekend's laughing stock.'

On an ideal pitch for run-making, the England XI were bowled out for a pitiful 43 in 75 minutes and 121 balls. It was the lowest score scratched against the Australians all summer – and also the lowest ever made at Eastbourne. Some 'venerable cricketers', remarked Cardus, 'watched the game in tears'.

As though attempting to comfort himself, he composed an elegy for a MacLaren innings that was over in an eye-blink. 'His hair is more than grey now; it is white. He holds himself with the old proud ease, though, and as he walked to the wicket the crowd cheered him and perhaps spared a moment for a wistful thought upon the past . . . He used the off bail to mark the right place on the crease, bent down on his bat, raised himself for another glance around the field – the imperial haughtiness was in it.' After these elaborately careful preparations, MacLaren played 'absurdly late' at a very fast and straight delivery from McDonald that was pitched well up. He was clean-bowled first ball. 'MacLaren flashed his bat as a man disgusted – impatient, maybe, that age can so hinder an eager spirit,' said Cardus. No doubt the words were meant to be consoling, but MacLaren comes across as someone too decrepit to be facing a bowler of McDonald's fire. Only Chapman, eking out 16, reached double figures. McDonald and Armstrong claimed five wickets apiece. This was not quite the worst of it for the England XI. While 'stealing a short run', said Cardus, Brearley wrenched his knee, making him unfit to bowl.

With 70 from Warren Bardsley, the Australians barely broke sweat to make 174 all out, believing – as did everyone else – that exerting themselves unnecessarily was a pointless waste of energy. The total would have been mountain-high if, breezing along at 83 for one, complacency hadn't unaccountably set in. Falcon, taking six wickets, and Faulkner, taking four, preserved some dignity for themselves and also for MacLaren. The Australians dismissed it as a blip, expecting to be on their merry way before lunch on the second day was served. At the close, with MacLaren batting again, the England XI were already eight for one.

It had been a 'farcical' performance, said Cardus. 'The match was, of course, as good as finished.'

Cardus said he 'felt ashamed' to write his report – 'a long column about an anti-climax'. The *Manchester Guardian*'s headline was chastising. 'A Disappointing Failure' was how the newspaper described it.

When the match resumed on the Monday, apparently doornail-dead, Cardus had already checked out of his hotel and sent his bag to the station. He planned to catch the 'express' train to London shortly before one o'clock and head to Lord's, where Middlesex were battling Surrey and closing in on the Championship. Indeed, he almost didn't go back to the Saffrons at all, doing so purely 'for sentimental reasons'. He wished to see MacLaren 'as he faced, for the last time, an Australian fast bowler'.

What Cardus got was only another glimpse of him. MacLaren had pushed and prodded five runs before McDonald, the 'lovely panther', cut down his stumps again. The stoop in his shoulders was noticeable as he left the crease. Cardus began to walk slowly towards the exit, where he lingered only because there was an hour to kill before his train left. The England XI were 60 for four – still 71 behind. Faulkner and Hubert Ashton were together now, attempting nothing more ambitious than saving face – since saving the match seemed impossible. 'I gently strolled over the grass, under the trees and their brown early autumn leaves,' remembered Cardus.

Faulkner was rather a heart-throb, a kind of Valentino in flannels: jet-black hair, stocky build, wide shoulders and sharp-featured, his nose like a blade. He was also recently divorced, and so received the clamouring attention of cricket's 'groupies' (or at least what passed for them). He'd fought for the British Army in the Great War, winning both a DSO and the Order of the Nile. In 24 Tests for South Africa, he'd taken 82 wickets with leg-spin and googlies and scored over 1,700 runs, including 204 against the Australians in Melbourne on the 1910–11 tour. Armstrong hadn't only seen this close up; he'd taken the catch that had eventually dismissed him.

Hubert Ashton was thin and whippy, 'impressive in style and sound in method', according to *Wisden*. He'd taken a century off Australia in that Cambridge defeat at Fenner's. More impressively, aged 20, he'd been awarded the MC in the last months of the Great War, destroying an enemy strongpoint under 'heavy shell and machine gun-fire'. Master Hubert needed no motivation. The England selectors had chosen to ignore him all summer – despite his hundred, despite his promise, despite picking an inferior assortment of other players out of desperation.

Cardus watched this unlikely pair gradually stage a fluttering come-back, and in the placid, near-empty Saffrons he 'heard their quiet strokes making echoes in the deserted place'. Cardus explained that he 'retraced my steps a little' and sat on a bench facing the pavilion. This is where he stayed. 'I did not go to London that day. Or the next.' Instead he witnessed the Miracle of Eastbourne, completely vindicating at the very last his faith in MacLaren.

More than any other game, cricket consistently produces outrageous reversals in fortune, so pronounced and so sudden as to seem wildly implausible. It always has. It always will. The mood and the mould of the match is changed because a catch is either taken or grassed. Or because a cluster of wickets fall in a noisy clatter. Or because a rapid flurry of runs, scampered or hit to the boundary, tilts the momentum. We sense it as unmistakably as we feel a change of temperature in the air. MacLaren, a Napoleon-like figure on the field, had once told Cardus: 'In every match, there comes a moment when the tide turns one way or the other . . . every captain should be on the look-out for that moment.'

That moment was upon him now.

The bare statistics testify to the improbability of what Cardus saw. The partnership between the veteran and the novice put on 154. Ashton made 75 at almost a run per minute. Faulkner, at the crease for three hours and 31 minutes, struck 21 fours in his 153 – his 'last great innings', as Cardus described it. The England XI reached 326, setting Australia 196 to win. It didn't seem daunting; especially when that target at the beginning of the final day was whittled to 171, leaving the England XI to somehow take nine wickets.

With his fast-medium swing, Clem Gibson had got rid of Herbie Collins the evening before. He claimed another five wickets. Gibson had been one of *Wisden*'s Cricketers of the Year in 1918, chosen with four other public-school players because the Championship was suspended during the War. That achievement, great as it was despite the circumstances, paled beside this one. He finished with figures of six for 64. Cardus, getting carried away, likened him to S. F. Barnes in his capacity to bowl deliveries that pitched on leg and swung violently to the off.

Falcon and Faulkner each claimed two (Faulkner outwitted Armstrong, trapping him leg before with a ball that Cardus said was 'whizzing with spin'). There were two prize catches. The first belonged to Claude Ashton, who Cardus believed 'saw the ball as a swallow sees a fly'. The second was Hubert Ashton's, chasing down a top-edge skyer that MacLaren, standing beside him in the slips, gladly delegated by folding his arms, turning his back and saying: 'I think you may have that one.'

The Australians, who with five wickets in hand needed only 93, were bowled out for 167 – defeated ignominiously by 28 'in a scene of heartbeats and shouts', according to Cardus. A small earthquake had occurred. As Cardus wrote: 'Who on Saturday could have got the faintest glimpse of such an end to the match, even in the wildest flight of fancy? . . . Why, the miraculous is here, black magic, the very imps of mischief.'

It was MacLaren's triumph, which is the only story Cardus wanted to tell. He gave due acknowledgement to Gibson, the Ashtons and Faulkner. He also recorded the 'profoundly sombre expression' on Armstrong's face as the drama tightened around him. He celebrated the 'fictitious England XI' as a group. But MacLaren was the master, the captain who 'put fielders in the proper places', gave his team 'hope and courage' and used his limited stock of bowlers astutely. It put 'the crown on his greatness', Cardus told his readers.

For him, all the imperishable memories of this 'glorious' match were of MacLaren. 'One will see him, white-haired and beautifully calm, standing in the slips beckoning a man to a more judicious place in the field. One will see him plucking at his trousers' knees in the old way, hitching them up before he slightly bends into the classic slip position. One will see him moving across the pitch at the over's end, taking now and then one of his bowlers by the arm and giving him a word of encouragement and advice. And if these impressions should fade in a while, surely one will never forget his walk to the pavilion at the game's end, the crowd pressing round him and cheering – MacLaren with his sweater over his shoulders, his face almost lost in the folds of it, looking down on the grass as he moves for good from the cricket field, seemingly but half aware of the praise-giving about him, seemingly thinking of other times.'

The passage is classic Cardus, encapsulating the differences between his writing and that of his contemporaries at the beginning of the decade. In four long sentences he does everything at once. He concentrates on the minutiae, showing you not only how MacLaren looks – emphasising again his white hair – but also how he appears and acts between deliveries: the almost inconspicuous push or wave of his hand, the dropped word in the bowler's ear, the tug on his flannels, which you suspect was done out of habit rather than necessity. Cardus tells you more than he can possibly have known. His MacLaren is lost in thought, seeing in this success flashbacks of every other that had gone before for him. This is an audacious presumption, but Cardus conveys what he himself was thinking and also what he felt others would think naturally too. He wrings from the picture every drop of emotion he can; and in doing so makes you really *see* it – even if you weren't there, had never been to the Saffrons and wouldn't recognise a photograph of MacLaren when one was shoved directly into your face.

Often we either loyally ignore the faults of our heroes or make excuses for them. We forgive or overlook their trespasses, indiscretions and mistakes because we want nothing to blemish our lofty ideal of them.

The perception you convey of someone also always depends on the angle from which you view them. Neville Cardus filtered A. C. MacLaren through those devoted and impressionably boyish eyes and his boyish acts of touching lamp posts and avoiding pavement cracks. MacLaren was his pin-up. He was the batsman, the suave amateur so superiorly sure of himself, who'd scored a century on his Championship debut, made a double hundred and a Test ton on his first tour to Australia, put together a first-class-record innings of 424 against Somerset at Taunton and also replaced W. G. Grace as England's captain. Even as 'The Great Man' aged and declined, the past still reflected off him and so something of his younger self remained imperishable in Cardus's mind. This explains the halo he bestowed upon him and then kept burnished. The rosy way Cardus saw MacLaren wasn't necessarily how others saw him. On the field, despite his talents, he was considered insensitive, bullying, grossly rude, unintelligent and also occasionally intransigent to a bloody ridiculous degree. His 'pep talks' were frequently exercises in spreading apathy or – much more damagingly – howling dismay. Motivation was not his métier. Like a lot of naturally gifted sportsmen, MacLaren couldn't work out why someone simply couldn't perform to his level. 'Gracious me! Don't tell me you're playing!' was typically his crushing 'hello' to those he scarcely rated. When, in 1902, England's selectors egregiously dropped the triumvirate of C. B. Fry, S. F. Barnes and Gilbert Jessop for the fourth Test against Australia, MacLaren bustled into the dressing room and declared aloud and in front of their replacements: 'My God. Look what they've sent me.' Off the field, he lurched from one inglorious business venture to another: hotelier (a little in the Basil Fawlty mould, apparently); stud farmer (knowing little about horses except how to bet on one); car salesman (entirely lacking the emollience critical to clinching a sale); magazine proprietor (without a bent for journalism); and manufacturer and supplier of sporting goods. He tried unsuccessfully to popularise inflatable pads. A keen customer was Sir Julien Cahn, who got one of his butlers to pump up his pair for him and always claimed that any leg-bye ballooning extravagantly off them had taken a thin edge.

The truth is that MacLaren wasn't good with people, his judgements of them often colossally wrong-headed. He had a bedside manner based on the barked order, a fact traceable as far back as his schooldays at Harrow. His fag was a 'quite useless' and 'snotty little bugger' unsuited to the sporting life, which in MacLaren's opinion made him the legitimate butt of ridicule and ritual cruelty. The fag's name was Winston Churchill.

Only three weeks after Eastbourne, perhaps still celebrating, MacLaren tried to board a moving bus in London. He was dragged seventy yards, tearing his left shoulder muscles and ripping the skin off his knees, which became badly swollen.

His reputation nevertheless continued to rise to a high tide again on the basis of outwitting Armstrong, the wilderness years and his failures before it ignored. Lancashire installed him as coach on an annual salary of £550.

The big and lasting beneficiary from Eastbourne was still Cardus. As he made clear: 'At this incredible match, at this consummation of a great cricketer's life, the *Manchester Guardian* was the only notable newspaper represented.' During that long weekend by the sea, he eclipsed his rivals, making them look like war correspondents who had gone to the wrong battle. Even *The Times* was so sluggish in politely hailing 'Mr MacLaren's Triumph' that it seemed the news had been relayed to them by a particularly ponderous pony and trap.

Virginia Woolf thought that 'nothing has really happened until it has been recorded'. In recording England XI versus Australia Cardus did MacLaren stellar service. He gifted him – and his unlikely comeback – to posterity. Without his first-hand account, MacLaren and the game would be a shadow in history, the drama and meaning of both extrapolated from the scorecard or imagined from fragments published in provincial newspapers. Cardus made them substantial. The grateful MacLaren would return the favour within a year.

Cardus, listening to the advice of his colleagues, published an anthology of his work on the back of the Eastbourne result. 'Apparently a writer is obliged to publish a book before he can expect to be taken seriously by the bulk of the people,' he said.

Grant Richards was one of those publishers who expunged the word 'afternoon' from the vocabulary. His days were divided into morning, lunch and late evening. He was a bit of a show-off, dressing flamboyantly. He wore a monocle and was nearly always seen with a huge handkerchief billowing from the top pocket of his jacket. Richards was once depicted as a combination of Oscar Wilde and Beau Brummell, resplendent in a velvet frock coat and a waistcoat with large, curved lapels. In the 1920s, when publishing was considered a gentleman's game and contracts were convivially signed in Mayfair clubs after the brandy and cigars, Richards still seemed to regret not having been around to publish Byron or Keats. He did, however, publish George Bernard Shaw and G. K. Chesterton, and would have brought out *Dubliners* too – if he and James Joyce hadn't squabbled over editorial cuts to navigate around the obscenity laws. One of his most notable books was A. E. Housman's *A Shropshire Lad*. Richards had one failing. He and money were parted too frequently and too easily, sometimes bankrupting him. *The Times*, twisting the knife into him, spoke of his 'recurrent lack of scruple', a tendency evenly weighted beside qualities of 'conciliation and cajolery' and a 'very real instinct for friendship'.

Whatever anyone thought of him, Richards never lost his eye for an opportunity. Cardus sent him a scruffy package of news cuttings. Enclosed was his mannered enquiry about whether he would like to

Grant Richards, a publishing dandy who knew and worked alongside some of the literary lions of London.

publish them. Cardus had gathered together match reports, profiles and some 'impressions'. He chose Richards because of his 'manifest love of books as things of the spirit and not commodities of trade'.

Richards was initially sceptical. 'It was one of those offers that do not immediately attract,' he said. The reluctant suitor was soon won over. 'I knew that cricket had some devotees . . . and, anyhow, whatever came out of the *Guardian* stable was worth backing on general principles,' he explained. So, while knowing 'nothing' about cricket, Richards agreed to publish *A Cricketer's Book*, a 256-page hymn to the game.

MacLaren wrote the introduction, which could not have been more generous. 'When one reads him in the armchair one is transported to the ground and sees the game again in actual progress,' he said of Cardus. Having begun with MacLaren, *A Cricketer's Book* appropriately ends with him too. He walks from the Saffrons after vanquishing Warwick Armstrong.

The *Manchester Guardian* review described Cardus as 'an idealist, an artist', who provided 'unique value' and had produced 'one of the few first rate books about sport'. The competition thought so too. The *Daily Telegraph* called it 'a landmark in sporting literature'. The *Sunday Express* thought it was 'a new classic . . . the kind of book we have been waiting for all our lives'. *The Bookman*, more used to devoting space to Bloomsbury, gave him a reference that glowed like a lamp: 'It has been freely rumoured that since Mr Neville Cardus began to travel with the Lancashire County cricket eleven as "Cricketer" for the *Manchester Guardian*, that newspaper has doubled its circulation. For the truth of this we cannot vouch; but we can at least declare that it deserves to.' One correspondent remembered that 'many times' he covered matches in which Cardus's reports elsewhere 'had been studied by every journalist' in the press box.

Cardus could swank around the editorial floor. Not long before, he had considered himself as a ' down-and-out . . . one of the rabble', who was full of 'half-baked aspirations'. His was a talent no one had wanted. Now, in barely three summers, he'd gone from nobody to somebody. The lowly utility reporter and gofer, whom his newspaper had slaved almost into dust, had become one of the country's foremost cricket correspondents. He had status. He had the admiration of his peers. He had become one of C. P. Scott's favoured sons.

His overnight success had been 20 years in the making, but the path of his flight was a wonder to behold.

Neville Cardus's life had changed in another regard. He had found himself a wife. Or, more to the point, she had found him.

A brief paragraph announced the news in the *Manchester Guardian House Journal*.

It gave an account of 'a gathering in the library' during which C. E. Montague made a presentation to 'N. C.' to commemorate his wedding to Edith King. The wedding, it said, 'took place a few days later'. Montague congratulated Cardus on the quality of his writing rather than the imminent nuptials. He had, said Montague, 'already embroidered his cricket articles with musical parallels, and nobody would be surprised if his skill did not contrive to adorn musical criticism with parallels from cricket.' There was a facetious final line, reporting that 'N. C.' replied to the compliment 'in a sensationally adequate speech'. Mr Cardus and Miss Edith Honorine Watten King became man and wife in June 1921 – less than two months before Cardus arrived in Eastbourne.

The journalist and playwright Keith Waterhouse, reflecting on the Manchester that Cardus knew, described 'young men' playing 'chess . . . in semi-basement cafés'; arguing 'philosophy under electric lamps on the steps of the Theological Institute'; attending 'mock Parliaments and Baptist Chapels'; escorting would-be brides 'up the clattering steps of concert halls and galleries'; and wooing the eligible ' in sooty parks on Sundays'. Waterhouse forgot to mention the Lyons' Corner House, one of a chain of tea and coffee palaces that were the Starbucks or Costas of their day. Waitresses, called Nippies, wore black uniforms and white caps and aprons. There were linen tablecloths, heavy and well-polished cutlery and thin china crockery. You could go into a

Lyons' anywhere and convince yourself you were being pampered. Cardus whiled away hours in these establishments either reading or talking to friends, mostly about the arts.

He met Edith in one of them. She used to claim she had come across him 'selling nails' in the street, the line actually the beginning of a racy music-hall joke.

Edith taught art at a girls' school and came from a family of school-masters. She was involved in the Unnamed Society, a group that staged avant-garde plays. Also fond of contemporary painting, she saw herself as both a bohemian, dressing brightly and decoratively, and a placard-carrying foot-soldier for Mrs Pankhurst, unafraid to state the case for suffrage on street corners.

Cardus once told John Arlott that he and Edith had first drifted into one another's orbit before the Great War. The two of them had mutual friends. Cardus couldn't remember exactly how the first conversation began. That was because Edith did to him what he'd later do to so many others: she talked him to near-death. There was nothing la-di-da about her. Her strong voice was several octaves lower than Cardus's and boomed out strong opinions in a distinctly Lancashire accent. She addressed loudly even those who were only a few feet away. It was as though she was speaking at a public meeting.

Edith was a manly-looking woman too. Cardus would once – and unforgivably – call her 'one of the most ugly . . . you ever saw'. Her face was a small oval. Her dark hair was tied back, but the fringe hung almost to her eyebrows. Her lips were thickish and she wore specta-cles, the lenses very thick. The gusto of her personality compensated for her plain appearance. She was brassy and boldly no-nonsense – exactly as Cardus's aunt Beatrice had been during his boyhood. Cardus was no matinee idol in the making. He revelled in telling a story against himself. A stranger offered to buy him a drink, which Cardus accepted. As the two raised their glasses, the man said: 'I've been

Edith Cardus, who was consumed by theatre and the arts and pushed her then fiancé towards the Manchester Guardian.

looking for years for an uglier man than me, and you win easily.' Someone meeting Cardus for the first time anticipated 'an imposing person' but found him plain and undistinguished – 'quite featureless', he said.

As well as sharing his passion for the arts, Edith encouraged his writing, often going over it before publication. 'If I put something in that wasn't right, she'd say: "Take it out. That's not you,"' said Cardus. She recommended the books of the 19th-century aesthete Walter Pater, author of *Studies in the History of the Renaissance* and *Imaginary*

*Though living apart during most of their relationship, Cardus
and Edith never lost their love for one another.*

Portraits, and also the plays of George Bernard Shaw. This was not a
traditional hearts-and-flowers romance, but the two of them slipped
into courtship and were quickly united in a specific common cause –
the advancement of his career. 'Write to the *Manchester Guardian*,' had
been one of her directives.

Cardus once said that he 'didn't know' why Edith had married him,
implying melodramatically that pity was the motivating factor. 'She
saw I was alone and bereft in the world.' He acknowledged, but didn't

dwell on, another factor. He wed Edith because 'I always said if I married anyone it would be her,' making it sound as though he was returning a favour.

The relationship was based on care, companionship and mutual understanding. It was also timely for both of them. For when the 'I dos' were finally said at Chorlton Registry Office, Edith was nudging 40 and Cardus was past 30. Edith was six years older than him, a fact she lied about – she is 33 on the marriage certificate, supposedly only two years his senior – and also afterwards on other documents. In a period when unwed women were considered to be old maids in their late 20s, and men who couldn't find a bride were thought of as ineligible bachelors, Edith and Cardus were 'on the shelf'.

You can build a straightforwardly hypothetical construction to explain the marriage, which was convenient for both of them. For Edith, because she was either asexual or a lesbian but was under social pressure to conform. For Cardus, because he was incapable of looking after himself, easily worn down and baffled by some of the chores of life such as paying bills and cashing cheques. The unconventionality of the marriage staggered those who didn't know them and even some of those who did. Each lived largely separate and independent lives while nominally being under the same roof. In no photograph does he ever wear a wedding ring. Edith remained in their flat – not far from C. P. Scott's home – and busied herself with drama and art.

She had none of the domestic skills that a wife was then expected to possess in abundance and execute without qualm or complaint. She had no intention of acquiring them either. She didn't cook. She didn't sew on buttons or darn socks. Once, Cardus arrived home late one evening to discover the pantry was bare; there wasn't even a loaf of bread in it. Edith uncharacteristically demanded to know where he had been at such an hour. That question had the same effect as flicking a lighted match on to a bale of straw. It flared into what Cardus described as 'the only quarrel' he ever had with his wife. 'When a woman asks me where I've been, that is the end,' he said bumptiously, marching out into the night. Cardus returned less than an hour later. He'd worked himself into a sweating panic, picturing a remorseful, woeful Edith with her head stuck in the gas oven. That is a remarkable conclusion to reach after such a minor kerfuffle in which only mild insults were traded and no crockery was thrown. What it does, though, is demonstrate the bond between them, however strange it seemed to outsiders, and also the dependency each felt on the other.

Whether or not the Carduses kissed in making up afterwards is a matter of conjecture.

Of his younger years Cardus once said that 'you didn't talk about sex any more than you talked about breathing'. He claimed to have 'no awareness' and 'no curiosity' about it either, insisting he fell in love 'only' with heroines of literature: Thackeray's seductive Beatrix Esmond, Fielding's Sophia Western, Hardy's Tess and Bathsheba Everdene. After them, he added, 'I went out into the street and I couldn't get interested in any of those ordinary-looking, pale-faced, Lancashire girls.' As an old man he'd insist that 'the history of my sex life' could be 'comprehensively told on a postcard'. He did, however, have dalliances; and Edith was stoically tolerant of them.

Cardus called her 'a very great woman' and said she 'understood' him. But, pressed about his marriage, he made one thing clear. It was a strictly platonic relationship. She was a 'wonderful sister' and 'nothing else', he said. Further lines clarified the arrangement: 'My wife and I remained great companions ... but we never shared sexual communication.'

Edith let him roam when and wherever he wanted and with whomever he chose, knowing full well that he'd always return to her. She had only one fault. She was wantonly extravagant with money, which melted in her hand. Edith bought whatever she liked and travelled first class. These were privileges to which she felt herself entitled as the spouse of one of the *Manchester Guardian*'s writerly lights. So whenever he was asked 'How's your wife?' Cardus replied with a single word.

'Expensive.'

4

WEARING A LOUNGE SUIT AT A BLACK-TIE BALL

NEVILLE CARDUS THOUGHT 'no game' lent itself more to the 'art' of writing than cricket, which is why his reports of it read like essays. Cricket, he said, moved so slowly that it not only allowed 'moments for reflection' but also enabled him to isolate 'performance and character for hours at a stretch'. Cardus had a manifesto for covering matches. He set out to 'unfold the game as a living activity set against the English summer' and reveal 'the mood and humours' of every player 'stroke-by-stroke' and 'over-by-over'.

Bluntly, but also rather arrogantly, C. P. Scott said that the *Manchester Guardian* readership must 'educate themselves up' to the level of the newspaper's critics and correspondents. Cardus took Scott at his word.

Allowed an unprecedented amount of space to focus on whatever took his fancy on the field or off it, Cardus admitted he wrote 'above the heads of the average reader' of cricket and also 'above the head of the game itself'. Whether everyone understood the classical, literary or musical allusions he dropped into his copy never bothered him. Those who didn't could go to the library and do some research.

Still afraid of disappointing his taskmaster Scott, who read everything fastidiously, Cardus took endless pains over his pieces, nearly always producing something which looked effortless – a sentence that fell softly on the ear or a phrase that startled the mind awake. As if he were a painter, Cardus described his early years in cricket as his 'yellow period'. The analogy with art is apt.

The painter J. M. W. Turner once swept into the Royal Academy to add a single daub of vermilion to his seascape *Helvoetsluys*. The annual exhibition was about to open and he walked in and out of it again in silence. He stayed barely a minute, but the small mark he left behind – placing a buoy in the middle of smoke-grey water – lit up the painting and made the competition, especially the John Constable canvas hanging beside it, look insipid in comparison. 'He has been here and fired a gun,' wailed Constable, enviously. Cardus had this sort of impact instantly on the sports columns of the *Manchester Guardian*, which had previously been so dour, and then on the pages of its competitors as well. He fired his own gun, and the game flared to life in newspapers as it hadn't done before.

Since no one else was doing it, Cardus looked for 'atmosphere and scene', which to him meant 'the shape of clouds . . . the shade on the trees . . . the sound of a church bell'. He treated the game as 'a spectacle as much as a contest' and attached himself shrewdly to those he identified as 'true characters' and 'artist cricketers', defining them as 'men who can get us interested in themselves'. He strove to capture the 'quiddity' and the 'essence' of them, creating his own National Portrait Gallery in pen and ink. His approach was straightforward. 'To go to a cricket match for nothing but cricket is as though a man were to go into an inn for nothing but drink,' he argued.

He detected minor things, which before had gone either unnoticed or simply unused, and then made something major out of them; something, moreover, that gave another dimension to a player, bringing him a few steps closer to the reader. He saw spectators abandon their drinks, left to stand half-supped on the Tavern bar at Lord's, to greet the arrival of Patsy Hendren, who always ran his first single 'hugging his bat in his two arms as though afraid to let it go from his possession'. He watched Johnny Douglas 'muttering to himself' as he walked back to his bowling mark – 'all the time rubbing the ball into the flesh

Hat at a jaunty angle, notebook tucked beneath his arm, Neville Cardus is already prosperous-looking and debonair.

of his left forearm passionately'. He studied the spinner Bill O'Reilly, who swayed to the crease as if 'running up the slant of the deck of a ship tossing in a heavy swell'. He described Percy Fender – 'the sun shines on his high forehead and gleams on his spectacles' – as no one else ever had, and also as though every gesture was microscopically examined. 'The sleeve of his shirt drops over his right hand after every ball he bowls,' wrote Cardus. 'As he walks back to his starting place he turns it up again, but probably without knowing that he does so, for the action has become habitual through long custom.' He celebrated the nimble prowess of wicketkeeper Bert Oldfield too. Every unfussy stumping was completed like 'an amputation done under an anaesthetic', the batsman mercifully unaware of it until the procedure was over. Oldfield removed the bails with courtesy – 'the ball in one hand, an apology in the other'.

Cardus had an acute ear for appeals. At Lancashire, the timbre of George Duckworth's was an amalgam of 'a denunciation of a batsman's delinquency, an order, even a command to the umpire'. Lol Cook's was full of the conspiracies against him, shouted in a high-pitched voice with 'desperation', as if 'he knew in advance that, once again, injustice was to be his portion'. At Surrey, Herbert Strudwick was diffidently courteous, 'as though saying . . . "So sorry. Pains me as much as you."' In particular, Cardus waited expectantly for the actorly routine Dick Tyldesley performed at Old Trafford. He was always pouring out a sob story designed to con an umpire. When Tyldesley first hit the pads, but was aware that any overture would be a waste of breath, he'd shake his head and say: 'Noa. Ah'm not askin' for that. It'd 'ave missed off stoomp.' When he did so for a second time, he'd vary the patter. 'Noa, not exactly. It'd 'ave gone over the top of leg bail.' This was merely preliminary throat-clearing for the third occasion, which brought a demand of such sure-fire conviction that denying it would seem tantamount to some gross miscarriage. 'Ow *is* it. Ow *is* it?' he'd yell. 'Usually he got the decision he wanted – the decision he had *conditioned*,' said Cardus, seeing one umpire after another fall for Tyldesley's bluff and likening each of them to 'Pavlov's dog' responding to the bell.

Umpires were prominent in a Cardus drama, frequent foils for highlighting the odd men out around them. Frank Chester, who had lost his right arm below the elbow in 1917 after sustaining a shrapnel wound in Greece, 'would give an lbw decision with finger pointing vehemently down the pitch, as though detecting in the batsman some really criminal practice'. Cardus suspected Chester had a judge's 'black cap' hidden away in his white coat pocket – 'just in case' he could actually send someone to the scaffold.

Cardus said he would point out, but never dwell too laboriously on, 'technical issues'. He presumed the knowledgeable and sophisticated reader didn't want a hectoring lecture from him. The role of the critic was to '*compensate* [his italics] all those who couldn't attend', rather than educate them officiously like 'a teacher'. That is a bit of a fallacy. Critiques were supporting beams in the structure of a lot of his work. You just don't necessarily notice them when you're lost in the loveliness of a descriptive passage.

In his youth, Cardus had watched Prince Ranjitsinhji – scorer of almost 25,000 career runs – as he batted 'with an ease which staggered the imagination'. No one for him, however, had conveyed adequately

K. S. Ranjitsinhji, who 'seemed to toss runs over the field like largesse in silk purses'.

in print his majestic flicks, sweeps and also his languorously luminous driving. When Ranjitsinhji got out, it annoyed Cardus to the very quick to read only that a 'good ball' had claimed him. What made it 'good' went unexplained. 'You will search the old cricket reports in vain for certain technical clues,' he said. He drew on his experiences as assistant professional at Shrewsbury School to provide them at last.

Neville Cardus was rather sniffy about some of the 'retired cricketers' who wrote for newspapers 'apparently ... without any training or experience at all'. He still revelled in describing himself as a one-time 'professional cricketer'. It was true up to a point – though the point in question was stretched more than a little.

When Cardus arrived inauspiciously at Shrewsbury School, his belongings tucked into a tattered tin box bound with rope, he discovered 'A Heaven down here below'. Mucky, back-to-back Manchester, noisy with rattling trams, was swapped for quiet country lanes, flower beds, clipped lawns, the peal of the chapel bell and the fat bend of the River Severn beside the Wrekin. The school's library was open to Cardus whenever he needed it. He'd retreat into the shade of an elm or a cottonwood to read the books he borrowed, educating himself with translations of Homer or Euripides, Euclid or Plato.

At this public school, he received a university education in cricket too. The senior pro, Walter Attewell, was replaced at the end of Cardus's first year. Ted Wainwright took over. Attewell had experience but no pedigree; he had played only one match for Nottinghamshire, his performance a calamity. He got a pair and didn't claim a wicket. Wainwright, a Yorkshireman, had prospered as an all-rounder under Lord Hawke at Headingley, taking over 1,000 wickets and scoring more than 12,000 runs, including a top score of 228. *Wisden* made him one of its Cricketers of the Year in 1894. Three years later he went

*The lush splendour of Shrewsbury School, where Neville
Cardus received a university-like education in cricket.*

on the MCC tour of Australia at a time when sailing there was
contemplated with awe, the Victorian equivalent of blasting off to the
moon. He was a stern-looking man in a blue-serge suit. He had a high
forehead, his hair swept back to reveal a widow's peak. His moustache
was like a scraggly English hedgerow. His eyes were as small as
marbles. Attewell had snored like the sonorous low notes of a tuba.
Wainwright got drunk every night, considering anyone who didn't to
be a temperance sissy. The relationship began shakily.

''Ave a drink wi' me,' said Wainwright. Cardus, abstemious then,
told him he drank 'only ginger ale'. Wainwright replied mockingly:
'Christ, tha'rt a reight bloody cricketer.' When sober, however, he
would talk about cricket and cricketers. So a top pro passed on daily
to the rawest of amateurs the subtle tricks and some of the tradecraft
seldom found in books. The two of them were soon playing together

under pseudonyms in a village match, picking up some extra pocket money, before the crude ruse was uncovered.

Cardus learnt how to recognise a good cricketer and also how to empathise with him, because of his own misfortune.

The first ball he ever bowled at Shrewsbury – 'panic abruptly seized me,' he admitted – slipped from his sweaty grip and bulged into the sides of the net. The second ballooned out of his hand and landed over the top of another net entirely. 'I heard a guffaw that filled me with shame,' he said. Worse followed. When facing the school's first XI, Cardus bowled off-breaks and was flogged repeatedly to the boundary, a public humiliation. He seriously 'contemplated flight', repacking his tin box for a moonlight flit. As a last resort Cardus decided to bowl fast, measuring out a long run before he 'tore along the earth' and 'hurled myself at the wicket'. His motivation was 'a single dread vision': an ignominious return to 'the endless squalor of Manchester'. The delivery, which was a full toss, exploded against the bails. In half an hour of assorted full tosses, long-hops, wides and no-balls, Cardus managed to take a further five wickets for 'about a dozen runs'. All the weariness of that effort fell upon him. He was 'broken-winded', taking his sweater and hobbling from the field, his shoulders so sore and stiff that the next day he was forced to find a doctor, who massaged them loose again.

A colleague on the *Manchester Guardian*, the soon-to-be novelist Howard Spring, later reported that Cardus's abilities with the ball did not improve with age. In one match, Spring picked out – 'with the tail of my eye' – a team-mate in distress on the boundary. He saw the player 'turn, vomit swiftly and then, with graceful stoicism, face the game again'. He hurried him into the pavilion and poured a medicinal brandy. 'Don't worry,' the player told Spring. 'I'm all right now. It was Cardus's bowling.'

Cardus's own misfortunes always reminded this most unlikely of 'pros' that the game was damned difficult. He made allowances for it in his criticisms. More significantly, Cardus leant on the accumulated knowledge Wainwright had shared with him to describe the anatomy of a player's performance. With his typical flourish, Cardus wrote that the Australian Clarrie Grimmett 'walks about the field on dainty feet which step as though with the soft fastidiousness of a cat treading a wet pavement'. But he could dissect the spinner's threat too, the passage revealing the minute observation which had taken place to make it. 'Grimmett is less a googly than a leg-break bowler. He uses the "wrong 'un" sparsely; he is content to thrive on the ball which breaks away and leaves the bat; that is the best of all balls. A straight ball, wickedly masked, is Grimmett's foil to the leg-break. He makes a virtue of a low arm; his flight keeps so close to the earth that only a batsman quick of foot can jump to the pitch of it.'

Even more perceptive is his analysis of Jack Hobbs, whom he watched with a gimlet eye in the nets, making 'stroke after stroke' with a 'beautiful white bat', the blade of which he examined afterwards as though 'reluctant to do it hurt'. Every one of those strokes produced 'a clean, solid noise, with no overtones'. Hobbs, said Cardus, was 'not in serious vein – merely improvising like the pianist who lets his fingers move irresponsibly and experimentally over the keyboard'. The science of his batting came next. 'From behind the net the technique of Hobbs is, so to speak, seen under a magnifying lens. Or it is as though one were looking at a painting with one's eyes almost glued to the canvas. You can see that now more of energy, even of roughness, goes into Hobbs's cricket than is apparent when watching him from a distance. He grips his bat in the middle of the handle as he waits for the ball, but frequently when he plays back the right hand drops almost to the bottom of the handle. This denotes strong right forearm leverage in Hobbs's defensive strokes. Immediately the bowler begins his run Hobbs seems to have some instinct of what manner of ball is on the way; rarely does he move his feet to an incorrect position. His footwork is so quick that even from behind the nets it is not always possible to follow its movement in detail.'

Cardus similarly broke down Learie Constantine's powerful approach. Constantine made 'the largest ground look small', he said, before explaining why. 'His strokes are always made late. He does not lift up his bat high behind him as the ball is coming ... Constantine waits until the ball is on him; then, swift as lightning and swifter, he cracks his bat like a whip ... He can cut from the middle stump, clean down to third-man, with a stab that momentarily takes away the eyesight of the slips. He will lie back on his right foot and crash the ball past mid-on – a good length ball too ...' Cardus was spellbound by one Constantine stroke. It was a six struck to leg – 'so fine that you were ready to vow that it went over the wicketkeeper's head'. He called it 'a piece of magic to everyone but the magician himself'.

Cardus claimed: 'If I ever went to a cricket match and wrote a dull article, it was not my fault; it was the batsmen or the bowlers who caused the dullness. Out of nothing, nothing can come.'

He could nonetheless construct a memorable account of an unmemorable day's play. Cardus began a report of a Canterbury Festival match like this: 'As soon as the cricketers came in to lunch I walked to the memorial which stands on a green bank and pays tribute to Colin Blythe, loveliest of all slow left-arm bowlers, who was killed in the 1914–18 war. As I stood in the August sunshine, with nobody near me, but all around, not far away, the white tents and happy animation of the Festival, time slipped back and Blythe was bowling for Kent again in Canterbury Week, spinning the ball and curving it through the air to his heart's content on an afternoon as sunny and radiant with English life as this. And at this very moment, as I stood there, a military band played a simple melody of Handel. Write me down as a maudlin ass, but the truth is that for a moment my eyes were misty. Then the band struck up a merry tune, and the brilliant day's activity was resumed.'

Memorials to Colin Blythe and Fuller Pilch at Canterbury.

He looked at the Essex–Lancashire match at Leyton the way Ruskin would have looked at a pastoral painting. 'The willows round the field, the white tents, the river with curved wooden bridges over it near the pavilion, the country folk in the crowd – all these things had to do with the game. For cricket is sensitive to habitation.' He even described his lunch: 'There was veal and ham pie, with ginger-beer to wash it down, and an old lady with a kindly face asking you with a curtsy if you wanted any more.'

Of a staid game at Leicestershire, an icicled wind blasting across the ground for umpteen hours, he wrote: 'The players were pretty immovable in sweaters. The real heroes were two spectators, who sat near one of the sight-screens all day, from noon to evening, exposed but never once leaving their seats. But perhaps they were only dead . . .'

And there was his valediction to a season in Kent. It was late August and the outfield 'lay silent in the evening sunshine'. He wrote: 'I stayed for a while in the failing light and saw birds run over the grass as the mists began to spread. That day we had watched Woolley in all his glory, batting his way through a hundred felicitous runs . . . It was all over and gone now, as I stood on the little field alone in the glow of the declining day. "The passing of summer," I thought.'

With modesty, Cardus reacted to questions about where his talent came from as though reluctant to admit he possessed any. What he never hid was the identity of the writer who had turned him into a writer too.

While taking baby steps in cricket journalism, Neville Cardus always went to Lord's feeling like a gatecrasher wearing a lounge suit at a black-tie ball.

He found himself treated as an outcast there. At the Eton–Harrow match, he encountered heavily perfumed ladies promenading in richly coloured gowns, which reminded him of 'a transcendental seed merchant's catalogue'. An 'overpowering dowager' bore down, demanding a scorecard from him. 'Quite naturally she took me for some hireling of the back stairs.' Cardus curled his lip at men in 'preposterous' collars, waistcoats, 'toppers' and spats, and boys with monocles. 'Next year,' he wrote, with absolutely no intention of return-ing, 'I really must take the precaution of wearing a tall hat to disguise my plebeian origins.' He saw it as *Debrett's* in visible motion.

Cardus was already fairly well known when he wrote that piece, which makes you appreciate how unsure of himself he must have been at Lord's – and also of how socially alienated and inadequate any relative newcomer of his status must have felt. He didn't try to pretend that his hosts had been hospitable. Or that there had been an attempt, even obviously specious, to put on a show of being pleased to see him. He had even been afraid of venturing into the press box.

'Unless one happens to be definitely of Lord's, and a member of the mighty MCC, one is outside the pale here,' he complained. 'You are inexorably kept at a distance. The place is a mass of signboards, teaching you your manners and position in life . . . A man from the unfashionable north, carrying with him a suggestion of real industry, feels that Lord's is all the time eyeing him curiously from a safe point of vantage . . . It is hard to imagine there is any place in the world where class distinctions are so firmly stressed.'

The unfriendliness of it 'forcibly' stirred one memory in him. He compared Lord's to Chesney Wold in *Bleak House*, a gloomy Gothic horror cold and unwelcoming.

Finding Charles Dickens in the library had sent him 'crazy' as a boy, he said. Dickens's novels were borrowed and read so often under street lamps and by candlelight that the pages almost dropped out. Cardus could quote verbatim pieces of description and dialogue. Whomever he saw or met was often likened to one of the 'life-size' characters he found in those books – from Nicholas Nickleby to Mr Pecksniff, and from Mrs Bumble to Miss Larkins.

When Cardus looked in the mirror, he saw David Copperfield staring back at him. Copperfield's 'Personal History', which is Dickens's in the flimsiest of disguises, seemed to Cardus to have been written specifically for him. 'The ordinary universe became unreal, hardly there,' he claimed after reading it. 'Copperfield so often behaved and thought as I behaved and thought that I frequently lost my own sense

The Grace Gates, Lord's.

of identity in him.' He instantly felt a bond with Dickens and his struggle out of poverty and on to literary achievement. 'We were both born in the same stable,' he said. Had Dickens still been alive, Cardus would have walked to Gad's Hill to speak to him. 'Discovering Dickens is one of the few really important events that occur in mortal life, like first love,' he explained. Cardus would read Dickens on a tram, so absorbed in a plot that his stop and half a dozen others afterwards would zoom by. He 'did not care'. He was occupied in 'a world more alive and dimensional than this world'. Dickens reduced real life to something 'shadowy' and 'unreal' and 'tedious', said Cardus. He taught him that '*all* objects and places, from fanlights to riverside docks, are likely to strike the imagination.' He made him want to write.

No one can possibly understand Cardus's approach to cricket writing without also understanding his absorption in Dickens. He labelled him 'the most real of story-tellers, almost a teller of fairy tales'. Cardus even indulged in this extreme view: anyone who didn't like Dickens 'should be avoided as soon as detected'.

From Dickens he learnt prolificacy. He learnt how to exploit plot and create and develop characters. He learnt that no writer – especially a cricket writer – should take himself 'too seriously'. He learnt the importance of lacing his reports with humour. 'Without it there is nothing,' said Cardus.

Dickens wrote episodically, the chapters of his novels peeled off the flat-bed printer and distributed in instalments. Cardus treated his journalism that way too. He saw his cricket reports as a daily drama, a soon-to-be-continued series in which the cricketers had their setbacks and their lows, their high achievements and their place on the honours board. Each fitted into the beginning and middle and finale of the season, the sweep of summer like one long story, which he called 'the game's great seasonal comedy'.

Cardus said that he could 'scarcely believe that all those juicy characters I came to know on cricket fields have actually existed'. To him they were 'all quite indistinguishable' from the fictional figures of Dickens.

References to his works, both explicit and implicit, appear throughout Cardus's writing. There is the bowler who pretends, like Mrs Gamp in *Martin Chuzzlewit*, 'not to deceive you'. There is the disconsolate fielder at third man, who on a freezing morning 'blew on his fingers and swung his arms' like 'the coachman' in the same novel.

Cardus borrows the word 'spificate' from Dickens, appropriating it to describe a destructive, wild innings. There is the comparison of the MCC with the windbags and prevaricators of the Circumlocution Office in *Little Dorrit*. Dickens even accompanied him on his first assignment to Old Trafford for the *Manchester Guardian*. In a lovely foretaste of the Cardus to come, George Hirst was likened to a character from *The Pickwick Papers*. Cardus, alighting on the sort of detail inconsequential only at first glance, noticed that Hirst, approaching 47, had shaved off his bushy moustache. A smidgen of vanity was one explanation for it. A declaration of intent was another. 'Is it that he is really only just about "to begin",' wrote Cardus, 'and has given us notice by assuming this youthful air, a sort of taking off his coat, like Mr Snodgrass, as a charitable warning of the fact?'

Cardus claimed he knew so 'little' about grammar that he 'wouldn't be able to pass an elementary school test' in it. 'I could not guarantee to detect an adverb, and what the gerundial infinitive is – I haven't the faintest idea . . . I know what a noun is, mind you,' he said. He nevertheless followed what he called his 'commandments' of composition. These owed much to Dickens too.

Dickens used a quill pen. Cardus used a fountain pen or pencil. He gripped a pen so hard that the skin of his right index finger and second finger were hard and smooth and occasionally sore, as though he'd bowled fifty overs of spin with them. He pressed on regardless because he disliked what Dickens had no opportunity to use, which was the typewriter. 'The noise of the keys,' he once moaned, 'is a shocking cacophony.' He tried to master the machine, forever failing. He could only peck slowly at it with each index finger. 'I could seldom find the letters readily . . . I was prepared to swear it was the typewriter that did not possess a letter P or, on another occasion, a letter Z.' Of writing itself, he added: 'Sometimes the *right* word comes and sometimes it doesn't . . . when it does come I like to shape it with a pen.'

Every morning Dickens was punctual and businesslike at his desk, never waiting for inspiration to tap him on the shoulder. Cardus followed that example, making it sound spiritual. He considered it a duty to 'go before the Muse every morning', he said. 'I have written and written for days and thrown everything in the wastepaper basket. But still, I've made my genuflexion before the Muse. Eventually She will come, and when She comes She dictates, and that is when grace descends upon you.'

So it went on. Cardus insisted that 'you must love writing as passionately as a man loves his mistress.' We know how passionately Dickens wrote; and now we know – which Cardus didn't – how passionately he loved his mistress too. Dickens was surrounded by his personal library. Cardus argued that 'good writing' always depended on 'good reading'. You couldn't hope to write if you didn't devour books. Indeed, he could be churlish about his cricketing summers when 'for weeks' he found himself 'in a world where nobody apparently ever read a book, or anything in a newspaper except for the sporting pages'.

He wasn't only talking about the players.

Then, as now, covering cricket meant everyone lived on top of everyone else – sometimes in a cramped space – for hour upon hour during day upon day. Reports were composed on squared telegraph paper, copy-boys ferrying a bundle of sheets to the post office for transmission. On a breezy day at Worcester one correspondent lost his entire report, which blew out of the copy-boy's hands on the bridge and was last seen floating down the River Severn with a flock of swans. Another correspondent, settling comfortably into his seat after filing an exclusive story, learnt that his newspaper hadn't received it because the telephonist couldn't read his scratchy handwriting; every line was gobbledegook to her.

Neville Cardus's attitude towards the job was unconventional, emphasising both his different approach and his detachment from those around him. During County Championship matches he treated the press box like a left-luggage office, dropping off his things there in the morning and returning only after tea, writing his pieces in one long sitting. Cardus 'preferred to stay in the fresh air', rather than be shut away, obliged to listen as other writers voiced their opinions, quarrelled between themselves or interrupted his own thoughts with remarks, few of which improved the silence.

The rivalries and seething antagonisms got on his nerves. In search of quietude, he'd stroll around a ground and light a full pipe before finding a vacant space and sitting anonymously among the crowd, to overhear them gripe and gossip. If a spectator happened to be reading the *Manchester Guardian*, so much the better; Cardus would be eager to hear whether he was being talked about, his own report quoted around him. Often he'd stand near a sightscreen, puffing away in smoky, contemplative silence, his hat pulled low over his eyes on the sunniest days.

Cardus always claimed a small corner to call his own. At Lord's, he sat on the 'Green Bank' and later went into the back row of the stand, so close to the clock that he 'could hear it ticking'. At Trent Bridge, he 'lolled' at the crown of the pavilion, high enough to see the distant scene – the blue-grey dome of Nottingham's Council House, the poky castle on its lump of sandstone rock. At The Parks, he claimed a striped deckchair, pleased whenever a friendly dog came close enough to be patted. And at New Road, he drifted far from the boundary and lay down. 'There is some enchantment about watching the movements of men in white through the sun's haze from a long way off,' he argued. Wherever Cardus went, he drank so much tea that he peed frequently. 'I soon found out that a wicket would certainly fall the moment my back was turned and I had entered the "gents"'. One cold summer I believe I was the first to "take" 100 wickets,' he said.

Cardus was a singular man. Not only did he like being on his own – even in a crowd – but he also found that some of his colleagues during the inter-war decades took things 'too seriously' and could be slightly annoying, irritable or 'over-bearing'. He could only cope with them in small doses – and vice versa, he supposed. Contact in moderation was the best way of assuring harmony. The gentlemen of the press – writing about cricket was a wholly masculine affair then – were an eccentrically diverse community, like characters in a situation comedy.

There was Sydney Pardon, the editor of *Wisden*, who had warts on his face, carried an expanding ear trumpet and watched every ball through a pair of ivory-covered opera glasses. He was so deaf that one innocuous but hopelessly misheard conversation with a colleague passed instantly into folklore. Pardon asked how he might get rid of a hedgehog at the bottom of his garden.

'Why not shove it up your arse?' said his colleague grumpily, possibly while in the high dudgeon of a hangover.

There's no guessing what Pardon *thought* he'd been told, but his plaintive reply was priceless enough to be repeated constantly afterwards: 'It's been there for a fortnight.'

There was H. J. 'Bertie' Henley of the *Daily Mail*, who carried a walking stick in the manner of Dr Johnson because of a lame left leg and watched most games from the bar. There was the big-bearded A. W. Pullin, 'Old Ebor' of the *Yorkshire Post*, whose lunch was always liquid, which meant that his early afternoons were spent in the snoring oblivion of sleep. He'd awake with a snap and ask: 'Anything happened?' There was A. C. M. Croome, correspondent of *The Times*, who had played alongside W. G. Grace for Gloucestershire and is said to have had his life saved by the good doctor after falling on to a spiked boundary railing that pierced his throat. And there was Croome's successor, Beau Vincent, who carried his false teeth in his coat pocket and once sailed to Australia only to sail right back again

Old Trafford as it once looked to Neville Cardus.

because of homesickness. Why Vincent agreed to go in the first place is unfathomable. He was generally reluctant to travel much further than Lord's or The Oval; he considered even the Midlands and the West Country as being practically overseas. He once turned up at a Test match without any paper and sat next to Cardus, who had turned up without a pencil. Fortunately Cardus had spare paper, and Vincent had two pencils. Vincent, a harmless but hapless chap, became one of Cardus's convivial allies.

Another of them was William Pollock, 'Googly' of the *Daily Express*. A former drama critic, Pollock had a jutting Roman nose like a beak, and in profile resembled a bald eagle. The little hair he did have was thin and blond and combed back to reveal a high pate, which glistened as if someone had given it a wax polish. Pollock was a roisterer, a leading light of festivities at London's Savage Club, where cricket writers and cricketers alike gathered, usually to get roaring drunk.

Every man has an enemy. Cardus's was the obscure B. J. Evans, of the London *Star*, who held a particularly low opinion of him. He

described Cardus as 'the **** who keeps pinching all my *******
epigrams', also accusing him of being 'a sneak'. Shortly before a match
at Essex, Evans went on a news-gathering expedition, leaving his wife
to do her knitting in a deckchair. When he returned, garrulously relay-
ing the gossip he'd gleaned to her, Cardus was sitting in another deckchair close by. He was accused of scribbling down Evans's intelligence
while pretending to complete the *Times* crossword. Why Cardus
would steal anything from Evans is a puzzle. As for the epigrams . . .
well, you only have to cursorily read Evans to realise he was a mediocrity, a pub pianist compared with Cardus, the concert virtuoso.

A frosty antagonism developed between Cardus and Pelham
Warner too. Each tried to pretend it did not exist, while barely
tolerating the other. Warner, dear old 'Plum' to his friends, wore a
variety of silk hats throughout his life: Championship-winner, Test
cricketer, tour manager, chairman of selectors, administrator, journalist and founder-editor of *The Cricketer*. Social status was blood
and breath to Warner. He was oleaginous towards those he believed
could advance his career. He was condescending to those he considered beneath him. When *The Times* commissioned him to contrib-
ute 'Cricket Reminiscences', Warner wrote anonymously, which
enabled him to conclude the first of them with this brazenly self-
aggrandising statement: 'Pelham Warner played a faultless innings
of 150.'

A Machiavellian streak ran through Warner like fat in streaky
bacon. He was also Macavity-like – always scheming for or against
something or someone, working paths that afterwards were difficult to
trace back to him. He kept a goodly distance between himself and 'the
crime'.

Cardus would flatter Warner, calling him 'my favourite Plum'.
Warner would flatter Cardus, calling him a 'lyrical writer'. The notion
these two opposites amicably rubbed along finally splintered apart

when Cardus castigated what he saw as 'bias' in selecting southern-based amateurs for England over professionals elsewhere.

He wrote, no punch pulled: 'Consciously or unconsciously, a "local" prejudice is at work; more than ever the amateur player well known in London is given preference over a professional player of equal or superior skill who comes to London only once every summer with his Northern, Midland or Western county.' The criticism, which stung and left a wound, homed in on Warner, who saw no conflict of interest in writing for the *Morning Post* and simultaneously being chairman of selectors.

Even without being specific about the beneficiaries of Warner's alleged favouritism, Cardus would have made him splutter self-righteously purely by raising the matter. In pinning down one player in particular, he not only guaranteed, but seemed to be deliberately seeking a High Noon confrontation at the Nursery End at Lord's. Cardus had been closely studying Gubby Allen, thinking he lacked the right stuff for Test cricket. As an MCC man, from the tip of his nose to the toe of his handmade shoes, Allen was an ideal candidate for selection. He was also much more than Warner's blue-eyed prodigy. Warner doted on Allen like a son. Some thought Warner *was* his father. The theory was based on his lifelong devotion to Allen's mother. The rumours about his parentage were not classified information either, making Cardus's criticism appear premeditated and personal.

Warner replied to him in the *Morning Post*, his article headlined 'A Critic Taken to Task'. Cardus's assumptions had 'no basis in fact', he said. Cardus took aim and shot back at him: 'No fewer than three Middlesex bowlers [Allen was one of them] played for England in the Test match at Lord's last June. There are not three amateur bowlers of international rank in the whole of England.'

An anonymous critic, contributing to the *Times of India*, said of Cardus and Warner what no British newspaper dared to suggest. Cardus 'does not particularly like Plum or Plum him, in spite of all the polite palaver in which they have been indulging'. Cardus could afford to antagonise the likes of Evans. Warner was different. He was powerful, vindictive and very patient. Revenge for this slight would be meted out cold.

More congenial colleagues than Warner emerged during the late 1920s and the 1930s. There was E. W. Swanton, J. M. Kilburn, Alec Waugh and Dudley Carew. There were also distinguished ex-players such as C. B. Fry, Percy Fender and R. C. Robertson-Glasgow. Swanton and Kilburn were austere and aloof. Kilburn, heir to Pullin, had handwriting so swirly that it almost counted as calligraphy. He'd apply the full stop to his report as soon as the day's final ball was bowled, hand it to a telephonist (he was too grand to phone over his own copy) and wish everyone a courteous but clipped 'good evening'. In charge of the seating arrangements during Test matches at Headingley, he once mischievously placed Donald Bradman directly next to Douglas Jardine in the press box at a time when the loathing between them was palpable. Barely a word was spoken. Barely a glance was exchanged. Swanton could be brusquely officious. Some of his match reports for the *Evening Standard* (he didn't move to the *Daily Telegraph* until 1946) were chloroform in print, capable of sending a reader to sleep faster than a hospital anaesthetist. Cardus said of him: 'He is a most likeable man when you come to know him; but he can't expect people who don't know him not to get the impression of self-importance and ... a certain pompousness.' He believed there was 'some sense of inferiority' in Swanton, who gave the impression of belonging to Oxbridge and Eton – without ever doing so – and became tightly entwined with the politics of Lord's.

Waugh, the brother of Evelyn, was hired by the *Sunday Times* on account of his reputation as a novelist, his writing often compared to Somerset Maugham's in style and intense productivity. Waugh was unquestionably a cricket man. The lead character of his then scandalous debut novel, the autobiographical *The Loom of Youth*, was called Lovelace, a semi-fictional portrait of the Nottinghamshire and England captain Arthur Carr. Waugh, who openly depicted homosexuality in the book, had an unrequited crush on Carr at Sherborne. His Test reports for the *Sunday Times* were remarkable insofar as the pieces were filed in between long stretches in which he seemed to see only glimpses of the play. At Lord's, he always found a cubbyhole in the pavilion and grafted at his latest novel there.

The monocle-wearing Fry, one of the greatest of Britain's sporting heroes, came across as something between a retired admiral and an unusually athletic Oxford don. Fry was so multi-talented that, after announcing he planned to tackle the Turf, he was asked: 'As owner, trainer or horse, Charles?' He seemed to be made of white five-pound notes too. He brought his chauffeur-cum-butler-cum-chief-factotum to games, ordering him to dispense champagne and food to all and sundry from a large wicker picnic hamper, which was stored in the boot of his Bentley. He wrote marathon match reports for the *Evening Standard*, some stretching to over 2,500 words, and appeared every morning in different garb, as though he were a walking advertisement for Savile Row tailoring. He was an impulsive man, always in search of a china shop to wreck. His voice also drowned out everyone else's. He warbled bits of opera, recited lines of poetry and discussed – whether anyone wanted to hear it or not – past events from his own career as Test cricketer and international footballer.

Fry still made less commotion than Fender. During the age in which the Remington portable typewriter counted as trailblazing technology, he provoked the ire of a Headingley member with his loud, repetitive tap-tapping. He was accused of spoiling the game. The upset member threatened to write a letter of complaint to the Yorkshire secretary and became more enraged than ever when Fender asked drolly: 'Shall I type it for you?'

C. B. Fry, the most complete sportsman and inveterate talker and storyteller.

Carew confessed that he had got his first assignment through nepotism – his stepfather was a chum of *The Times*'s sports editor – and because he'd written a novel. Like Cardus, he worked himself into such a terrible state of 'stage-fright' about covering his first match at

Lord's that he sat in the Mound Stand, a scorebook laid across his knees, and never dared to move. 'The Press Box was out of the question,' he said. 'It was a most anxious day.' His first cricket book, *England Over*, a snapshot of the summer of 1926, was written to avoid 'a bad nervous breakdown' and is Cardus-like in spirit, the matches less important than the places and the crowds.

Robertson-Glasgow resembled a youngish John Betjeman. He was bald-headed, quietly spoken and courteous, a man to whom other men gravitated. He was also Cardus's artistic brother, a highly refined, wry writer for whom brevity became a trademark. Robertson-Glasgow insisted he was 'more than half in love with indolence', which accounted for his preference for pen portraits and miniature sketches rather than the brand of long-form essay that defined Cardus. But, first for the *Morning Post* and later for *The Observer*, he brought the know-how of his former life as a Somerset medium-quick and welded it to the craftsmanship of pure writing. He was affectionately christened 'Crusoe', the genesis of the nickname worthy of repetition even if you've heard, or read about it, two dozen times before. It has the Essex batsman Charlie McGahey returning to the dressing room and indignantly telling his captain: 'I've just been bowled by an old bugger I thought was dead 200 years ago – Robinson Crusoe.'

Cardus respected anyone who could 'really write' and eschewed the statistical minutiae. That is why he was so drawn to Robertson-Glasgow and so fond of him too. How could you not be fond of someone who described the weather at Worthing as being 'windy and warm, like bottled lemonade', or claimed that Sir Aubrey Smith, the cricketer and Hollywood actor, was gallant enough to have ridden beside King Arthur and become captain of Camelot's First XI?

Robertson-Glasgow was the one cricket writer Cardus wholly respected and read regularly with envy. He admired the shape of his mind. Each, celebrating beauty, also saw something buried deep in the other, strengthening the affinity between them. The merry 'good morning' Robertson-Glasgow gave to everybody, and also his garrulousness, seldom hid his troubles. He was bipolar, suffering breakdowns far more awful and prolonged than his friendly rival's own.

Cardus retained his eminence despite the competition. If a successful life is partly dependent on time and chance, then he arrived with almost split-second punctuality. County cricket was focused suddenly on those twice-yearly battles between Yorkshire and Lancashire to which most other correspondents were considered outsiders and consequently irrelevant. The Roses matches were 'special occasions' for Cardus. He knew that what he said – and how well he wrote – would get him noticed and even talked about.

He considered himself 'on show as much as the players'.

5

SPOILING EVERY BLOODY BANK HOLIDAY

THE COUNTY CHAMPIONSHIP became a clash of clans squabbling for northern supremacy. Between 1922 and 1939, Yorkshire won 11 titles, surpassing even Lord Hawke's success during the early 1880s and the late 1900s, and Lancashire claimed five. 'One way or the other,' said Neville Cardus, the Roses match became 'more important than the Ashes' to anyone who found it impossible to be impartial about them.

He saw every day of every Roses match then, casting the fixtures as both 'a combative blood feud' and 'the ancient bone of contention'. Defeat, either home or away, severely bruised all winter the pride of whichever county suffered it. Summing up the formalities, rather than the pleasantries, Roy Kilner distilled the boiling rivalry into two often-quoted sentences: 'We shake hands on t'first morning and say "How do?" Then we say nowt for three days but "howzat?" ' He ideally thought Yorkshire–Lancashire games 'should have no umpires – but fair cheatin' all round in conformity wi' the law'.

The crowd was 'part of the event', said Cardus. Photographs prove it – from Old Trafford to Headingley, and from Bradford's Park Avenue, once described as 'cricket in Hell', to Sheffield's Bramall Lane, where a pall of smoke hung between earth and sun, partly obscuring sullen tenements and squat chimneys. You look at each picture and examine with astonishment the heaving masses, banked steeply and thickly around the boundary, before the eye eventually settles on the field itself. There seems scarcely enough room to exhale. Some matches attracted 30,000 to a single day, the play happening on a 'tiny island of green in a vast black sea', explained Cardus. Spectators spilled beyond the ropes and had to be pushed back into stands that were choked. Cardus liked watching spectators arrive and jostle for the best position. Lancastrian and Yorkshireman alike came 'with a garden of roses', red or white, pinned to their coat, pledging allegiance silently but obtrusively. For them it was a holiday from the warehouse, the factory lathe or the mill, the day off celebrated with flasks of tea and 'snappin' tins of sandwiches. The air would be filled with the great noise of insults and encouragements from every part of an unsegregated ground.

The jagged rise of the Pennines split the counties geographically and the long-ago disputes of kings, once and future, allowed everybody to cite history as an excuse for enmity. The accents and dialects were different too. But Cardus believed Lancashire and Yorkshire liked one another – and had more in common – than either cared to publicly admit. The Lanky and the Yorkie came from fundamentally the same soil, the same industrial backdrop, and also had the same mindset. Recognition of this, as well as the affection one cloth-cap, working-class county had for the other, went unsaid and unacknowledged only in case accusations of 'soppy softness' were levelled against whoever dare make it. Cricket gave both of them an identifiable sense of self and put a swagger in their step. Cricket made them dependent on each other too – for who else was there to gripe about or struggle with? Cricket united them with a smack twice a season, the contest frankly 'nowt' to do with anyone else. The tale, often told, of the man caught applauding each side with equal fervour underlines that:

'Are you Lancashire?' he was asked.

'No,' he replied.

'Are you Yorkshire?'

'No,' he replied again.

'Then shut yer clapper and mind thi own business.'

Standing in a shilling enclosure, binoculars pressed to his face, Cardus once made a similar error of judgement. There was a long, throaty Yorkshire shout for lbw, which he said 'ten thousand' of the faithful instantly amplified. 'Impulsively, and without knowing what I was about', he spoke aloud the thought that came instantly to him – 'not out, not out'. He became 'suddenly and curiously aware' of someone behind him. Cardus turned around, to find a man fixing him with a wide, wild stare. 'What's the matter with thee? And what do thee know abaat it?' he asked, accusingly. For safety's sake, Cardus pretended to be a Yorkshireman before making his excuses and sloping off towards the neutrality of the press box.

He thought the Roses matches could 'not be understood in the South of England'. He considered the Home Counties 'too suburban and too genteel' to appreciate the 'hard seriousness' and introspection of the cricket. Or how much the result 'mattered' in both Lancashire and Yorkshire, where the perfect nonsense and serial absurdities elsewhere in the world were put aside until the match was settled. The significance of the result had a longevity which would have dumbfounded those who thought sacrilegiously of cricket as 'nobbut a game'. Weeks, months, years 'and decades too', said Cardus, could go by, but specific results were brought up and boasted about to gain bragging rights – even by those inconveniently born too late to have actually seen them happen.

The games Cardus witnessed, which seldom escaped a dousing of rain, were 'spiky with antagonism', and revolved around 'impassioned arguments' and 'dour temper' and sheer 'cussedness'. Watching them, he stressed, could be 'a rack of torture on which we were stretched hour by hour'. Every one was fought in 'a tenser air' than anything else the Championship offered, and the play was slow on principle – and even grindingly dull – because it was governed by the fear of losing. Too much was at stake for any 'foony stuff', added Cardus, who remembered the instruction to batsmen: 'No fours before lunch.'

When Arthur Morton, an ex Derbyshire all-rounder, umpired in an embittered Roses match, Cardus reported his exasperation at the chelp and chunter of fieldsmen around him. 'For goodness sake,' moaned Morton. 'Stop this chatterin'. Ow does th' expect me to umpire in a parrot house?' Mostly, however, appeals for lbw were 'the signs of waking life' Cardus saw, the sessions a comedy of non-communication. He deplored the tedium with some fine grumbling. 'We have not seen ten minutes of batting worth walking a hundred yards to see ... Not more than an hour of the bowling has touched first class quality.' Only half in jest, Cardus claimed that newspapers preset two headlines on the printer's stone the day before any Yorkshire–Lancashire match began.

Dour Struggle at Headingley
Slow Batting by Lancashire

The strategy of painstaking caution and parsimony was too obtuse for the bored A. C. M. Croome, who looked at the tens of thousands who had turned up to witness in rapt silence another attritional game and then enquired irritably of Cardus: 'Why are all these people *here?*' Croome said it in an offhanded way, as if questioning their sanity. He found it incomprehensible that someone would pay to watch something so leaden, so inanimate. Cardus said that Croome didn't appreciate that the unadventurous approach was actually 'a suspicious searching for position' and 'a calm that hints bodefully of the brewing storm to come'. He forgave him for it; after all, Croome had been born 'below the bend of the River Trent', which accounted for his ignorance of such matters.

Lancashire versus Yorkshire was 'every year like a play and a pageant', he said. Cardus was convinced that 'every action' and 'every movement' in them exposed the character of the 'North of England', which explained why more sensitive southerners, such as Croome, observed them in puzzled incomprehension. The games were a 'struggle for existence', he explained. It was different at Lord's, at The Oval, at Canterbury and beneath the church towers at Taunton too. Matches there – unless Yorkshire and Lancashire were involved, of course – could be expansive and appear sometimes even flighty, as though victory was a distant second to the pleasure derived simply from entertaining the customer. As Cardus pointed out, such an attitude was not only deplored where he came from, but also judged intolerable. Only one thing mattered: grinding the opposition underfoot.

'Magnanimity and fair do's is all very well between Somerset and Kent or Middlesex or Surrey. But the Roses matches are another matter entirely. We want no nonsense about "May the Best Side Win".'

The best side was usually Yorkshire. Of the 42 Roses matches fought between the wars, Lancashire won only five, which is why Neville Cardus regarded each of them as dressed 'majestically in history'. The sweetest he saw came in 1924 at Headingley. 'I still dream about it,' he said long after the event, consecrating it in his memory.

The game didn't begin promisingly for Lancashire. Day one brought the 'old, old story' of 'damnable iteration', said Cardus – a morning of stifling Yorkshire maidens, the scoreboard stuck as if broken, or changing only to register a snatched single. Lancashire were attempting to creep up on the enemy, gaining territory in miserable half-inches. Just 39 runs came in one hour and three quarters. Every one of those tedious minutes, added Cardus, was like being given 'glimpses into eternity'. In the afternoon Lancashire, as though their own lethargy had wearied them, sagged to 113 all out.

On the second day sparks flew everywhere.

Cecil Parkin bowled with pop and spit; Cardus called him 'a Spofforth incarnate'. He was the early tormentor, ripping out most of the top and middle order. With equal assuredness, Dick Tyldesley moved in to mop up the tail. It was scarcely a fight. The final six Yorkshire wickets disintegrated for 43 in a total of 130. Cardus went from pessimist to optimist, experiencing the light-headedness of hope. This didn't last long. In front of '30,000 souls', most of whom were 'magnificently Yorkshire to the marrow', Cardus said Lancashire's second innings was 'born into a world of trouble'. The pitch was now 'treacherous', bad enough to make the best look 'childlike on it'. Against the triumvirate of Roy Kilner, Wilfred Rhodes and George Macaulay, eagerly capitalising on easy pickings, Lancashire shrivelled, too timidly afraid that every ball was a forked devil. Each wicket prefaced a roar so fiercesomely loud and partisan that Cardus likened it to 'the savagery that must have been in the noise of the multitudes in days of old – as innocents were driven to the slaughter'. Lancashire were rolled over for 74, the total embarrassing Cardus, who condemned the batting as 'spineless' and conceded defeat. He received in reply a postcard from a furious Lancashire patriot, dismissing him as a disloyal clot – though the language used was fruitier than that. 'You ******* fool,' it said.

With Yorkshire needing a measly 58 to win, Cardus considered writing a short lament from his hotel room and asking the *Manchester Guardian*'s sub-editors to tag the scorecard on to the end of it. But, hearing an echo of that cheering at the Saffrons for A. C. MacLaren, he dragged himself to the last rites. He saw a Roses finale like few others before – and fewer still since. What the pair of Parkin and

*A bird's eye view of Headingley, an oasis of green in
a smokey landscape of terraced housing.*

Tyldesley produced with clever fingers were 'thunderbolts out of the
blue sky of everybody's complacence', he said.

Yorkshire anticipated a nonchalant stroll of a morning, the shedding of sweat unnecessary. A few pushed shots, a streaky edge and the
odd straight-driven four would see them safely home. Expecting the
same, Cardus went to sit at the Kirkstall Lane end, squeezing himself
among a knot of supporters already in celebratory mood. Then Herbert
Sutcliffe went to the third delivery of Parkin's second over, the ball
breaking back and trapping him lbw. Percy Holmes fell almost immediately too, a cannily disguised top-spinner from Tyldesley that 'sped
from the turf sinfully' and rapped hard against the bottom roll of his
pads. While Yorkshire were still absorbing those misfortunes, another
shook them to the core. Maurice Leyland was bamboozled, tamely
chipping a dolly drop into Tyldesley's hands. 'There was something
combustible in the air now,' wrote Cardus, who, like everyone else, was
an 'incredulous' onlooker. Yorkshire imploded, scarcely able to rationalise the collapse, let alone halt it. Wilfred Rhodes, reckless and

desperate, played a 'Heaven help me' sort of shot to Tyldesley and perished leg before. 'He was an unforgettable picture of an old war-horse at bay,' said Cardus, watching him thrash the air in vain. Edgar Oldroyd, reckoned to be the 'best sticky-wicket batsman in the world', came and went again in a finger-click; Parkin clean-bowled him with 'a stinging off break'. Not even a shower of rain, leaving Lancashire the unwanted legacy of a greasy ball, disturbed the momentum. Only Roy Kilner, a 'Death or Glory' expression on his stern, pained face, clung on, his bat 'militant' against each fresh disaster. Chaos swam around him. Lancashire fielded in a frenzy, leaping and diving and denying boundaries to Yorkshire that were worth 'guinea gold', said Cardus, who found his heart palpitating 'unpleasantly' and a 'hollow' opening up in his stomach. Worried that Kilner would take the game away from them with a few pugnacious slashes and swishes, Lancashire began starving him of the strike and weeded out the rump of the middle order and then the tail.

Yorkshire went from three for three to six for 16 and then to eight for 32. The man sitting beside Cardus got up and, in a voice admirably controlled, bade him good day. 'I'm off,' he said. 'Who'd a thowt it?' When the last wicket crashed, the total was only 33. Kilner, though unbeaten on 13, 'was foiled', said Cardus. 'Down into the abyss he had to go with the rest.'

Yorkshire had succumbed in just 23.5 overs. Tyldesley had taken six for 18; Parkin three for 15.

Cardus was unable to contain himself. 'We have been led out of the wilderness. We have entered the Promised Land ... Not even the annals of Lancashire cricket contain a page more thrilling, more splendid ... Old Trafford will talk about this famous day till the end of cricket's history; men of a ripe age will sigh, in the presence of tomorrow's chil-dren, for the good old times ...' He saw in the glow of the players' surprised faces 'the posterity awaiting them' in the record books.

Cardus admitted that he had 'rarely been moved so much to a sort of adoration for cricket and cricketers'. What caused it was not only the victory, but also – and predominantly – Tyldesley's 'faith and composure' and his 'true magnificent doggedness' in assuring it. To him, Tyldesley had been 'heroic' in a 'moral battle'. Knowing the non-cricket follower might scoff, thinking the assessment crassly excessive, Cardus qualified it in his own defence: 'It was only cricket, you might insist, only a game. But the testing times of this life are just what a man makes of them.'

How much the match meant, both to victor and vanquished, became apparent after Cardus left Headingley. He leapt on a tram heading to the railway station and saw the conductor approaching, whistling and jaunty and about to claim his fare.

'What ha' they won by?' he asked Cardus.

'They haven't won. They've lost,' he replied.

The conductor wasn't satisfied. 'Ah mean t' cricket match. Did they lose any wickets?'

Cardus assured him that he'd been referring to 't' cricket match'. The guard listened and then turned his back and walked solemnly to the front of the tram, where he passed on glum tidings to the driver. He did not return. He issued no ticket.

In Leeds city centre Cardus found the news had travelled before him, the story already assuming its full scale. 'You could see the effect on most faces,' he said. He went into the café at the railway station, bought a pot of tea and waited for his train to Manchester. A Yorkshireman plonked himself at the same table and struck up one of those pass-the-time conversations that usually lead nowhere and are forgotten five minutes later. Cardus, though, would remember this one. Often he scolded fellow Lancastrians for believing 'the old super-stition about the essential Satanism of all Yorkshiremen', who he insisted 'really are nice, cheerful and hospitable folk'.

Well, most of them are . . .

'Hey, this is a reight do. Fancy Yorkshire being put out for fifty,' the man moaned, more in pain than infuriation, before spotting that Cardus didn't appear at all disconsolate. 'Tha doesn't seem to be takin' it to 'eart very much?' he said. Without hesitation, Cardus disclosed his place of birth. The man stared at him differently now. 'Oh, so tha comes from Lancashire? And tha come specifically to see t' finish this mornin'? Ah suppose tha's feelin' pleased with thissen. And tha's goin' back to Manchester . . . Well, ah 'opes tha drops down dead before thi gets theer.'

Cardus thought about the man when Yorkshire shook the defeat off, regained their equilibrium and went on to take the title six weeks later. It allowed Cardus to call them a 'side that moves like a machine invented with the purpose of winning Championships'.

It seemed unlikely then that the same thing would be said soon enough of Lancashire.

When Neville Cardus became the *Manchester Guardian*'s cricket correspondent, Lancashire hadn't won the title since their undefeated summer of 1904.

The Championship was still constructed as though Heath Robinson had designed it while slightly tipsy. It was a weird and unwieldy contraption of arithmetic. The counties didn't play the same number of games. The bonus points system was cockeyed. There was a percentage system that could only be understood if you'd won the Nobel Prize in mathematics. In its 'Miscellany' column, the *Manchester Guardian* compared the mechanics of the Championship to the British Constitution. 'It has grown up more or less by haphazard,' the paper stated. 'It contains some things hardly to be defended by exact laws or logic.'

However the table was calculated, Yorkshire had begun to top it regularly. The balance of power tilted from white to red rose only when Lancashire imported the pace of Ted McDonald from Australia. As Cardus admitted: 'Everybody loathed us because, as Yorkshiremen declared, we let a "foreigner" play for us.' McDonald wore well the sobriquet of 'The Silk Express', his scary speed delivered with a gracefully gorgeous action; he was the Michael Holding of the 1920s, always scratching out his mark with a long rake of his boot.

McDonald was a compelling figure, but an aberrant, Chinese box of a man, who squandered what he possessed unfathomably. It makes his career seem in retrospect like a series of comebacks. He made only 11 Test appearances, preferring to chase money as an English pro. The wealth he accrued – Nelson alone paid him £500 per season, plus perks, to play in the Lancashire League – was flung away hedonistically. Money always brought out the beast in him. McDonald had to constantly pester Lancashire's committee for cash advances to cover debts, each replaced with another almost as soon as the cheque cleared.

He was a rake, a bounder and a wastrel. He was 'obliged' to leave his first job, as a clerk for a Tasmanian insurance company, after the management discovered an unsophisticated embezzlement. He drank like a blue whale. He gambled so compulsively and crazily on long shots that today's punts on spot-betting look in comparison like gilt investments. He smoked cigarettes by the packet, consuming them at such a rate that his voice sounded like a car's back wheels uselessly spinning on gravel.

Lancashire's title successes were nonetheless based around his phenomenal pace. Even if McDonald didn't take a batsman's wicket, he could frighten him into giving it to someone else.

In 1926, playing only his second full season at Old Trafford, McDonald was no spring chick. He was 35, but the smoker's creases around his mouth and the telltale bags beneath his eyes made him appear a decade older. Age and all his louche living still didn't weary him; he took 163 Championship wickets. In 1927, he claimed 143. In 1928, celebrating a hat-trick of pennants, his tally was 178. Lancashire had a big-gun battleship in McDonald. Everyone else – apart from Nottinghamshire, who could call on Harold Larwood – had a cruiser.

To read Cardus is to suppose that Michelangelo must have sculpted McDonald from a piece of unflawed marble. He admired him in paragraphs that were almost heart-shaped with love: 'We never have need to argue the fact of greatness. It knocks you over at first sight,' he said of him. 'His long sinuous movements to the wicket, a glide rather than run, and that beautiful flexion of the wrist, just before he lets the ball go, has a snake-like pose and a hint of venom.' His 'scary pace', even observed from a safe distance, made Cardus flinch. His right arm was 'a wheel of war', he said.

Cardus rated McDonald 'a Lucifer of his craft'. There was certainly something devilish in and about him. A quick bowler can afford to be boastfully arrogant; he can play the playground bully with impunity. McDonald still overdid the privilege, making himself loathed rather than merely unpopular. He would saunter cockily into an opposition dressing room to intimidate teams, telling the captain to 'ring up the Royal Infirmary' and order a 'few stretchers'. Not even Larwood – appreciably faster and more accurate than McDonald – had the audacity to be so brazen. Larwood had too much respect for cricketers forced to make a living against him, doing so in anticipation of a bouncer that could crack their skull or a brutish ball capable of crushing a finger. He didn't have to threaten anyone verbally; simply turning up was threat enough.

'There was never a cricketer of loftier disdain,' announced Cardus, which is about as close as he got to condemning McDonald's many defects. He even tried to pass them off casually as Nature's fault, as though McDonald was blameless for his own irresponsibly rank

Ted McDonald, approaching the crease and caught in a pose that makes his sobriquet 'The Silk Express' seem so beautifully appropriate.

behaviour. He possessed an 'incalculable spirit', declared Cardus, and did not 'seem to understand the comings and goings of the forces within him'. The marvellous thing about a line with a double meaning is that it can only possibly mean one thing. Anyone who read that assessment of McDonald, and also knew McDonald personally, was aware that Cardus had summed up the player's personality as much as his cricket.

Spectacular though his figures were, McDonald could have improved on them. Lancashire's slip fielding was woefully inept; Cardus thought a stiff tutorial on the basics of catching from A. C. MacLaren was long overdue. McDonald was also commander-general of the awkward squad. Lancashire's captain, Leonard Green, understandably anxious to exploit his prime asset, was guilty of over-bowling him. McDonald totted up more than 1,200 overs per summer. But he had a tendency to dissolve into sulky truculence when upset and became uninterested when his mood turned black. 'Tricky to handle' barely covers it. McDonald was insolent and contrary, and as volatile as nitroglycerine. 'There are moments when he will not spend his energy on the small fry of batsmen,' said Cardus too compassionately. No one could stir McDonald out of what Cardus termed his 'majestic indifference'. He'd see him toss up slow off-breaks to the frailest middle-order and tail-end batsmen – and do so 'sardonically by the hour' – in protest and out of spite. After growing tired of his own indolence, he'd then 'sweep these weaklings out of sight by sudden strokes of speed', added Cardus, 'as though he had impatiently said: "Out of my way, scum".'

It was as if there were two McDonalds far different from one another. No one could say with certainty which of them would play. That point was sharpened in Lancashire's first Championship-winning season of the 1920s. Against Kent at Dover, McDonald loitered around the boundary with a couldn't-care-less slouch, which became gradually more pronounced.

Cardus's match report evokes the quintessential England of high summer. You read it and realise he was joyously glad to be there. His words are a shouted celebration. He picks out the white 'tents and wavering colours' all around him and the 'green lawns and terraces rising high behind the little pavilion'. He basks in the 'sunlight everywhere' and the sky as a 'dome of glass all stained blue'. He gives himself up 'with lazy delight' to 'the delicious changes in the passing hour – the full light of noon, the soft silent fall to mellow'.

In the beginning, McDonald doesn't share Cardus's enthusiasm for either the match or the surroundings. He is grumpy, withdrawn, a bit sour and stubborn. He goes through the motions petulantly. Cardus spots that he does 'not seem in a conquering mood', sending down bumpers desultorily because he can't be bothered to do anything else. And then, after fluking one wicket – a top-edged skyer to the leg side – he snaps awake, interested and alert at last. 'McDonald realised, in the style of the good opportunist, that he was in fortune's good books,' explains Cardus, who is soon watching him get faster and then faster still. Purely because of McDonald, the game stops drifting and instead veers dizzily Lancashire's way. He takes seven wickets for 81.

That effort seems to exhaust McDonald. When Kent go in again, requiring 426 after a Lancashire declaration, he is subdued and silent. He dawdles around the field, as if not remotely caring whether a Frank Woolley century will make the mammoth target reachable. He experiments bizarrely, bowling leg-spinners round the wicket. Leonard Green tries tact and cajolery and some pleading too. Nothing gets a spark out of McDonald who, like a recalcitrant diva, won't sing. Lancashire look 'rather broken' to Cardus, and 'every other ball bowled' is being 'hit to the distant parts of the ground'. At tea Kent are 341 for five. Cardus seeks out Green: 'What in God's name is the matter with Mac?' he asks. 'Has he a strain or something?' Green sheepishly replies: 'No, he just won't bowl fast.' Cardus tells him: 'You should order him to.' Green, more sheepishly still and like a parent incapable of controlling the tantrum of a child, wails: 'I've tried, and he just won't. He says the wicket's too slow.' Green urges Cardus to 'go and talk to him', because 'I'm damned if I can do any more.'

Cardus finds McDonald quietly drinking a glass of whisky, which Green has poured for him. He implores McDonald to put some spine into his bowling. He explains that if Kent get the runs, the Lancashire committee will 'play Hell' with Green for declaring. McDonald 'snarls' at him – Cardus emphasises that word – and then says: 'Very well.'

Whether the alcohol or Cardus's pep talk was the antidote to his lethargy is unknowable. But McDonald, fit and fortified now, steams in, bowling with 'havoc' and 'beauty'. Cardus sees him 'smash' the tops of the stumps and claim a hat-trick. 'Thus a sudden heave of the game's great wheel landed the laurels in Lancashire's grasp,' he says. A brass band, on the lip of the grass, surreally begins to play the madrigal out of *The Mikado* as McDonald, as if resurrected, takes his haul to five precious wickets for the innings and a dozen in the game.

'And so,' concludes Cardus, 'a noble match was nobly won' after 'the changeful hurly-burly'. Cardus promises to 'think of that summer afternoon ... on my death-bed'.

His Lancastrian roots didn't make Yorkshire despised opposition to Neville Cardus. He looked on them enviously but kindly. He excused their intolerance of Lancashire as 'simply the measure of the Yorkshireman's pride in his county's genius for cricket'. In admiration of their domination of the title – and their obsession with it – he also proposed: 'Let us forthwith make Yorkshire Honorary Champions For Ever ... the rest of us can then get on with the game undisturbed.' In Yorkshire, cricket was 'one of the finer passions of life'. Yorkshiremen saw it romantically – even though they kept 'quiet about it', he said.

He claimed to have overheard two men at Headingley selecting the next Test team, which under them consisted entirely of the Yorkshire XI: 'It was too much for me. I interposed,' he said. 'Sorry,' I said, 'but I couldn't help over-hearing you. May I draw your attention that in picking your England XI you have left out the name of Jack Hobbs?'

The amateur selectors considered the thought momentarily.

'By gum, so we have,' said the first.

'Aye,' agreed the second, 'so we have – but how could we get 'im in?'

The story seems too good and too perfectly tidy to possibly be true; but, then again, in the 1930s Cardus was so enamoured with Yorkshire that he urged the same thing, which would have meant elbowing aside Denis Compton and Bill Edrich: 'People laughed at the idea and said it was one of my little jokes. I was serious . . .' He had just seen them rout Lancashire by an innings and thought: 'The great thing would be to keep the Yorkshire team *as* a team.'

Cardus said he found 'something likeable, even lovable' in Yorkshire and felt 'at kin' with the likes of Wilfred Rhodes, Herbert Sutcliffe, Percy Holmes, Maurice Leyland and the glumly unglamorous Arthur 'Ticker' Mitchell. He would quite gladly have followed them the way he followed Lancashire. For Yorkshire offered a far richer and seemingly inexhaustible source of material for him, begging to be mined.

Len Hutton arrived in the side, solemn and sallow-faced but precocious in his shot-making. So did Hedley Verity, a white neckerchief tied around his throat as he bowled some of the wickedest spin ever seen; Cardus christened him 'the Professor'. There was also the gawky, bespectacled Bill Bowes, with his whipped quiff of blond hair, and Brian Sellers, a passionate captain who had a hobnailed practicality about him. Once, sitting with Sellers as a Yorkshire hopeful batted, Cardus heard him say: 'No, he won't do. He's not ready yet.' The batsman, as though responding to the put-down, suddenly cover-drove

What the bowler saw. Herbert Sutcliffe's compact, solid stance signalled the indomitability of his approach to batting.

Hedley Verity, a bowler as 'secret and self-contained as an oyster'.

gloriously. 'Well,' asked Cardus, 'what about that stroke? There's beauty for you.' This was a moment of one-upmanship, and Cardus waited for it to settle. He expected Sellers to nod his head and accept that he may have been hasty in his original assessment. Not a bit of it. Sellers simply snapped back: 'Aye, but we can't win championships carryin' a ruddy Art Gallery about with us.'

Cardus nonetheless saw art whenever he saw Yorkshire.

The distinguished Rhodes, trying to pretend he was 'nivver a star' but 'just a good utility player', created a dilemma for him. 'He was a man to be afraid of and prayed against,' he said, alluding to his destructive powers, which were turned so frequently on Lancashire. Of the 'curving line' of Rhodes's left-arm flight, Cardus asked: 'Is there anything in cricket, or in any other game, more lovely to see?' He liked the plain simplicity of Rhodes's approach too: 'The same familiar walk

Wilfred Rhodes, the craftiest of bowlers and shrewdest of tacticians. He possessed a ruthless intolerance of failure.

to the bowling crease, a few quick but easy steps, a little effortless leap, then the body comes through after a beautiful sidelong swing ... no fuss, no waste ... conservation of energy and perpetual motion.' He believed 'the beauty' of it – 'the monotonous rhythm ... as ball after ball comes through the air dropping, dropping, dropping' – ensnared the unwary. Rhodes's skill was to benumb the batsman 'minute by minute', making him think each delivery would always plop 'on the same spot ... at the same pace', when actually the length and speed were infinitesimally but crucially different. 'Every ball like every other ball, yet somehow unlike; each over in collusion with the rest, part of a plot; every ball a decoy, a spy sent out to get the lie of the land; some balls simple, some complex, some easy, some difficult; and one of them – ah, which? – the master ball.'

Sutcliffe matched Rhodes in Cardus's affections. 'If I had to choose a batsman to play for my life in a Test match, I would nominate him confidently, and then go and find an insurance company to take out an old-age endowment policy.' His partner, Holmes, was 'volatile, unpredictable of mood', but 'always alive by instinct', which made him interesting. He was a 'bobby dazzler', an 'artist' who liked to improvise and throw himself at the mercy of Fortune. Holmes also had a rubbery face which betrayed his emotions, ideal fodder for descriptive passages. Sutcliffe was a different type of man – cool, undemonstrative, unruffled – and a different class of batsman.

'Though he did nothing in particular with his bat, he did it very well,' said Cardus, who catalogued him among the 'close-cropped Roundheads' and 'the Puritans'. He arrived at the crease and left regally, scarcely a hair out of place or a mark or blemish on his pressed flannels and shirt. Cardus called Sutcliffe 'His Lordship'. His 'air of foppishness', which Cardus highlighted, was combined with a 'bold, not to say arrogant hint of assurance and self-possession'. Sutcliffe was also as 'hard as nails'. Cardus saw him struck flush on the knee when

Yorkshire's prolifically reliable opening pair, Herbert Sutcliffe (left) and Percy Holmes, leave the pavilion at Scarborough.

fielding in the leg trap. He winced but abruptly waved away the fieldsmen who rushed towards him like emergency medics. It was as if, remarked Cardus, he had told them: 'We Sutcliffes do not suffer pain.'

What Sutcliffe always gave was the 'zeal for dependable service', eschewing the ostentatious for the orderly, his opener's tasks carried out with unflappable concentration. He didn't belt the ball; he placed it smoothly. He progressed to centuries rather than raced to them. No one went to see a pyrotechnical performance from Sutcliffe.

In one Roses game a supporter became exasperated with his reluctance to offer a shot and his statue-like stillness, which suggested his boots had been cemented to the crease. 'Coom on, 'Erbert,' he yelled, 'what dost think thi are – a ruddy War Memorial?' In another, almost

*Herbert Sutcliffe, a 'hard as nails' and undemonstrative
Yorkshireman, his batting never rushed.*

400 runs were made on the opening day at Headingley, and two sixes
were struck in the same over. Tongue pressed firmly into cheek, Cardus
expressed appalled horror at such cavalier insouciance, shaming
Leyland – 'the cricketer thus to abuse an austere tradition' – as if he
had committed a felony. Normal order was soon restored. 'Sutcliffe
saw to it that honour was done to the proper and ancient spirit of the
occasion,' he wrote. 'He batted two hours and twenty minutes for 40.'
He'd abstain from making a stroke by withdrawing the bat suddenly,

the backlift so extravagant that he seemed 'likely to stun himself' with a blow on the head. He took time between deliveries, patting the pitch 'like a boy at the seaside making sandcastles', and picked up 'a foreign body' that was discernible to no one else. He bored the spirit and then sapped the life out of bowlers.

The memory of one Sutcliffe innings – 195 in a Roses match in 1931 – lingered for Cardus. 'Seldom have I seen batsmanship as certain of itself,' he said. Sutcliffe batted in a manner that suggested he 'would have smiled indulgently at you if you had reminded him that the game is full of uncertainties and that there are several ways whereby a batsman can occasionally get out'.

The officer class of cricketer always sent Cardus into rapture, but he got more column inches out of the rank and file, the support troops on the periphery. Mitchell was typical of them: the dourest and sternest of cricketers, who wore his cap at such a pronounced angle that it often covered the top of his right ear. He communicated only through sarcasm and rebukes. He rarely praised anyone, a chill wind of antagonism blowing from him on the sunniest days. Mitchell was the sort of man of whom it was said: 'If he went riding with the Four Horsemen of the Apocalypse, he would not noticeably enliven the party.' Mitchell deplored ostentation. A team-mate, diving to take a spectacular slip catch, was reprimanded as he lay sprawled across the turf: 'Gerrup, tha's makin' an exhibition o' thissen.'

Mitchell and Cardus bumped along together. He said of Cardus: 'Aye, 'e's all right, but a bit too flowery for my liking.' Word of that comment filtered through to Cardus.

Mitchell's mild ribbing of him produced mild ribbing in return. A week later Mitchell was struck squarely in the box – 'between wind and water', as Cardus put it – while batting for the Players against the Gentlemen, a fixture Cardus renamed the Workmen versus the Great Unpaid. In his report Cardus recorded Mitchell's misfortune: 'Mitchell, while showing good form, received a fast rising ball which struck him violently in the stomach. If he will allow me to use such flowery language.' The private joke formed a surprising bond between them.

Wisden described Mitchell as a man for a crisis, which was another way of saying he clung to the crease like a barnacle to a ship's hull. He had a reputation as a dreadful stick-in-the-mud, capable of dead-batting for an eon and spreading gloom. Mitchell could 'hit like a mule and be as obstinate as a mule', said Cardus. He spent six hours over one Roses century and four hours – a canter in comparison – to reach another. He showed 'grim imperturbability' and 'impressive immobility', according to Cardus. During the second hundred a spectator, incandescent to the point of wanting to shoot either himself or Mitchell, leapt from his seat after yet another maiden got pencilled into the scorebook. He broke the dead silence with a raving soliloquy.

> Every bloody year. This Mitchell, 'e cooms an' spoils Bank Holiday. I says to mi missis this mornin' 'Ah'm goin' to Old Trafford. An' Mitchell'll be there agin, spoilin' Bank Holiday.' An' there 'e is. Every bloody year, Mitchell – an' ah'm speakin' to thee, so don't pretend tha can't hear mi. Every bloody year ... thi spoils Bank Holiday.

Mitchell had qualities that were the opposite of magic. He was not endowed with great skill. His game was about frustrating the opposition and fatiguing them through hard grind and sweat of endurance. In this, he was not alone ...

6

AN ENCYCLOPAEDIA
IN LOOSE TROUSERS

N O ONE EMBODIED the absolute essence of Neville Cardus's writing – his approach, his style, his characterisations – more than the 'grizzled, squat, bandy-legged' Yorkshire all-rounder Emmott Robinson. Cardus called him 'a glorious gift' to his journalism. Out of a minor cricketer he created a major figure.

Robinson was a jobbing journeyman, a bits-and-pieces chap beside the elite of Wilfred Rhodes and Herbert Sutcliffe, Len Hutton and Maurice Leyland. Statistics confirm it. Robinson didn't make his debut until 1919, aged 35. He took 100 wickets in only one season and reached 1,000 runs just twice before retiring in 1931. He never claimed the double or came close to being chosen as one of *Wisden*'s Cricketers of the Year. He didn't challenge for a place in the Test team either; not even in those parlous summers of the early 1920s. The sum total of his contribution was respectable enough – 9,744 first-class runs and 902 wickets – without being exceptional.

'Of the average cricketer there is little to be said that the scorebook cannot tell you with a casual glance of it,' stressed Cardus. He vehemently believed Robinson was different. While not 'a great cricketer in technique', Cardus rated him as a 'unique' player, 'whose value could not be assessed by figures' because 'his blood and temper' had absolutely 'nothing to do with arithmetic'. Cardus argued: 'He might take no wickets, hold no catches, and make no runs ... and yet win a match for Yorkshire by his knowledge of how and when to attack.'

*Emmott Robinson, for whom cricket was a way of
living, a mission and also his religion.*

Robinson had 'shrewd eyes' and a 'hatchet face' and became to
Cardus 'the personification of Yorkshire cricket in one of its greatest
periods'. In print and in conversation he affectionately referred to him
as 'the old Emmott'. He saw in Robinson intense dignity, inexhaustible passion and an unmatched professional pride. 'Few,' he said of him,
'absorbed the game – the *Yorkshire game* – into their systems, their
minds, nerves and bloodstreams.' Every breath he took was for

Yorkshire. 'It was for him a way of living, a mission and also his religion,' added Cardus.

To Robinson belongs one of the best lines Cardus ever composed. Everything you need to know about him is contained in the emotive image Cardus plants in the mind: 'I imagine that he was created one day by God scooping up the nearest acre of Yorkshire soil at hand, then breathing into it saying, "Now, lad, tha's called Emmott Robinson and tha can go on with new ball at t'pavilion end."'

It has been said, ad nauseam, that Nottinghamshire's committee had only to whistle down a pit shaft to summon half a dozen strong-backed fast bowlers with biceps and forearms bulging like Popeye's. Yorkshire were better off than that. Whenever Cardus was in the county and saw 'a baby boy in a perambulator', he would mutter to himself: 'There goes one of their cricketers of the future.' Cricket was played everywhere – on scrubland, on cobbled streets beneath lamps, in backyards and gardens. The pool of talent was miles wide, fathoms deep and spread across the four ridings.

The Bradford League served as a finishing school for those who aspired to wear the cloth crown of a Yorkshire cap. It was hand-to-hand combat. You had to be mentally strong as well as immeasurably skilled to survive there in an atmosphere that could be sulphurous, so seriously were results taken. The league was formed in 1903. In the first four decades of its existence, the novice could find himself pitted against Jack Hobbs or Frank Woolley, Herbert Sutcliffe or the immortal S. F. Barnes, Learie Constantine or Len Hutton. Thousands paid to watch them, the pros picking up a lucrative salary supplemented by pass-the-hat donations for every half-century or five-wicket haul.

Robinson spent most of his early career in the Lancashire League, where he took more than 300 wickets for Ramsbottom, before Bankfoot, Pudsey St Lawrence and then Keighley enticed him over the border. Here Robinson learnt what Cardus described as 'no risk' cricket. 'He had no use for the flashing bat school,' he said. 'He dismissed it with one good word: "Swashbuckle."'

His swing bowling and dogged batting, every innings a rearguard action, earned him a belated call-up to Yorkshire. He was seen as a temporary solution to a short-term problem, which was filling one of those tragic gaps the Great War had created. Without that war, Robinson wouldn't have broken into the Championship at all. Without Cardus, he'd have been largely forgotten after getting there, a footnote of some vague curiosity in the club's history.

His move out of the Leagues and into the Championship brought Robinson renown, but not much more money. That fact rankled with Cardus, the plight of the under-paid county pros paramount to him.

In the mid-1920s one of the most pompous and patronising books ever published about the game, *A Searchlight on English Cricket*, was written anonymously by 'A County Cricketer'. The author was soon unmasked as E. H. D. Sewell. His grandfather had been a knight. His father had been a colonel in the army. Sewell had played briefly for Essex. One of his later books was called *From a Window at Lord's*, which was the prism through which he filtered most of his cricket. He was very much a gentleman of cricket's establishment – and very much a gentleman journalist too. He saw himself as a social arbiter of the game's dos and don'ts.

He believed two things. The first was that hard-handed pros shouldn't share dressing rooms, gates, trains or hotels with amateurs. The second was that most of these sons of toil would agree with his argument. To even campaign for equality would stir up 'restlessness and lack of discipline' among cricket's proletariat, claimed Sewell.

He saw sinister politics at work in 'the whole crusade against any so-called dividing line between amateur and professional'. He

*Emmott Robinson uncharacteristically posing as though
he was a flamboyantly attacking batsman.*

thought it was 'Communistic, if not Bolshevist, in tendency'. He had
a distaste for pros 'chit-chattering' to reporters too. A ghosted article
any of them submitted to the racy end of Fleet Street was in 'breach
of good custom' and then further condemned as 'this evil'. You can
only wonder how preposterously far Sewell's definition of 'evil' actually
stretched.

In the most priggish passage, which was a know-your-place finger-
wagging, he warned pros against what he saw as 'too great a tendency'

to 'demand' instead of 'request' better pay, better accommodation and better travel arrangements. Sewell also expressed acute personal disgust that some of them had been 'heard to ask for a glass of sherry after lunch', as though this was presumptuously uppity. He regarded the average pro as the hired help, the below-stairs servant, there only to fetch and carry uncomplainingly for his master, the amateur captain. He dismissed them as socially ignorant and uncouth, so uneducated in manners and etiquette that most would use a napkin as a handkerchief and wouldn't recognise the fish fork. No doubt, after reading *A Searchlight on English Cricket*, Sewell expected them to doff a flat cap, thank him profusely and then offer to shine his shoes.

Cecil Parkin made a more pertinent observation, which Sewell either hadn't read, given his intense dislike of paid cricketers hiding behind ghosts, or wouldn't quote because it punched a pavilion-sized hole through his arguments. 'Can anybody live decently and bring up a family on six pounds a week?' asked Parkin, who wanted 'a living wage the year round'. He was speaking up for himself and his ilk, which included Robinson.

Sewell was not alone in his Victorian attitudes. Cardus was fond of cheekily calling Lord Hawke 'the Dr Johnson of Cricket' on account of his lofty pronouncements, made as though he was sitting on top of Mount Olympus – a peak which Hawke gave the impression he alone was fit to occupy. Cardus thought his Lordship's notorious 'Pray God no professional will ever captain England' speech was typical of someone who belonged to 'a less democratic administration of the game'. Those who protested that Hawke had either been misquoted or misinterpreted were deluding themselves. Cardus knew a pro could lead a side because he'd seen Wilfred Rhodes do it unofficially at Yorkshire, and he felt, unlike draconian traditionalists such as Hawke, that the sight of him doing so officially wouldn't cause some cosmic upheaval.

What the Yorkshire pros earned (eventually raised to £11 for home games, £15 for away matches – plus win bonuses and talent money) seemed parsimonious and also feudal to Cardus.

There was even a huge discrepancy between what was pocketed by the top pros, among them Jack Hobbs, and the salary of labourers such as Robinson. Hobbs advertised cigarettes and energy drinks, fountain pens and breakfast cereal. He endorsed tailored suits. He made enough cash – annually banking around £1,500 – to buy a sports-goods shop. Robinson didn't own a car, travelling everywhere by train or tram or on foot. In the close season he'd scrape together a living from winter coaching, sometimes overseas, or from speaking engagements at dinners.

Jack Hobbs was so popular and so famous that John Tussaud sculpted a bust of him for Madame Tussauds wax museum in 1930.

When he at last got to know them, Cardus related easily to the county pros – though, admittedly, he did not always tell them why. Like him, they'd come from terraced homes with outside toilets. Like him, they'd grown up among men who, lacking much of a formal education, did manual labour or menial jobs because nothing else was available for them. Like him, they'd known what it meant to be poor or properly hard up, always fearing that late-night rap on the door from the rent-collector or the bailiff. Cricket had been a way of escaping all that.

Dick Tyldesley was once shown a report in which Neville Cardus slated him for 'some loose bowling'. He threw the *Manchester Guardian* on to the floor after reading it and snorted: 'Ah'd like to bowl at t' bugger.'

Emmott Robinson took a more conciliatory approach. At Bradford's Park Avenue, during a spotless day in 1920, he influenced the outcome of the Roses match unexpectedly and sensationally. Yorkshire were in disarray. Lancashire needed only 52 to win and had six wickets in hand. In broiling sun, Yorkshire's supporters disconsolately filed away, not wanting to listen to Lancashire gloat afterwards, and so missed Robinson tear through the middle order and tail, his bowling a blizzard of unplayable deliveries. He made the ball bend boomerang-like in the clammy air and took nine for 36. From a state of plush comfort Lancashire sank into miserable calamity. Their last six wickets fell for 24 runs. 'It was cricket almost too painful to watch,' said Cardus, disconsolately. He became so apoplectic about Lancashire's sudden and abjectly appalling collapse – sourly attributing it to supine batting – that he failed to give Robinson sufficient credit for his feat.

'I do not, of course, forget Robinson's excellent work,' he wrote, a little reluctantly, before compounding the error with three observations denigrating it through implication. Robinson hadn't bowled particularly well. The 'co-operation' he received from the batsmen guaranteed his success. Yorkshire hadn't won the match; Lancashire had lost it. He conceded 'bad luck alone' had denied Robinson all ten wickets – Roy Kilner claimed the other – and that his 'immense grit and determination' were primary in his personal triumph. The phrases still weren't fulsome enough; there was something distinctly grudging about them, as though Cardus couldn't believe Yorkshire had won and resented the fact.

A few weeks later Robinson ran into Cardus and complained to him. 'Ah suppose if ah'd tekken all *ten* wickets ah'd have convinced thi,' he said.

Contrite and embarrassed, Cardus accepted that he'd been unfair. From then on Robinson 'won my heart', he admitted. He began to look at him with 'the eyes of the lover to the beloved'. For Robinson, who had previously kept his distance, 'Maister Cardus' became a pal overnight, regularly sought out for company.

Robinson became more important as Cecil Parkin declined, a question mark of unfulfilled potential hanging over him. A man's personality will determine his fate and being your own worst enemy makes others superfluous. So it proved for Parkin, his career cut short in the mid-1920s after he made the mistake of trusting a ghostwriter. He gave him carte blanche to make up whatever he wanted in a signed piece for the *Weekly Dispatch*. Parkin saw the words attributed to him only when the newspaper was delivered – less than an hour before a queue of reporters began banging on his door. Beside his name were two columns of scalding criticism of the England captain Arthur Gilligan, lambasted for 'snubbing' him in a Test match against South Africa at Edgbaston. England had won at a stroll, but Parkin – top of the national averages then – had bowled only 16 overs, an admiring spectator as Gilligan himself claimed match figures of 11 for 90. Parkin's sanguine response at the time – he accepted the hard pitch suited Gilligan rather than him – became steaming outrage in print. The ghost quoted Parkin as being 'humili-ated' and then exacerbated the sin by inventing a spicier claim still: the threat to 'never again' play for England. The article was like a detonation blowing up beneath him. Even though Gilligan was magnanimous, supporting him publicly and privately, the MCC ostracised Parkin, a semi-broken man because of it. He went on a downhill slither, the japes wearing thin, before his first-class career petered out. He loved his cricket so obsessively that he once told Cardus: 'When me playing days are done, I'll do as those Roman Emperors did. I'll get into a hot bath and cut me ruddy throat.' Metaphorically at least, he did cut his own throat. The blade was ever-higher wage demands, a few more obstinate and intemperate newspaper articles and the tendency to be a belligerent nuisance – far too much of a misfit for Lancashire's liking.

Cardus spotted in Robinson what he'd originally recognised in Parkin – endless comic possibilities. He really did look and act – and walk and talk too – like someone who had fallen fully formed out of the pages of *The Pickwick Papers* or *Nicholas Nickleby*. Had Dickens met Robinson before Cardus did, he'd have based an entire work around him. He was only 5 ft 5 in tall. He had an impish face, small, sunken eyes and prematurely greying hair. His countenance was that of the gravedigger, and he shambled around the field in a shirt, sweater and flannels that looked as though he'd slept outdoors in them for a week. His awkwardness attracted Cardus. Like Arthur Mitchell, he wore his cap crookedly. His baggy trousers, awfully creased and grass-stained, were so loose that Cardus expected them to drop around his knees at any moment. He resembled a musical-hall comedian searching for a cheap laugh. 'You were getting ready to see them fall down altogether when he would remember them in time,' said Cardus, watching Robinson vigorously hitch his belt towards his narrow belly with his thumbs and forefingers before retightening it. The process would be repeated on several occasions throughout the day. So was the 'rolling up' of his trouser legs. For some reason unbeknown to anyone, Robinson bought his flannels a few inches longer than his legs and then turned them up above the ankle, which made him look like a holidaymaker about to paddle into the sea.

Once Robinson, much to Cardus's astonishment, arrived wearing brand-new kit. Before lunch he seemed stiff and uncomfortable in it, as if trussed up in a formal suit. But after tea, following some diving about in the dust, no one would have known that his clothes had been fresh and pill-white only that morning. He appeared again as cricket's vagabond traveller, dishevelled and wrinkled, like a bundle of dirty laundry.

Cardus normally liked to convey the pomp and circumstance of his favourite cricketers to his readers. With Robinson he preferred to show 'the eloquent droop of the man in his hours of impotence'. He said Robinson was 'at his best' when 'suffering frustration' because he'd be about to do 'something' that could be turned into a treasurable paragraph.

After one of his screaming pleas to an umpire, Cardus wrote: 'Emmott Robinson has just appealed for leg before wicket. You probably heard him.'

After another, which was rejected, Robinson's eyes turn into 'daggers' and he becomes 'so discommoded' at the over's end that he walks into the wrong fielding position.

And after an uncharacteristically rapid 23 scored in 15 minutes – for Robinson was usually a batting slowcoach – Cardus rebukes him with the sarcasm: 'The innings must be regarded as the one blemish in an otherwise unimpeachable career.'

Robinson was 'eternally trying hard' and 'always living vitally in the game', said Cardus. His hair was honourably 'silvered' and the 'keen lines graven on his face' were the consequence of constant worry as much as experience. 'He was one of the richest characters and most unselfconsciously humorous men ever to put on flannels,' explained Cardus, who then added: 'He would have been outraged at *any* suggestion that he was really being humorous. The great Yorkshire cricketers of character and comic genius never *tried* to be funny. On the contrary, they were terribly serious men.'

Cardus never pretended that cricket was the puritan's game. Or even that a high moral code always motivated those who played it. There was a lot of skulduggery going on. Bowlers coated their hands in resin. Wicketkeepers used bird lime on their gloves. Slip fielders waited until neither the umpires nor the batsmen could see them before unobtrusively jamming a long, hard fingernail beneath the seam to lift it. Some picked it until their fingernail bled. There were run-scorers who refused to walk even when the nick was loud enough to rattle the windows of the press box. 'There is gamesmanship *and* gamesmanship,' wrote Cardus, his use of italics differentiating what he called 'witty subterfuge' from 'malicious sportsmanship'. The former, he said, 'could be practised equally by both sides within the law'. The latter gave 'the opponent no opportunity to retaliate'. Cardus broke down the categories further. 'Then there is the way it is all exploited – whether with humorous relish or sour frustration.'

Cardus credited Robinson with one piece of jiggery-pokery that was 'fit to make all the watching gods on Olympus laugh their halos off' – even Lord Hawke.

He had pads as wide as barn doors, and knew how to use them. His motto was 'Nivver take a risk if you can win without.' When Lancashire required two wickets in three overs to gain precious first-innings points, Robinson plunged into defensive mode, hiding the bat so well behind his pads that he seemed to be playing without one. All went according to plan until five minutes to six. Misjudging the line, he got himself trapped leg before. 'He did not immediately "walk",' said Cardus. 'He

cocked his ear at the umpire as though temporarily afflicted by deaf-
ness,' and waited 'in case some mistake had been made'. Eventually,
with the umpire's finger still raised, he turned and began plodding to
the pavilion like a 'shirehorse after a wearying day of ploughing'. It was
'artful' and also 'a masterstroke', one of the most drawn-out retreats 'in
the history of cricket', said Cardus. Robinson was so deliberately slow,
first in leaving the crease and then walking towards the pavilion, that
he seemed 'not to be moving at all'. The tactic misfired. The last man,
Abe Waddington, impetuously came down the pitch, swung and
missed and was stumped comprehensively.

Months afterwards, in the depths of a northern winter, Cardus met
Robinson at a cricket dinner. 'At once he spoke to me as he sat by my
side at the groaning table. "Fancy," he said, "fancy Abe gettin' out like
that, *stumped*, in a Yorksheer and Lankysheer match with game in *that*
position." Then he smote the table, causing glasses, knives and forks to
dance. "Before anybody 'ad got ME out stumped ah'd 'ave died first."'

'What is more, he meant it,' said Cardus.

Emmott Robinson was generally a medium-pace outswing bowler,
who 'bowled as though nothing in the world existed' except the batsman crouched in his stance.

He began his run with a peculiar, one-legged 'dog kick' and ran the
floating new ball away, even as the perfect, inviting length lured his
victim forward. He liked a green wicket. At the beginning of a match,
Neville Cardus regarded it as 'a joy' to see him 'inspecting the turf,
pressing his fingers into it, feeling it and talking of the "texture" like a
shrewd buyer of cloth testing material'. He was paranoid about retaining the shine, preserving it by carrying the ball in 'cupped hands', as
though it were 'the Holy Grail'. If anyone thoughtlessly threw it in
short or along the ground, Robinson would be driven into a frenzy of

irritation and then 'seem almost to cross himself at the sight of an act of blasphemy'.

Even in his late forties, he insisted on fielding in close, almost suicidal, positions that began with 'silly' or 'short'. A batsman once told him he was 'a bit near, old boy' and asked him: 'Don't you think you might get hurt?' Robinson simply growled back: 'Thee get on wi' thi' laikin'. I'll tak care o' mesen.'

When a match was going badly, he would stand with his head down and his balled fist resting beneath his chin like Rodin's *The Thinker*. When it was going well, he would 'natter away', a constant dialogue that Cardus said would flow like the 'dirt-brown river Aire'.

His shambolic looks, as well as the broadness of his accent, could deceive the unwary into regarding him as an unsophisticated dolt. But Cardus acknowledged his remarkable tactical foresight with the compliment 'What a scourge that eager brain could be.'

He was a walking encyclopaedia, chiefly because he compiled his own, voluminous *Cricketing Britannica* and carried it around with him from ground to ground. Every evening Robinson wrote down notes of the day's play in a black, oilskin-covered book, a compulsive accumulation of intelligence which he said comprised 'Wheer t' batsman got runs, how they got out, their best shots, state o' t' wicket an' stuff like that.'

There was a charmingly eccentric zealotry about him too. Herbert Sutcliffe covered himself in a pungent eau de cologne, which made him smell like the soap counter at Harrods. Robinson liked to wait until Sutcliffe had sprayed himself and put away the bottle before entering the dressing room. He'd make a pantomime-show of sniffing the air before asking with a mischievous disdain: 'Who's bin usin' this muck?' He'd then stare inquisitively at each player in turn, always turning his gaze on Sutcliffe last of all.

He once hiked across the high-ridged toe of Yorkshire to deliver a brown paper parcel to Bill Bowes, recently married. The present had been bought especially for the groom. Whether Mrs Bowes wanted it didn't seem to matter. 'I've bought you a weather glass, Bill,' he said, spoiling the surprise before the unwrapping. 'It's the same as mine, an' tha wants to look at it night and morning. It's seldom that I've been let down, an' it's nice to know when there's a sticky wicket in t'offing.' He wasn't being flippant. As Robinson saw it, the barometer was the bowler's philosopher's stone. On the doorstep, he began regaling Bowes with an analysis of matches in which, like an infallible oracle, it had been decisive in determining a result. His parting shot to Bowes was 'Be sure that tha makes good use of it.'

A sign of how swiftly Robinson proved himself, despite his Championship inexperience, is that Wilfred Rhodes trusted his opinions. Rhodes was never discreet with his criticism. If he didn't like a player, he told him so. If he didn't rate him either, considering the man a liability, his backside wouldn't touch a bench in the dressing room. Almost immediately, Robinson became known as 'Wilfred's lieutenant'. His shrewdness made him indispensable. His ruthless intolerance of failure was quintessential Yorkshire; he could have been Lord Hawke's bastard son, so obsessed did he become about exploiting any advantage to win. Rhodes had complete confidence in him. He and Robinson were like-minded and inseparable, always talking or thinking about strategy and always speaking as one. One Sunday, Cardus came across the two of them strolling together through Hyde Park. The previous day, at Lord's, Yorkshire had totted up more than 300 runs. The Sabbath had unfortunately been spoilt by an early thunderstorm, now replaced with dazzling sun. '"A lovely afternoon," I said to them, in greeting,' recalled Cardus, who expected a jaunty, pleasant reply. Instead Robinson, his mind on the game, snapped: 'Aye, and a sticky wicket wastin' at Lord's.'

Rhodes and Robinson were responsible for giving Bowes and Hedley Verity their cricket education. At the end of every evening on an away trip there would be an informal coaching session before lights out. A shaving stick, a toothbrush, a hairbrush and other toiletries were positioned on a lumpy eiderdown to denote the fielders. 'All our mistakes,' said Bowes, were then 'discussed in detail'. Verity and Bowes once made the grievous mistake of going to the cinema, returning to find Robinson and Rhodes waiting for them in the hotel foyer. That day Verity had taken seven wickets for 26 against Hampshire. Robinson proceeded to chastise him for giving away a 'fower' – and not finishing with seven for 22. 'Whativver wa't' doin?' asked Robinson, telling Verity that he needed to be thriftier.

Robinson, despite being impecunious, always offered foundlings in Yorkshire's team the tantalising incentive of a five-shilling bounty for scoring a fifty or grabbing five wickets. He did so even when it meant robbing Mrs Robinson's housekeeping to pay for it. At his benefit match, as the hat was passed for contributions, Cardus saw a man clutching a shilling to give to the collector. The collector, however, didn't hear his shout and passed on. The man slipped his shilling back into his pocket. Aware of how much any sum, modest or not, mattered to the beneficiary, Cardus promptly made an appeal in the *Manchester Guardian* for the shilling to be handed over. 'In the interests of Emmott Robinson,' he wrote, 'this Yorkshireman ought to be rooted out, wherever he lives . . . A shilling's a shilling.'

Cardus didn't say whether he made a donation that day, but Robinson deserved far more than a shilling from him. 'I was lucky in my epoch to have before me, every day, material for my work,' said Cardus. Robinson provided a lot of it. No wonder, after his retirement, Cardus lamented 'the sorrowful gap' he left behind. 'Not soon are we going to look upon his like again,' he said.

In his first match report of the following season, he ruminated on Robinson's whereabouts. 'I wonder where the man is at the present moment. What is he doing? Probably saying "how's that?" involuntarily and by habit.'

The Yorkshire team would 'never look the same' to Cardus without him. But the fact Robinson wasn't playing didn't prevent him from making occasional guest appearances in the *Manchester Guardian*. No excuse to name-check him was ever wasted.

A green pitch would have made Robinson 'cry like a baby' to own it, said Cardus. At the sight of a risky cut, Cardus would picture the 'appalled expression' across those squashed features, as though the rashness of the stroke had imperilled the very future of cricket. An unlikely result, a headline-making innings or a fantastic display of bowling, pace and spin alike, would provoke the wistful thought 'What a pity we cannot interview Emmott Robinson about it.'

Improbable though it seems, Cardus got what he obviously wished for: he was able to write about one more Robinson appearance for Yorkshire. He was drafted in as a fielding substitute during a Roses match after Verity fell ill. In the third over, Robinson appealed for lbw from silly mid-on. The umpire shook his head and then addressed him directly, evidently in no mood to hear again hour upon hour of such badgering. 'Thee keep thi mouth shut,' he said, 'tha's not playin' in this match, really.'

For once, Robinson was speechless.

William Makepeace Thackeray asked of the novel: 'What if some writer should appear who can write so enchantingly that he shall be able to call into actual life the people whom he invents?' The opposite applied to Neville Cardus. The characters he wrote about could seem fictional, fashioned wholly from the imagination but allowed to breathe beside the living and against the backdrop of real places. Even Emmott Robinson got confused between how Cardus saw him and how he saw himself. A young Brian Close, meeting him a decade and a half after his retirement, said he found Robinson 'living up' to the character everyone supposed him to be.

Robinson's fidgety mannerisms and idiosyncrasies became more pronounced after Cardus highlighted them. He wore his scruffiness like a stage costume. He accentuated his own Yorksheerness, broadening an accent already as thick as a limestone slab. Much as an actor can never shake off a part he repeatedly plays, so Robinson couldn't detach himself from his depiction in the *Manchester Guardian*.

Robinson once said to Cardus: 'Tha' knows tha' made me oop?' Cardus denied it. 'I didn't, really,' he said. 'I *enlarged* him.'

This is what Cardus's explanation meant.

A wet morning at Headingley is followed by an afternoon of strong sunshine. Around three o'clock Robinson and Wilfred Rhodes inspect the pitch. Cardus has Rhodes pressing the turf with a forefinger and predicting: 'It'll be "sticky" at four o'clock.' Robinson then goes through the same procedure, as though the veterans are Tweedledee-Tweedledum twins, before he announces: 'Nay, Wilfred ... *half past*.'

What Robinson really said was simply: 'Aye, Wilfred.'

Cardus added in the 'half past' for the purpose of comedy, a leg-pull. Knowing Rhodes, and especially knowing Robinson, the exchange was not only plausible, but also characteristic. This was enough to make it permissible for Cardus. 'I didn't invent,' he insisted. 'My imagination drew out of him what was natural and germane to his character.' Cardus argued that afterwards Robinson would 'firmly' believe 'that he had said what I made him say'. Robinson even pinched the story, using it verbatim, for after-dinner talks. In the end, he convinced himself that the dialogue had left his lips as reported – and also that Cardus had absolutely nothing to do with it except acting as a reliable stenographer to his wit.

Where quotes were concerned, Cardus didn't necessarily burden himself with the inconvenience of having to be strictly factual. He couldn't resist – indeed, he seemed to see his interference as a duty – adding a pithy punchline to a speech that lacked one.

The other prime example came during a Roses match. Dick Tyldesley smartly takes an edge in the leg trap. He sportingly tells the umpire that the ball flicked the grass before he pouched it. The umpire recalls the batsman, who has turned and begun to walk off. Cardus congratulates Tyldesley in print and then in person. 'A fine piece of sportsmanship, Dick,' he says. 'Thanks, Maister Cardus,' replies Tyldesley. 'Westhoughton Sunday School, tha knows.'

The second sentence was another piece of Cardus's lovely embroidery, irresistible to someone who saw every game as a plot and every cricketer as a performer. 'In it was crystallised a portion of Lancashire's entire social history that throws a revealing light on the way Lancashire county's lads were brought up,' he said, referring to the Methodist Chapels prominent in most communities. As with Robinson's 'half past', Cardus tacked on 'Westhoughton Sunday School, tha knows' because he felt it was what Tyldesley *ought* to have said – and also precisely what he *would* have said if the thought had occurred to him.

Cardus gave reality a little push and pleaded 'guilty, m'lud' to that, offering an argument rather than excuses. 'I used to feel that these characters in cricket were not always communicative enough,' explained Cardus. 'They didn't say the right things. I thought something must be done about this ... I attributed to them the words I thought God intended them to say ... to make them articulate.' Cardus, writing a 'transcript of life', called this 'the Higher Truth'.

The benevolent will judge it as poetic licence, harmless entertainment that doesn't libel or belittle the subject and is written in the key of sympathy. The critical will damn it and his mitigation as abhorrent, arrogant, airy flimflam to cover a deliberate distortion. Whether you care and which side you take will largely depend on how much, if at all, you admire Cardus and his writing. He certainly was not a serial mythomaniac like the playwright Lillian Hellman, of whom Mary McCarthy said: 'Every word she writes is a lie, including "and" and "the".' Nor was he like the *New Yorker* writer Joseph Mitchell, who concocted composite characters who didn't exist. He certainly wasn't the *Daily Express* sports writer Desmond Hackett, overheard dictating quotes from a sent-off footballer even before the miscreant had left the muddy pitch. Cardus had more in common with the portrait painter John Singer Sargent, who told one sitter that he was widening the brim of her hat 'for compositional purposes'.

Cardus condemned those who condemned him as po-faced 'solemn upholders of prosaic fact', who were 'actually happy to kill a good story dead'. He knew cricket was full of good stories that weren't true but ought to have been, which is why they were published in the first place and then took root so deeply that everyone came to think of them as authentic. Human nature wants to believe, after all.

No, George Hirst didn't famously whisper to Rhodes 'we'll get them in singles' in the 1902 Ashes Test at The Oval. Bobby Peel didn't urinate against the sightscreen after Lord Hawke curtly dismissed him from the field for bowling in a beery fug for Yorkshire. And most of the anecdotes about W. G. Grace were wishful thinking, misremembrances or deliberate fabrications. Grace's *Memorial Biography* was sanitised to satisfy his wife's desire to immortalise her husband as a decent chap rather than an autocratic cad who considered the laws of the game as the basis for negotiation strictly on his own terms. Pelham Warner insisted to a friend that 'none' of the quotes attributed to Golden Age cricketers was true; but then Warner, never as close to W. G. as he wanted others to think, was brazen enough to dream up sufficient 'personal reminiscences' about the old man to persuade the BBC to make a programme about them.

Nowadays Warner wouldn't get away with a fraud like that. Nor would Cardus dare attempt to embellish a quote. He'd be found out instantly and excoriated for it. For what once could only be verified as genuine or exposed as fake by poring over big, dust-ridden bound volumes – and then cross-checking other big, dust-ridden bound volumes – can now be achieved with a few clicks of a computer mouse and a subscription to half a dozen newspaper libraries on the internet.

Something else was different in Cardus's day. Even some of the most famous faces in cricket weren't quite famous enough to be stopped on the street away from their own towns or cities. Those on the margins, such as Robinson, had the slimmest chance of being identified a hundred miles from home.

The photographs and caricatures published of them in newspapers or as cigarette cards were too small to make their features generally recognisable to anyone who didn't see them play regularly. A lot of film was shot, but most of it stayed in the can and wasn't shown. Eventually Pathé News put together profiles of each county club, which meant players who were normally seen no bigger than a couple of inches tall on newsprint were suddenly smiling at the cinemagoer on a shining screen 40 feet high. The viewer could compare Cardus's physical descriptions of them with the evidence of their own eyes.

He said that cricketers such as Robinson and Rhodes, Cecil Parkin and Dick Tyldesley simply set his 'humorous or picturesque imagination free to go its way'. Cardus was an impressionist painter – not a documentary photographer. He wrote about what he saw, but this might not necessarily have been what the writer beside him had seen. In the scant, short strips of film that exist of the players he doted on, it is noticeable nonetheless how accurately Cardus drew them – their walk, their run, their faces are exactly as he portrayed them to his readers.

The admissions Cardus made about tampering with quotes damages him irreparably as a scrupulous nuts-and-bolts news reporter, but never as a critic – and certainly not as a master of descriptive prose. John Arlott, who made a thorough study of him and subsequently buttressed it with anecdotal research, reached two important conclusions: Cardus's exaggerations had themselves been 'exaggerated' and they were of 'little consequence'. He hadn't made up nearly as much as he'd been accused of – and there were cricketers' autobiographies and an assortment of club histories to confirm that. Arlott also thought his audience preferred Cardus's Higher Truth to the Literal Truth.

'No one treasures a "Cricketer" article more than the cricketer about whom it is written,' said J. M. Kilburn. Another reliable witness put it even better and more comprehensively than that.

'Ah ewsed to think 'at he took t'mickey aht o' me sometimes be what he said abaht me when we wor laikin' Lankysheer, but noa-body injoyed it moore nor Ah did. They wor reyt happy days, and na-body did moore nor Neville Cardus to mak''em happy days.'

So spoke Emmott Robinson.

Lancashire managed to win another County Championship – in 1934 – but Neville Cardus knew why Yorkshire eclipsed them so often, taking three titles immediately before that summer and another four after it. 'The county ignored the genius on the doorstep,' he said.

Cardus frequently quoted Dr Johnson's judgement of Edmund Burke to explain why a particular player appealed so strongly to him. 'If you met him for a few minutes in a shed while sheltering from the rain you would say: "That is a remarkable man."' Learie Constantine fell into that category.

Cardus was never given enough credit for his staunch practical support of Constantine, who told John Arlott of Cardus's kindnesses. He was always offering 'to help' in any way possible and recommending (as he did for others) books and music. In return, Constantine called him 'My favourite cricket writer'.

Constantine put into perspective, rather politely, what it was like to be black in Britain between the wars. He had to 'walk delicately', he said. 'If I am introduced to a white person, I have learned now to keep my hand at my side until a white hand is plainly offered to me. A good many times of holding my hand out and having it ignored has taught me what I must call "Negro-in-England" manners.' Appalling prejudice was commonplace and considered acceptable by those who perpetrated it – and too many of those who saw it happen.

In 1929 Constantine signed lucratively for Nelson in the Lancashire League.

The bulk of Pendle Hill rose distantly beyond the club's boundary. If you could see its contours, the locals claimed, then it was about to rain. If you couldn't, it was already raining. The town was choked with mills, terraced houses and smoke, the 40,000 population predominantly working class and almost exclusively white. Constantine was the only black face in Nelson apart from a man who collected refuse in an old pushcart.

Constantine described himself as a 'coloured curiosity' there. Most of the community into which he settled couldn't have picked out Trinidad, his island, in an atlas and had only the vaguest notion of where the Caribbean Sea lay.

As well as hiring him on £500 per summer, paid in weekly instalments of £25, Nelson handed Constantine a guinea for every half-century and each haul of five wickets or more. There were travel expenses, too, and the largesse of 'The Collection', the size dependent on the munificence of the spectators. Nelson arranged digs for Constantine and his wife, Norma, which is how one of the highest-paid sportsmen in Britain found himself boxed into two rooms beneath the beady eyes of a battleaxe landlady. Her greeting was hardly warmly welcoming. She made it abundantly and undiplomatically clear that 'nobody else would have us', said Constantine. The couple were both pestered and shunned. Some peeked voyeuristically through their front window to catch sight of them, as though husband and wife were a just-discovered species in some zoo's glass cage. Racists crossed the road to avoid them. Or pointed. Or whispered abuse. A young boy approached Constantine and asked innocently: 'Has ta' bin down t' coal 'ole, mister?' Another shook his hand and then looked at his own palm, expecting some trace of inky blackness to have passed on to it. A third, whom Constantine befriended, dissolved into tears after his friends mocked him. 'Uncle Learie, you never told me you were coloured,' he said, bewildered. The post brought hate mail, the poison-penmanship usually anonymous. One letter began 'Dear Nigger'. Away from Nelson, he was refused tables in restaurants and rooms in hotels. At one cricket dinner he heard a woman proclaim loudly: 'I see they've let the jungle in on us.' A team-mate, run out on Constantine's call, chastised him as 'a black bugger'. What Constantine called other 'incidents' and 'a few nasty moments' with Nelson and elsewhere were 'mostly hushed up', he admitted.

Even after Constantine had established himself, becoming the respected local champion, he felt obliged to quote 'a medical expert' who had analysed and compared the blood of every nationality, concluding categorically that 'the coloured man' was biologically no different from any other. There were dissenters who refused to believe it, the blinkered sort who, seven decades earlier, would have scoffed at Charles Darwin's declaration about evolution.

Cardus went to watch his debut for Nelson at Accrington. Everyone was there for one cricketer, one purpose. The tramcars were 'packed to a tightness that made the occupants for the time being bosom friends, intimately connected', said Cardus. It was a freezing Saturday, the turf heavy. Cardus spoke to the elderly tea lady, who sympathised with Constantine's wintry introduction to the season. 'I'm sure he's feeling cold,' she said, staring out of the window at the low, mottled clouds. 'She saw him not as a great cricketer,' explained Cardus, 'but as a lorn, lost native, far from home.' Constantine took three wickets, claimed one catch, scored 27 runs, including five fours, and, according to Cardus, who heard a 'buzz' from the crowd when he batted, set 'the imagination aflame' with his 'adventurous heart'. Without him there was no show. 'At the fall of Constantine's wicket,' said Cardus, 'hundreds of spectators got up and went home to tea. I was one of them.'

Cardus considered him to be 'the most original cricketer of the present day'.

As a bowler, he was 'hostile' and expected to take a wicket with 'every ball'. He ran in 'as though for dear life', his cap sometimes blowing off his head during the galloping, bouncing approach, before a 'sideways leap' and then the delivery, his arm 'beautifully high'. As a batsman, 'no man, living or dead, had ever hit shots more fiercely or cleared such distances'. It was as though a Constantine innings was like a meteor shower. 'One of these days he will lose a cricket ball for ever; no one will ever find out exactly where it dropped,' he said. As a fielder, he 'should be given first refusal on all catches from deep long leg to third man', because his sprinter's speed, beyond human reckoning, would allow him to swoop and gather it first 'wherever it is skied'.

Cardus was utterly apolitical, so engrossed in the aesthetics of life that social struggles around him – the General Strike, the Wall Street Crash and subsequent Great Depression – didn't penetrate the rarefied bubble in which he breathed. General elections came and went without his cross appearing on any ballot. The news in newspapers was barely glanced at. Only the arts pages were properly read. His unawareness of, and almost total lack of interest in, serious events and issues of the day – as well as anybody else's response to them – could be spectacularly bad. Ideally no explanation should be ruined by an excuse, but ignorance led Cardus into errors of taste and judgement.

Learie Constantine, his every innings like a meteor shower of shots. 'No man . . . had ever hit shots more fiercely or cleared such distances,' said Cardus

Constantine asked him to write the foreword to his book *Cricket and I*. As Ramachandra Guha has pointed out so trenchantly, the page and a half Cardus submitted 'presented a stereotypical view of cricket in the West Indies'. He thought Constantine's game grew from 'impulses born in the sun and influenced by an environment and a way of life much more natural than ours'. His cricket was 'racial', added Cardus. Another piece, appearing the following summer, reads now as unforgivably insensitive. Cardus first criticised Constantine for being too flamboyant. 'It will be a pity,' he went on, 'if Constantine allows his crowd to endow him with the irresponsibility of a "jazz" coon cricketer.' You can hardly credit that Cardus, an educated man, failed to comprehend the insult he was hurling; or how hurtful Constantine would find it. As he did with so many slurs, Constantine let it pass.

The inside of Old Trafford's pavillion, which Cardus knew so well. A painting of his hero, A. C. MacLaren, hangs to the right-hand side of the fireplace.

Cardus was lobbying Lancashire's committee to recruit Constantine. He admired his dignity and his poise, and campaigned for him as though quietly electioneering for a candidate, knowing Constantine was 'eager' to go to Old Trafford. Constantine acknowledged, and was grateful for, Cardus's influential support. The plan still broke apart. Constantine was content to say an 'unpleasant disagreement because of my colour' was responsible. Just how unpleasant that disagreement had been became apparent decades later.

Wisden described Len Hopwood as a 'utilitarian cricketer' of whom no spectator would ever claim nostalgically: 'What fun he was to watch.' It was Hopwood who revealed that the prospect of Constantine wearing the Red Rose cap and sweater had brought the dressing room into near-revolt. 'The thought of a coloured chap playing for Lancashire was ludicrous. We Lancastrians were clannish . . . We wanted none of Constantine. We would refuse to play . . . A black man taking the place of a white man in our side was anathema.'

Cardus had been wasting his time. 'Imagine what he could have done for Lancashire,' he said.

7

THE TEN-SHILLING NOTE

CARDUS DEVELOPED WHAT he called 'two different personalities' on the *Manchester Guardian*. There was Neville Cardus as 'Cricketer' and Neville Cardus as music critic. When the first went into hibernation, the second took over. To him it was as straightforward as shedding one set of clothes and slipping on another. To others, especially those he most wanted to impress, these disparate disciplines seemed not only incongruous but also wholly incompatible, like displaying bookends that weren't a matching pair.

Cardus protested: 'I used to be asked – and I am still being asked – "How can you reconcile cricket with music?" Why shouldn't one write about any two subjects if one has an affinity for them?' He said that possessing 'two related or complementary subjects' was 'therapeutic', enabling him to 'refresh' himself by moving from one to the other. He'd add that even 'great artists have had some ordinary enjoyment'. Mozart played billiards. Strauss endlessly shuffled cards, duelling in games of 'skat'. Toscanini watched wrestling. Shostakovich liked football, often writing about it in his diary. Cardus saw music and cricket to be exactly alike in one respect. Each was equal as 'a form of human expression'.

It was a nuisance for him to have to constantly explain this. It was also an irritation to have to defend himself to music aficionados, who believed his relationship with cricket was somehow sullying, and to cricket devotees, who thought he ought to specialise, concentrating exclusively on their sport. Lastly, it was wounding to discover that, however much he ached to be recognised primarily as a writer on Brahms and Beethoven rather than on Len Hutton or Walter Hammond, Cardus found himself nonetheless more widely regarded as 'a cricket correspondent who pops along to concerts'. He wanted to be taken seriously – too seriously, perhaps – in his judgements of music. But irrespective of how many fine reviews and notices appeared – more than 2,000 in the *Manchester Guardian* alone – Cardus still had to overcome the suspicion that his summer job would always devalue, and even taint, his winter one. The prejudice continued to rankle with him. 'The music critic who relaxes now and then into, say, cricket is at once eyed dubiously,' he said, as though talking about someone else while acknowledging his personal problem.

Summer Place hadn't been a musical household. It didn't contain an upright piano, which a lot of homes inherited and retained for decoration, using the top as a plant stand. As a working-class chap, who played cricket on the brick crofts, he said he risked being derided as 'a sissy' for taking an interest in music. But 'music', explained Cardus, 'came to me by grace' all the same. This epiphany occurred in his late teens, listening to the light opera *Tom Jones* in Manchester's Prince's Theatre. He sold some cherished books, enabling him to return time and again to hear it in the same week. From then on he was 'determined to have a long love affair with music'.

The gramophone record was a rare and expensive thing. Most recordings were on cylindrical phonographs, the reproduction more crackle, hiss and spit than gorgeous sound. Cardus remembered: 'If you heard a wonderful piece at a concert, and you went home ... haunted by the lustre of the music ... you were filled with sadness at not being able to afford to go and hear the piece again, for months or even years.' Cardus was lucky, discovering he had the equivalent of an eidetic memory for sound. He could 'remember music without effort', recalling it again flawlessly in his mind, as though a needle had been dropped on to a record playing beside him.

As with his education in literature, Cardus was predominantly self-taught in music. He queued for the shilling area to hear the Hallé Orchestra. He took singing lessons. He copied out 'great tracts' of scores. He began to learn the language of music 'exactly as a boy learns everyday speech'. Oddly, given his musical bent, Cardus failed to master an instrument; he was a rotten pianist just as he was a rotten typist, one keyboard as trying for him as the other. Music still became part of him. 'I think that in all my life,' he said, 'I have made a good and thorough job of only one thing – listening to music.' He cultivated 'the art of listening', he added, which allowed him to 'live the life' he 'wanted most of all' – being paid eventually to attend concerts from Salzburg to Vienna, from the Three Choirs Festival to the Edinburgh Festival and from the Free Trade Hall in Manchester to the Queen's Hall in London.

On the basis that 'nobody respects a deputy', Cardus claimed to be 'not particularly anxious' to go into music criticism in Samuel Langford's long and formidable shadow. Langford had unselfishly shared his intelligence, never attempting to either discourage Cardus or indulge in one-upmanship against him. But Cardus wanted first to 'come to some confidence in myself as a writer' and work 'more or less a seam of my own' before attempting to compete on the same level. Cricket gave him that platform.

In 1927, Langford died in the same timbered house and in the same bed where he had been born 64 years earlier. He'd been so ill that his last notices were written in private boxes during the intervals of concerts. Cardus, acting as his messenger, took his copy to the office and then put him in a taxi. Langford's final column was composed while he was propped up on a pillow. Cardus collected it, arriving to find his dear friend 'exhausted', his head lying sideways so that he could peep at the sky and look at his garden from a small window. Outside, a tree was beginning to leaf. 'The last he would see of the light of the world would come through the same latticed window,' wrote Cardus.

He succeeded Langford as chief music critic as though by hereditary right. From the start, and thanks to Langford, he had a confidence in his music criticism which he didn't possess in his earliest cricket writing. He was certain his reviews were 'good'.

Walter Pater had set down a route map for critics, the signposts of which Cardus followed. It applied to cricket and music equally and was governed by the gut. Pater wrote: 'The first step towards seeing one's object as it really is, is to know one's own impression as it really is, to discriminate it, to realise it distinctly ... What is this song or picture, this engaging personality in life or in a book, to *me*?' The quote underlines how much Pater's philosophy became ingrained in Cardus; even the use of italics is a bow to Pater. 'I cannot describe what Beethoven's Fifth Symphony means, as an object outside my own mind,' wrote Cardus. 'But I can at least try to describe what it means to *me*.' His favourite saying became 'A critic should have a score in his head, not his head in the score.'

The *Manchester Guardian*'s calling card gave Cardus authority and influence. Few newspapers anywhere gave as much space to music. Cardus used it well. He approached concert criticism the way he had previously approached cricket reporting. He didn't think too highly of a lot of his colleagues, who sat stern-faced in their reserved, cushy seats. 'I hated the bulk of English music criticism for its dryness of nature and parsimonious good-mannered use of the language ... I decided I was going to enjoy myself,' he said. Cardus didn't want to be stuffy or buttoned up, which is how he saw the more sombre and scholarly reviewers, who submitted pieces that read either like a wet, sorry day at a cricket match or as though repetition made the music dully familiar to them. If these men had been books, Cardus wouldn't have turned a single page of them.

He believed music was poetry – 'the language through which men of genius reveal themselves' – and he intended to 'always' bow his head to 'the miracle of it'. BBC broadcasts were making classical music more accessible to the masses than ever before. There was a new audience even for Covent Garden opera, and Cardus sought to appeal to it. As he had done with cricket, he also sought to imbue his columns with some 'romanticism', defined as 'imagination with a sunset touch', and some character too. He'd quote Mahler – 'what is best in music is not to be found in the notes' – to emphasise that he was searching for the soul of a conductor or a soloist in the same the way he'd searched for it in a cricketer such as Emmott Robinson. He wanted to be read by people who had only a minuscule interest in music. 'If I were the editor of a newspaper, and only musicians read the notices of my music critic, I would sack him.'

A writer's style is like his fingerprint, and so you can read Cardus on music and recognise the loops, arches and whorls, belonging uniquely to him, that had already dominated his cricket writing. The reader isn't drenched in the technical detail of the musicologist. He would say, quoting Lord Chesterfield's advice: 'Wear your learning, like your watch, in a private pocket. Do not pull it out and strike it, merely to show that you have one.' Cardus liked to linger on what he described as 'a single aspect of the passing show', which allowed him 'to hail the flying moment'. You know he's locked on to what he called those 'certain' words, which aren't 'just plain and as battered as current coin', but evoke the essence of a performance. The violinist who could 'transform silence into the very air of melancholy'. The pianist whose playing 'inspires pulsations of the aesthetic senses', so that 'he and the piano are one and indivisible'.

Langford had passed on a slice of advice that Cardus stored away: 'Never write anything about a performer that you wouldn't be prepared to say to him face to face.' He did damn one concert nevertheless as a series of 'orchestral bowel releases (without odour)', and responded to the critical reception given to another with an elegant slap: 'Somebody was heard to remark that the tone here and there became thin. And our expert will no doubt stride into Heaven one day, and his first comment will be that an angel's halo is not level over the head.'

Cardus's main competitor was Ernest Newman, another Lancastrian, whom he called 'the Aristotelian' of the *Sunday Times*. Theirs was a rivalry-cum-friendship that survived 'many acrimonious arguments' in print. Langford had taught him to 'feel and translate'. Newman taught him to 'observe and analyse'. Newman wore a homburg hat and a long dark coat. He had heavy lips and lidded eyes and 'flavoured every word he uttered', said Cardus. There was respect but also wariness between them. Cardus thought Newman had a 'blind spot' for Mozart which, in cricket, was the equivalent of being unable to recognise the superiority of Jack Hobbs or Victor Trumper. Cardus was a Mozart man; to him, he represented 'the very spirit of music'.

'What is a critic to say of Mozart at his most felicitous?' he asked. 'The purer the music, the less there is to be said about it.' Newman grumbled that Cardus was dreamy and besotted about composers and conductors, a tendency that knocked the edge off his critical faculties. 'The trouble with you, Cardus, is that you are too in love with music,' he told him.

Cardus took the insult as a compliment, never diluting his response to what had moved him. Bach was 'music's great sane head'. Beethoven was 'its storm-tossed heart'. Schubert was 'kindly and humane'. Of Wagner, he celebrated someone whose 'mind worked on two planes . . . he saw with his ears and heard with his eyes.' Mahler was that 'daemon-driven seeker, and ultra-sensitive barometer of mankind's vicissitudes'. Elgar, who made music like 'the perfect gentleman', told of 'a way of living and thinking' that was 'indigenous to the part of our land that nurtured him'. Of course, you had to hear his 'greater works' in cathedral cities such as Worcester, where his music 'gives a tongue to the

*New Road Worcester, from the pavilion. One of
Neville Cardus' favourite grounds.*

place's very stones'. And Toscanini's 'pursuit of beauty' was 'fanatical'.
He 'suffers for it', said Cardus, and serves the work of the masters 'like
a priest'.

References to music appeared frequently into his descriptions of cricket
and cricketers because Cardus was still thinking about a concert or a
performer whenever he watched a game, including a Test. He said he
studied Wally Hammond in 'much the same way that I listened to the
Jupiter symphony of Mozart'. Cardus saw him bat majestically at Lord's
and then went that evening to Covent Garden, where he felt 'a certain
lowering of the aesthetic temperature'. Nothing he heard there, during
some bawling Italian opera, compared to the uplifting sight of
Hammond's strokes. Significantly, however, cricket doesn't spill at all into
his collected essays and reviews on music. Hammond could be likened to
Toscanini, but Toscanini could never be likened to Hammond, because
he thought such a reference would have been inappropriately vulgar. On
this, he could be stuck-up-snooty, directly contradicting his earlier asser-

tion that – in artistic expression – music and cricket were equal partners.

Cardus confessed: 'If anyone had ever told me that I was destined to make a reputation as a writer on cricket, I should have felt very hurt.' The comment is so derogatory that he might as well have rubbed the disparagement in, claiming he slummed it at Lord's but lorded it with the Vienna Philharmonic. Instead, he said something worse. He made it sound as though cricket had been nothing except a ladder, useful for taking him to a higher place from where he could look down on it a little disdainfully. 'My cricket,' he said, had been a 'means to an end – that end being always music'.

Cardus would later recant, but the fact he said it at all is indicative of how much he had changed. His first publisher, Grant Richards, found him 'austere' and 'sensitive', someone who would 'not believe his stuff is worth reprinting'. His second, Rupert Hart-Davis, whom *The Times* described as 'the king of editors', remarked that 'applause' to 'some extent' had gone to Cardus's head.

Hart-Davis was being a mite diplomatic. Cardus became a ubiquitous celebrity in the circles in which he moved. He wasn't shy of reminding everybody about it.

Arnold Bennett was one of the few writers who could make a fortune with a single book in a single day. His annual earnings before the Great War topped £16,000 – worth in excess of £1m today. After it ended, he stopped counting. He owned a Queen Anne country house and a yacht. He travelled luxuriously in Europe and America. He prolifically produced novels and plays alongside essays, reviews, polemics and other assorted non-fiction. Neville Cardus admired Bennett's work, especially *The Card*. He saw himself in its comic protagonist, 'Denry' Machin, the archetypal self-made man, who through chutzpah rises from washerwoman's son to mayor and wealthy entrepreneur. Bennett, like Cardus, was a provincial lad. The squat, bulbous kilns of the Potteries were the landscape of his childhood.

In his cub days on the *Manchester Guardian*, Cardus was sent to the first night of a Bennett play. He spotted the author, 'a pouter-pigeon of crinkled shirt-front and tails'. He boldly went to introduce himself, one question pre-prepared. 'I asked him,' said Cardus, 'if it was possible for a writer to live for long in the provinces and come to anything.' Bennett had a crippling stammer. Saying 'hello' was difficult enough. Saying his name was sometimes trying unless enormous pressure was put on the tongue, his facial features contorting so dramatically that his eyes bulged. Cardus could mimic the impediment. Bennett 'doubted' that anyone shut off from the smart salons of London could prosper as a man of letters. But he warned him: 'D-don't c-c-consider leaving the *M-Manchester Guardian* for j-j-just a few p-pounds extra. M-Money is n-no use, my boy, except in l-l-l-LARGE quantities.' That final, clinching statement was stammered out in a 'high explosion' of breath, said Cardus.

The 'applause' Cardus constantly heard on his behalf, and which Rupert Hart-Davis had spoken about, grew steadily in volume. Editors flocked around him like birds pecking after breadcrumbs. He wrote so much and so widely that you suppose he seldom slept. He contributed to *The Listener*, *The Field*, the *Empire Review*, *The Spectator*, *John Bull Magazine* and an assortment of other periodicals – general titles, some specialising in music and others in sport. The BBC invited him to give scripted talks, privately warning producers to 'balance' the microphone because his ill-fitting dentures had a tendency to 'rattle'. He'd recently had 22 teeth removed.

His piece 'Cricket Fields and Cricketers' was prestigiously chosen as one of *The Hundred Best English Essays* by the Earl of Birkenhead. On this literary scorecard, spread over more than 900 pages, Cardus went in to bat beside Hazlitt and Macaulay, Conrad and Wilde,

Strachey and Churchill. Another essay, 'Cricket and Cricketers', was picked for *Prose of Our Time*, part of the Teaching of English Series for schools. Again, Cardus kept exalted company. Other writers in the collection included D. H. Lawrence, J. B. Priestley and Virginia Woolf. He found his selection amusingly ironic. His education had been rag and bone; now he was going into classrooms as a torchbearer for writing. As a valuable learning guide, the rump of the book offered students a brief analysis of each writer's style. Cardus showed 'lyrical joy', it declared. He was 'cultured' and 'epigrammatic'; and his 'Plutarchan use of anecdote' was expressive and perceptive.

It posed questions too. The first was: 'Is the general effect at all impaired by the rhapsodizing passages?' The second asked: 'Discuss and give examples of Mr Cardus's habit of treating the game and its conditions symbolically.' Cardus said he 'didn't have a clue' how to answer either of them. He did have *every* clue when it came to exploiting his profile, something no one else writing about sport could then hope to attain.

In the late 1920s and early 1930s the orderly queue for Cardus's services snaked down Fleet Street.

The Observer's editor J. L. Garvin tentatively proposed the newspaper should 'borrow' Cardus every Saturday because the *Manchester Guardian* didn't need him. Rebuffed in that approach, Garvin attempted to take Cardus on to his staff. So did the *Sunday Times*. So did Lord Beaverbrook's stable of newspapers – especially the *Evening Standard*. The salary would be £1,500 per year (a six-figure sum today). There was one catch. Cardus would write exclusively for the *Standard*, forgoing lucrative freelance contracts.

While basking in the courtship, Cardus admitted privately that he had 'no intention, deep down' of ever leaving the *Manchester Guardian*. Music, rather than cricket, was the reason for this. 'You had only to tell any musician in Europe, any man of letters, artist – anyone who was anyone, in fact, that you belonged to the *Manchester Guardian* and at once they met you not as a pressman, not as a journalist, but as a writer, free and civilised.' The newspaper also bent submissively to his whims. He could submit a column half a yard long and expect to see it published uncut. He could cover whichever cricket match or concert he chose.

He still made expert use of the leverage rival offers provided. He even wrote to Garvin, the letter containing flirting, flannel and a lot of flattery. 'The only paper for me in London is yours,' he declared. While ostensibly pleading for guidance about Beaverbrook's approach to him, Cardus was really making a negotiating move. The rigmarole was necessary to squeeze more out of the *Manchester Guardian*. Cardus collected offers as easily as philatelists collected stamps. Each offer was outlined to his editor. C. P. Scott or his successors prevaricated – Scott always claimed he'd never 'stand in the way of any man's advancement' – before folding to the unspoken demand of a salary increase, the newspaper unable to afford losing him. Cardus would be given a further 'one hundred pounds per year'. His salary shot to £1,100 – plus the kind of expenses that Mr and Mrs Ordinary could have lived on comfortably. He was the only person on the *Manchester Guardian* to earn four figures through 'writing alone'. With his freelance work too – turning down more requests than he could ever accept – Cardus counted among Britain's swell well off. At the beginning of the 1930s, when purchasing power was considerably higher than today, the average annual wage amounted to £195. At the end of the decade, it was still only £214. You could buy a three-bedroom house in London for £350.

Garvin's reply to Cardus is lost. The next letter to him from Cardus comes four months later. He apologises for taking so long to respond to Garvin's advice. He gushes that 'I regard you as an adopted father – and I've never had one of my very own.' He repeats the claim that

The Observer is his paper of choice. He is 'content to wait' for the chance to work for it. As well as dripping with insincerity, Cardus's letter angles for another tasty offer he can use as blackmail.

Cardus held an image of himself as a distinguished and privileged literary gent and man about town. It was gleaned from two now long-forgotten novels by J. M. Barrie, both of them predating *Peter Pan*. The books, *When a Man's Single* and *My Lady Nicotine*, were about 'pipe-smoking and lodgings' and 'letters from editors commanding more and more articles' and upright Chesterfield armchairs in wood-panelled gentlemen's clubs from where the old boys' network traded favours over goblets of brandy. Cardus was unknown, unconfident and past 30 before he saw the side of London that Barrie had described for him. He wanted it permanently for himself.

Cardus came to believe 'the word culture was seldom pronounced' in Manchester. The city became too insignificantly small and provincial to contain him and his ambitions.

In London he could seek out those who admired him, hobnobbing with writers and poets such as J. B. Priestley, Siegfried Sassoon and the now-knighted Barrie. He soon cultivated a coterie of influential music friends, among them the conductor Sir Thomas Beecham, fellow Mancunian and creator of the London Philharmonic Orchestra. Their relationship, initially spiky, became so close that Cardus would become his biographer. There was also Arthur Bliss, composer of *Morning Heroes*, which he wrote to rid himself of recurring nightmares about the Great War, and Malcolm Sargent, for whom fame as a conductor arrived early and never left. The affinity between them stemmed at first from a shared background. Sargent came from emphatically working-class stock too; his father had been a coal merchant.

Lord's also ceased to be the inhospitable place that the self-styled 'callow' and 'unfashionable northerner' had instinctively recoiled from and wanted to rebel against. Cardus's conversion was so miraculous that the St John's Wood Road, running outside the Grace Gates, should have been renamed the Road to Damascus.

He felt crowds ought to go to The Oval by bus – 'the democratic way' – but regretted that hansom cabs were 'not run specially for men of sentiment' who wanted to ride stylishly to Lord's through Regent's Park. On sunny mornings, Cardus would take the Tube to Baker Street and stroll the rest of the way, using a rolled-up umbrella like a walking stick. He would cut through Dorset Square, past Marylebone Station and along Lisson Grove.

Lord's was now 'my headquarters', he said, switching swiftly from outsider to insider. The stewards, whom in the beginning he had regarded as stuck-up and unfriendly, practically bowed and gave a tug of the forelock whenever he appeared. He was soon maintaining that 'the ends of the earth' came to 'a resting point' at Lord's for every 'good cricketer'. Also, he thought every cricket-lover, 'wherever he may be at the fall of a summer's day,' should turn his face religiously towards it. Already eyeing MCC membership and the benefits it would bring, Cardus promised 'the name of Lord's' would be found 'graven' on his heart. He came to see it as a 'haven of peace in an unruly world', basking in the 'aristocratic pleasure' of the place.

He celebrated the ground as 'a microcosm' of the city too. The Tavern side was 'the East End'. The Long Room was 'the West End'. When the lunchtime promenade on the grass took place, he thought the 'Seven Dials was free to move with Belgrave Square' in a display of social equality. This was spurious nonsense, of course.

Life increasingly meant London for him. In 1931 he even took 'Town Membership' – four guineas per year – and long-term residency in a snug room at the National Liberal Club. The club, which Gladstone had first established in neo-Gothic, high-ceilinged splendour at the beginning of the 1880s, had grand bars and a spacious dining hall, a panelled library and a riverside terrace. Members included literati such as George Bernard Shaw, H. G. Wells and G. K. Chesterton.

Cardus once said: 'I can't work in a domestic atmosphere. I must have a place with no distraction.' His room, which was rather like a monk's cell, provided this. There was a single bed, a wardrobe, a bedside table and a desk. Cardus refused to clutter the space with pictures, books or 'gramophone' records because he disliked possessions, which he considered as a burden.

This was still the apotheosis of pleasure and decadence for him. Uniformed staff opened doors and nodded greetings. Every morning, Cardus was brought tea and toast and his newspaper. He didn't have to shop for food or cook for himself. He didn't have to launder or press his clothes. He didn't even have to tidy up: someone made his bed and arranged his razor and soap in the bathroom. Every evening his mail and messages were waiting in a neat pile on his desk. He could solicit company and conversation when he wanted it – there was always someone hanging around the bar or the dining hall – or hide away in silent solitude after borrowing a book from the library. Small things mattered to Cardus. He made full use of the club's free stationery, pretentiously aware that its embossed paper showed not only where but also how comfortably he was living. A Whitehall location was ideal for him too: a cab, hailed by a flunky, would take him to Lord's or The Oval, to Covent Garden or the Queen's Hall.

Of course, one person was conspicuously missing from the swirl of Cardus's very ordered, very civilised and very aesthetic existence in London.

His wife Edith was barely seen at all.

The details of everyone's sex life seem pruriently funny – apart, of course, from your own. Neville Cardus was the perfect example. He was a virgin until his mid-forties.

He was the sort of man who flirted and fell in love easily, gadding about with what his wife called 'his little girls'. Edith didn't complain. 'It makes him so much better tempered when he comes home,' she said phlegmatically. When Cardus couldn't find a suitable partner to accompany him to a function, Edith would chide him for being too picky: 'Eh, Neville. You're getting too particular about your girls.'

The 'girls' were always younger than him and always acolytes of his writing. The relationship he struck up with them was always platonic too. Cardus quoted the love letters swapped between George Bernard Shaw and the actress Ellen Terry. He thought one phrase of Shaw's was particularly relevant to him. 'All my love affairs end tragically because the women can't use me.'

But Cardus's marriage was almost a decade old when he became infatuated with a woman he considered to be 'the most beautiful in the world'.

It changed his life.

The postman began the affair, bringing Cardus a fan letter that was written in pencil on a page ripped out of a notebook. The writer said she had strained her ankle. She was unable to leave her home in Kent to watch Frank Woolley bat at Canterbury. 'You will surely understand the deprivation I am undergoing,' she said. Cardus, always susceptible to coquettishness – especially when it was dug over with a spade – found hers irresistible. 'I replied suggesting that one day we might meet.'

That day came only 'a month or two later'. In what seems like a prequel to the teary *Brief Encounter*, each 'described roughly our individual appearances' and arranged a date that began beside the bookstall at Charing Cross station. It was not a success. For one thing, she was ten minutes late. For another, Cardus was confronted by someone slender, who could have passed for a milk-pale 'suburban office-girl', rather than the voluptuously alluring figure his imagination had prepared him for.

She asked, almost immediately, to borrow ten shillings. She'd laddered her stockings and had 'forgotten' her purse. He thought this was a polite way of picking his pocket, which cast a further pall over him. The two of them spent an hour in 'more or less conventional talk' before a lie followed. Cardus relied on the oldest excuse – another appointment awaited him – and left, regretting the time he had squandered.

Next day she returned the ten shillings in an envelope, the accompanying message imploring him to believe that she 'really' had left her purse behind absent-mindedly. The trusting Cardus agreed to take her for dinner at a hotel on the Embankment. 'I hadn't the heart to let her think that one look at her had been enough for me,' he said. There and then, Cupid's Arrow, as straight and direct as a Woolley off-drive, struck him with a thwack. She arrived in a small grey hat. Her hair 'coiled' about her ears. 'In my dying hour,' he said, 'I shall remember the radiance which now emanated from her.'

As another writer said of a different woman: 'So quickly did he fall for her that no one in the room even heard the sound.'

Cardus wrote about her as though putting together an outline proposal for a romantic novel, the heroine such a beauty that one of the Pre-Raphaelite Brotherhood – Millais, ideally – would have made her his muse. The suburban office-girl was somehow transformed. Cardus went into rapture. 'Her eyes were more lustrous (and alluring) than any I had ever before seen. Her high cheekbones were vivid ... Her lips were rose red ... She walked with a suggestion of a swaying side-way motion ... She burned a flame of sex and being.' On Cardus inexorably goes – hooked, smitten, lost in a depth of emotion he hadn't experienced before and can't truly articulate, the prose turning a little purple in a failed attempt to convey it.

'At dinner she talked as if she had known me for years,' he said. When Cardus asked why she had looked so different to him at the

Charing Cross bookstall, she replied without demur: 'Engine troubles,' a euphemism combining discretion and delicate wit.

Her name was Hilda Ede. She was known as Barbe.

She was 37 years old. Her marriage, which took place in 1917, had brought three children. Asthma made Barbe brittle, her gaspings for breath sometimes terrifying Cardus. Without ever specifying them, he also said she had been through 'some troubles' before meeting him. In an example of one trait universally exercised – exaggerating the qualities of those we love – Cardus claimed she possessed a sure 'instinct for the best music, poetry and literature', honed during a convent education in France. Her 'sense of words was gorgeous'. She 'loved Dickens', a fact important to him, and 'knew much of Shakespeare by heart'.

Usually so careful about making certain one part of his life never strayed into another, Cardus made an exception for the bewitching Barbe. He paraded her everywhere, as if showing off a trophy, in front of music, cricket and publishing friends alike. He took her to Lord's and also to concerts in Salzburg, Vienna and Paris. C. B. Fry addressed her as 'Milady', a term redolent of airs, graces and elegance.

Cardus said there was 'no artificiality' about Barbe. She once interrupted Sir Thomas Beecham in mid-flow with the sharp rebuke 'Balls, Sir Thomas.' She would cry during an opera. She would complain of the 'bloody shoulder-straps' on her dress. In one wonderful line Cardus summed up her ability to be cockney flower girl one moment and society lady the next. 'She was Eliza Doolittle before and after Professor Higgins had taken her in hand,' he said.

Cardus further defined Barbe like this: 'When she projected herself it was not done to impress others, but to get the best out of herself in a given situation or scene. I would watch her when she wasn't aware that I was watching. Like a young girl, she would review herself in front of a wardrobe mirror, swirling around, showing herself to herself.'

In hotels, either in London or elsewhere, he would book separate rooms, slipping into her bed and sharing it chastely. What Cardus almost shyly described as 'my awakening' didn't occur until three years after the couple's first meeting. He and Barbe, staying at the Charing Cross Hotel, had been to a concert of Sibelius's Seventh, the composer's one-movement symphony, which is hardly a passionate or erotic piece.

He went to extremes for Barbe, eventually renting what the saucier Sunday newspapers used to describe as a 'love nest'. Edith knew about the flat, but not the ulterior motive for acquiring it. On Ebury Street, a five-minute stroll from Victoria Station, its tucked-away rooms were convenient for a mistress arriving by train from Kent.

The geometry of his relationship with Barbe could not be described as a love triangle only because he'd ceased to think of Edith romantically – if he ever had. She remained in Manchester, continuing to paint, collaborate on theatrical productions and socialise with friends, some of whom knew Cardus only as a vaporous presence, more away from the city and the marital home than part of it.

She did, however, find out about Barbe before Cardus confessed his adultery. Edith's brother, a builder and general handyman, had been asked to do plumbing work at the rented flat. He arrived unannounced, discovering Barbe, rather than Cardus, at the door. Edith didn't order him to stop seeing her. Her main concern wasn't the security of the marriage – neither wanted a divorce – but rather the protection of his reputation. Afraid some grubby nosy parker would see it as a scandal worth reporting, and fearing then for his position on the *Manchester Guardian*, Edith colluded with Barbe's spouse, ensuring no scene was ever made.

Since everyone of note who knew Cardus also knew about Barbe, the precautions she took look unnecessary. Elton Ede, the husband, wasn't predisposed to kick up a fuss either. He'd served in the Royal

Navy, gone into bookkeeping and accountancy and paddled about in the shallow end of journalism, which included writing about cricket for local newspapers in Kent. He was also a church warden and a front-line member of the Church of England Men's Group. Salacious publicity would have damaged him through his innocent association with it.

In the end, Ede got as much out of his wife's liaison as Cardus did.

In 1932, after trying for three years to yank Cardus away from the *Manchester Guardian*, the *Sunday Times* appointed a cricket correspondent. He was someone with no apparent pedigree for the post suddenly given to him.

It was Ede.

Arthur Conan Doyle put these words into the mouth of Sherlock Holmes: 'When you have eliminated the impossible, whatever remains, *however improbable*, must be the truth.' The inescapable conclusion is that a supporter, both generous and influential, pulled a string or two on Ede's behalf. Nor does it take a vast imaginative leap to settle on the most plausible candidate.

Ede began sharing a press box with his wife's lover. Neither man seemed remotely bothered about this.

Reviewing an anthology of cricket writing, Ede even insisted: 'When we turn to Neville Cardus it is with the same delighted anticipation that we feel when Woolley, who has scored 20 overnight, goes on with his innings. And when he mentions Emmott Robinson we cannot restrain a shout of joy any more than when Woolley hits a six.'

Few cuckolds have ever been so generous.

8

FORTY BOUNDARIES AND NOT A SPOT OF PERSPIRATION

THE CARTOONIST H. M. Bateman made such an eloquent state-ment about inter-war cricket that his pen-and-wash commentary on it became a popular print, bought to be hung in homes as well as club pavilions.

In the higher echelons of over-stuffy England, where it mattered to dress correctly for dinner, Bateman made his name satirising minor social gaffes in a series called 'The man who ...'. In these classic cartoons, such as 'The man who ate his luncheon in the Royal Enclosure' and 'The guest who called the foie gras potted meat', some poor, ignorant sap commits a ghastly faux pas that shocks his onlook-ers or sends them into a fit of apoplexy.

When it came to cricket, Bateman lampooned the game's prolific record-breaking. As the game's Golden Age receded, reclassified as the recent past, every newspaper he read seemed to contain something extraordinary that stripped the glitter off what had gone before and diminished it in comparison. Performances with bat and ball alike were pyrotechnical.

Between the start of the century and the Great War, bowlers took 1,000 wickets only eight times. In Neville Cardus's first decade as the *Manchester Guardian*'s cricket correspondent, the same feat was achieved 15 times. Tich Freeman, who Cardus described as 'a balding little man' capable of achieving 'sinfully seductive flight', snared more than 300 wickets in 1928 alone. On a 'sticky', bowlers were rampant. Gloucestershire's Charlie Parker claimed 17 wickets for Gloucestershire, facing Essex, and hat-tricks in each innings against Middlesex. Taking all ten seemed dully commonplace. Freeman did it. So did Gubby Allen, A. S. Kennedy, Clarrie Grimmett and S. F. Barnes, who was then a sprightly 56.

Otherwise, runs came in floods. Against South Africa at Lord's, England became the first team to rack up 500 in a day. In 1925 Jack Hobbs scored sixteen hundreds, including the 127th of his career, overtaking W. G. Grace. Cardus argued that Hobbs 'did W. G. a good turn', because the 'old man' was being talked about again rather than neglected. The following season, Hobbs made the highest score ever seen at Lord's – 316 not out for Surrey against Middlesex.

So it went on.

Sussex and Kent produced 1,451 runs between them at Hastings, where the lithe, silky K. S. Duleepsinhji, nephew of K. S. Ranjitsinhji, made 115 in the first innings and 246 in the second. In a cyclone of batsmanship, Percy Chapman totalled 260 in 185 minutes in one match for Kent. In another, for the Rest of England, he and Frank Woolley went wonderfully mad, rattling up 124 between them in less than three quarters of an hour. And, during 27 explosive days in May 1928, Charlie Hallows went past 1,000 runs, getting there on the month's last morning. You'll have to read the next sentence at least twice to convince yourself that the printer hasn't made an error in setting the type. That summer, five batsmen scored over 3,000 runs; another 14 scored more than 2,000; and 72 scored 1,000-plus. Some players did everything. In one match, Hampshire went puce at the sight of Middlesex's J. W. Hearne, who made 121 in the first innings, carried his bat through the second for 37 and also took seven for 24.

Those were the days.

In response to all this, Bateman drew what he titled 'The Test Match that did not produce a record'. Solemn-faced and shoulders slumped, the slightly embarrassed players troop off below the press box, each reporter unable to disguise either disgust or boredom or both. It's as if the teams have let themselves and everyone else down, because a game lacking some statistical ornamentation is meaningless. Bateman went to matches and mixed with writers such as Cardus. To add a little piquancy to his drawing, he depicted some of those he knew in the press box or on the fringes of it. One, with crinkly hair, turns away disdainfully, smoking his pipe. This is Percy Fender. A second, rather jowly and wearing a bow tie, is asleep, the narrow brim of his trilby pulled below his eyes. He's Beau Vincent as Bateman saw him. A third, a couple of seats along, is C. B. Fry, recognisable because he alone in the picture is actually working, head down and scribbling. Bateman is commenting on the industrial rate at which Fry cranked out words. The figure sitting on the extreme left of the second row is Cardus. He wears a big pair of round spectacles, the extravagant downturned curve of his mouth showing displeasure at something barely worth recording.

In truth, Cardus agreed with Bateman wholeheartedly. He didn't much care for records and couldn't remember them anyway. Even when he witnessed the smashing of one, his match report wouldn't necessarily acknowledge it. 'Newspapers,' he said, 'go on too much . . . about the breaking of records.' Keats believed that Isaac Newton diminished 'the poetry' of the rainbow by explaining it scientifically. Cardus believed that harping on about records diminished the poetry in a game. Cricket wasn't 'all about the figures', any more than music was 'all about the notes', he said.

What really counted for Cardus was interpretation and style. He went in search of a game imbued with 'the joy of life in summertime'

ANOTHER RECORD.
THE TEST MATCH THAT DID NOT PRODUCE A RECORD.

and preferred to see 'a single, glorious shot' from Woolley or Walter Hammond than a century by an inferior who occupied the crease as though fossilised to the spot. He had a fondness for bowlers such as C. S. 'Father' Marriott. 'To watch a leg-spinner endeavouring to deceive a great batsman on a good wicket is a *connoisseur*'s delight,' he said, arguing that crowds would 'flock to see a bowler of rare manipulative skill', because 'whether he is getting wickets or not getting wickets, he compels constant attention from the onlooker.' Cardus would gladly have watched Hedley Verity tweak the ball at medium pace towards nothing but a solitary stump or against chalk marks on a brick wall, so entranced did he become by the 'wheeling up of his overs' and the sun shining on his high forehead 'as though from some illumination sent out by his intellect'.

He still fretted that groundsmen were producing bland pitches to create statistical landmarks. The glut of them, said Cardus, was a threat to cricket's future because 'drama cannot be felt unless . . . conflict hot and bitter is present.'

A glimpse of what was lost. Hedley Verity's bowling action is freeze-framed in 1939, the last such sequence to be taken of him before his death during the Second World War.

After watching Surrey pummel Lancashire's bowling at Old Trafford in 1928 – amassing 567 – Cardus went as far as composing a lament. 'Alas, poor cricket, where now its hazards, its surprises?' he asked. So dominant were batsmen becoming that he feared: 'Some fine day a sparrow's nest will be found, built beautifully, between middle and off stump on a county cricket field.'

For him, newspapers were too full of 'records in every edition', which meant the spectator could not 'easily be astonished'.

He was rather premature about this. The greatest record-breaker of them all – the man who said 'one does not go seeking records; they simply just happen' – would prove Cardus spectacularly wrong.

There is a photograph, taken near the midpoint of Australia's tour of England in 1930, which shows Donald Bradman at the factory of his bat manufacturer, Wm. Sykes Ltd of Horbury, a small village outside Wakefield that scarcely seems a fitting backdrop for a superstar. He is in a bare, stone-floored room. The brick walls have been whitewashed and the bats are stacked against them. Bradman is in his civvies, wearing a three-piece suit with fashionably wide lapels. He's signing one of the bats and looking directly towards the camera.

You notice two things immediately. Firstly, the bats, compared with today's chunky hunks of wood, look like matchsticks. They are thin and clean and white, the sort you might buy in miniature from a seaside novelty shop and use on the beach. You wonder how a blow from one them, even hit plumb out of the middle, ever reached the far outfield, let alone crossed the rope. Secondly, Bradman, his face partly in shadow, appears older than someone who arrived in England aged 21. He was described then as an unassuming, non-smoking teetotaller and 'shy with girls'.

He looks already a seasoned statesman, a future leader for certain. That impression is reinforced when you hear him being interviewed a month or so later. Bradman speaks to his newsreel inquisitor with a focused, rational maturity. If you didn't know better, you'd dismiss the date on his birth certificate as fraudulent. He is calmly sure of himself and also of his place in the world. You understand how, despite the cargo of expectation he carried from Australia, Bradman was able to turn 1930 into what Neville Cardus considered his 'Wonderful Year'. He said of it: 'I doubt if he subsequently equalled, for verve and complete mastery, his batsmanship.'

Bradman had already made two Test centuries before putting a foot on damp English soil. At the start of the year he had also hit a world-record 452 for New South Wales against Queensland, scoring faster than a run a minute. The advance publicity promising the sight of this phenomenon was feverish. As Cardus wryly observed, Bradman consequently attracted crowds 'who did not know a leg break from the pavilion cat at Lord's'. He was the 'Run-Scoring Machine', the 'Cricket Robot', the 'Colt from Bowral'. He seemed too perfect to be true.

Cardus first watched him in the nets at Lord's, noting his 'fair hair and sturdy shoulders'. He saw him loosening his limbs and sniffing the unfamiliar air. The turf, said Cardus, was 'too soft for serious practice', but nevertheless 'a single stroke' – which was a quick late cut, 'powerful at the wrists' – announced his 'quality' to him.

On the surface, the Australians were a callow lot. In the 19th century there were matches between Smokers, such as 'the Demon' Spofforth and Lord Harris, and Non-Smokers, including Arthur Shrewsbury and Johnny Briggs. The Smokers were often photographed with pipes sticking out of their mouths or cigarettes dangling nonchalantly from their fingers. Those who regarded cricket as a mode of Victorian morality and tobacco as a smelly evil hoped the Smokers would not win. Some saw those first Ashes Tests of the 1930s as the beer-and-whisky brigade versus the abstainers. Like

Bradman, few of the Australian team drank. Even Bradman's cuppa was a tepid concoction – a third of milk, half an inch of tea poured directly from the pot and a large topping of hot water. To the British male public, who boozed, the Australians didn't suggest strength or manly endeavour.

Only four of them – the captain Bill Woodfull, the wicketkeeper Bert Oldfield, the spinner Clarrie Grimmett and batsman Bill Ponsford – had toured England before. Bradman was the head lamb among a small flock. Stan McCabe was only 19. The willowy Archie Jackson was 20, impressing Cardus immediately with 'that instinctive movement of his feet which proves the born batsman'. Jackson attracted Cardus's fancy for 'batsmanship' rather than mere 'batting' because of the fluidity of his strokes. 'You do not require to watch a batsman all day in order to convince yourself of his culture,' he said of him. 'An accent can be savoured in a single sentence – and from one stroke a cricketer's pedigree may be guessed.'

It was Bradman who nonetheless packed grounds and press boxes alike. At Worcester in April, where he made his public bow, the shack-like facilities accommodated a maximum of 16 journalists. Three dozen seats in a stand were set aside as an overspill area. It wasn't enough; 60 pressmen turned up.

Bradman would stress that the light in England, appreciably duller than Australia's even on a bright, blue morning, made it difficult for him to 'see the ball properly' during the tour's opening weeks. No one at Worcester would have believed that. He made 236: 'So busily did he score ... that I got the impression he was batting at both ends at the same time,' said Cardus.

At the tour's beginning, Cardus questioned whether Bradman was of the same rank as Jackson. At the tour's end, after that vintage summer in which he dealt only in high numbers and in the mass production of runs, his total superiority was inarguable. Bradman made bonfires of good attacks.

'In every art or vocation,' said Cardus, 'there appears from time to time an incredible exponent who in himself sums up all the skill and experience that have gone before him.' Bradman seemed to him to contain elements of Jack Hobbs and C. B. Fry, Victor Trumper and even W. G. Grace. He adapted them to his own brilliant ends.

He played 'with the sophistication of an old hand and brain – too old for Bradman's years and experience,' added Cardus. He demonstrated that a 'batsman can hit forty-two boundaries in a day without once giving the outfielders hope of a catch'. Cardus thought he could 'write a text-book on him with comprehensive and thoroughly enlightening diagrams' to demonstrate 'technique *in excelsis*'. His new admirer concluded: 'A number of Bradmans would quickly put an end to the glorious uncertainty of cricket.'

Bradman always looked unhurried – whether playing a shot, waiting for the next ball, even walking out of the pavilion gate. He moved slowly to the crease, allowing his eyes to adjust to the light before getting there. He placed the bat, its face closed, between his feet rather than behind the right toe, where it remained almost still until his backlift began. There was no frantic tapping of the bat for Bradman and no deep blockhole dug as though he was about to bury something. He had small, delicate hands, which were close together on the handle, the thumb and first finger of each forming an inverted V. This grip allowed his pick-up to begin smoothly and naturally anywhere from point to second slip. Looking around him, he saw the gaps between the fielders rather than the fielders themselves. As the ball was delivered, he detected – almost from the exact moment it left the hand – the speed and trajectory of delivery. It was as though in a nanosecond what his eyes saw was computed and calculated infallibly in the brain

Even Donald Bradman carried his own bag and his own bats, but looked as immaculate off the field as on it.

and appeared before him with the precision of some draughtsman's drawing. How else could you explain the sure-swiftness of his foot movements, gliding him into an ideal, if sometimes unorthodox, position? The method did not necessarily match the biblical-like instructions found in the MCC's coaching manual. The means could look a little crude and indelicate, making Cardus wince, but the ends were richly profitable; for no scorer added runs with their pencil for artistic merit. It was, as Cardus said, an established fact that Bradman 'belts the hell out of every ball he can reach' and treats 'everything as an excuse for a boundary'. He could catch too. 'I have seen him . . . hold a spinning mishit while his body was swivelling round like a top released from the whip.'

Cardus believed wholeheartedly that cricket was 'a game in which there was time for a man to develop and reveal his personality'. The batsman was 'a soloist exposed', which allowed you hours in which to 'get many insights' into him. Any Bradman innings confirmed it. Detectable was a trait setting him apart from his contemporaries. This was his 'singleness of mind and imperturbability'. He would do no more than flick the bowler a look with calm eyes, impervious to sledging spoken in a stage whisper. The shouting of the crowd, whether friendly or otherwise, never disturbed him either. Cardus once asked Bradman to explain his 'secret'. He replied unhesitatingly: 'Concentration. Every ball is for me the first ball, whether my score is nought or 200. And I never visualise anybody getting me out.'

Had a bomb gone off at long leg, Bradman would barely have registered the boom it made, so locked was he into what modern sportsmen call The Zone, a state in which everything is done instinctively and unconsciously. Cardus said it enabled him to stay 'at the wicket longer than most of the brilliant stroke-players ever dreamt of staying'.

In that famous summer, Bradman became only the fifth batsman – and the first Australian – to reach 1,000 runs before the end of May. His average then was 136.28. Drawn by the promise of witnessing something magical, 'crowds came from far and near to see him, and departed in disappointed droves when he got out,' said Cardus. Bradman needed a police escort to shelter him from the overenthusiasm of his own fan club, also joining 'the choice and limited number of men that would be recognised almost at first sight if they crossed Piccadilly Circus'. At the end of August, celebrating his 22nd birthday, sackfuls of cards, cables and letters were sent to him, a scale of worship unprecedented for someone who wasn't a singer, an actor, the Prime Minister or a member of the royal family. In the evening, rather than socialise, he would conscientiously write replies in his hotel room.

That Australia came from behind to deservedly win the series 2–1 was almost immaterial. The effect Bradman had on the season and the senses, as he totalled a mammoth 2,960 first-class runs at 98.66, remained in the memory longer than the result. There was a century at Trent Bridge, a double hundred at The Oval and his world-beating 334 – 309 of them in a day – at Headingley, where 'no shadow of fallibility fell for a moment on the gleaming surface of [his] bat.' This wasn't entirely factual. Harold Larwood was convinced that Bradman had snicked a bouncer before getting off the mark, the noise loud enough to be heard 'all over the ground'. Even Jack Hobbs, who didn't appeal unless he thought it justified, joined in. Bradman didn't 'walk' and the umpire shook his head. Larwood stomped silently back to his mark, storing up a grievance that would be articulated soon enough. England chased leather hopelessly for three sessions.

Even Cardus said he 'grew a little tired' of perfection – the repeated rat-a-tat-tat of fours that Bradman stroked or flogged to all parts

*A pastoral Trent Bridge in 1930. Bill Woodfull and Bill Ponsford
sprint for a run on the fourth day of the first Ashes Test.*

irrespective of what variety of ball was bowled to him. He went to
the highest point of the ground and stared down at him from
there, guessing as a delivery was released where the genius would
send it. As Bradman came off, Cardus looked closely at his face.
He was hardly sweating – 'forty boundaries and not a spot of
perspiration', he said. There was 'not a trace of weariness in his
expression' either. He looked 'cool and neat, as though fresh from
the bathroom'.

Next morning, as soon as Bradman was finally out, Cardus went to
congratulate him. In his eagerness to reach the dressing room – even
leaping over packed benches of spectators – he tripped and fell down
a number of steps, grazing his skin so badly that he needed treatment
and bandages.

The crowd, thickly packed, watch Jack Hobbs and Herbert Sutcliffe on the first morning of the fifth Ashes Test at The Oval in 1930.

The innings was statistically the greatest, outstripping everyone before him. But Cardus preferred the 254 Bradman hit in 341 minutes at Lord's, which he called 'a symphony' of a Test. 'If some good fairy were to ask me to pick out one match of all I have seen, to relive it as I lived at the time when it was played, my choice would be easy,' he said. He believed it met some 'Platonic idea of cricket in perfection' and ought to have been staged 'in heaven'. He also saw it then and afterwards in the 'glorious sunshine', which 'blessed every moment'. There were 1,601 runs scored in under four days; and England, despite making 800 of them, lost by seven wickets. Cardus said he watched it 'in an eternity of content'.

England reached 425 and K. S. Duleepsinhji, on his Ashes debut, made 173 of them. Woodfull almost matched him in an Australian

Donald Bradman was so successful at Headingley that
Yorkshire awarded him Honorary Membership of the club.
Here, he is mobbed after his 334 there in 1930.

reply that made the scoreboard operators bone-weary. His 155 and a
partnership with Bradman was the backbone of the tourists' 729 for
six declared. Cardus then saw Grimmett – 'his arm as low as my
grandfather's' – wheeling in artfully with his tricky leg-breaks to take
six second-innings wickets. The ball, he said, spun 'with the noise of
wasps' from his hand. He also saw Percy Chapman, one of A. C.
MacLaren's heroes from the Saffrons, make 'one of the most gallant
and dazzling and precarious innings which has ever cocked a snook' at
Australia.

That last day see-sawed. What seemed at first like a foregone
conclusion of Australian success offered instead a wisp of a chance for

England as Chapman – 'in beatitude' and batting as though in 'a trance' – made 121 in front of Grimmett's 'wild incredulous stare'. It wasn't quite enough. England were all out for 375. Australia, after briefly struggling, made 72 for three and broke hearts to win.

Chapman got Bradman with a catch in the gully that left Cardus gasping. The shot was a laid-back cut, struck with belting force. The crowd turned automatically towards the boundary, unable to understand why the ball was nowhere to be seen. Chapman had taken it 'an inch from the grass', so nonchalantly that almost no one noticed until he tossed his prize into the air. Cardus was sitting in front of the Tavern beside J. M. Barrie, who waited until Bradman was halfway to the pavilion before asking: 'Why is he going away?' Cardus looked quizzically at his friend, not grasping his meaning. 'But surely you saw that marvellous catch?' he replied. 'Oh yes. I saw it all right,' said Barrie. 'But what evidence is there that the ball which Chapman threw up into the air is the same ball that left Bradman's bat?'

For Cardus, Barrie's piece of whimsy encapsulated 'this great and enchanting match', during which 'victor and vanquished emerged with equal honour'. At its end, he sat on the Green Bank to compose his match report. It began:

> There is a passage in *Tom Jones* where Fielding, having got his plot terribly complicated, calls on all the high Muses, in person and severally, for aid; because he tells us, 'without their guidance I do not know how to bring my story to a successful conclusion'. As I write this report, I feel also the need of inspired and kindly forces. The day's play, in the old term, beggars description . . .

Cardus was able to recall this Test at will, as though the sights of it were stored kaleidoscopically. What shone out was Bradman's assault in the first innings. 'The advent of Bradman,' he wrote, 'was like the throwing of combustible stuff on fires.' It was 'a massacre', a 'cool deliberate murder' of the bowling, in which 'every shot dead in the target's middle' was 'precise and shattering'.

Bradman made his intentions clear from the off. Against slow left-armer J. C. 'Farmer Jack' White, whose cheeks were said to be ruddy-redder than a pantomime dame's, he 'leaped yards out of his crease and drove it to the long-on rails' without a flutter of self-doubt. The stroke was 'just one flash of prancing white and yellow, with a crack that echoed ... and sent the pigeons flying'. Bradman made his first hundred in 105 minutes. 'There were not enough fieldsmen available' to shackle him, said Cardus, who thought 'soon his bat must be red hot and catch fire.' The innings was 'beautiful and yet somehow cruel' and 'the most brilliant and dramatically incisive' of his career. Bradman agreed with Cardus. 'Technically [it was] the best innings of my life,' he said later.

Bradman once complained that Cardus had sometimes been 'quite harsh' in his judgements of him. The comment suggests extreme, if not paranoid, touchiness. The reviews Cardus gave him were rhapsodic. He was 'the killer' at the crease. There was 'no mercy in his play'. His cut 'had a battleaxe strength'. His hooks 'were savage'. A drive or a pull 'affected the bowler like a pugilist's knockout blow'. Cardus made it sound as though every contest was Man versus Superman in which anguished bowlers beseeched Bradman to stop pummelling them with the pitying look of the downtrodden. One of them, when asked to outline the 'best ball' to bowl at him, replied in frustration: 'There's no bloody best ball – it doesn't exist.'

Bradman went after his runs with an ambition far beyond the 'avaricious dreams' of anyone else. 'A hundred runs is nothing to him,' said Cardus, who liked to tell of walking along Whitehall and seeing a newspaper bill comprising two words in thick, black capitals:

BRADMAN FAILS

Cardus bought the paper, turned to the back page and discovered the joke hidden in the Stop Press. Bradman had made *only* a half-century.

It was argued even then that Bradman could seldom master a 'sticky', the worst of which reduced science to nonsense. Cardus spotted another weakness, the ramifications of which would ripple into the next series. He asked Ted McDonald to assess Bradman. McDonald would not countenance – 'at any price', said Cardus – that Bradman was 'another Victor Trumper'. Already newspapers were forecasting that, though his talent was still forming, he would shatter 'all Test records'. This didn't impress the curmudgeonly McDonald either. 'Maybe he will,' he told Cardus, 'but there's only been one Trumper and there'll never be another.'

McDonald, as though he'd been given a challenging dare, wanted to demonstrate what he meant. The Australians faced Lancashire at Aigburth, a chocolate-box ground of tall, wide trees, tents, candy-striped deckchairs and a Tudor-looking pavilion. McDonald stoked himself up for the occasion. This was his Test match. He bowled very fast on the line of leg stump. When Bradman, who had made only nine, backed away and moved across to off, attempting to swish McDonald audaciously square, he found himself beaten for pace. The leg stump went 'spinning', said Cardus. He'd later swear that Bradman had 'flinched' against the ball. Cardus also said McDonald's satisfaction at claiming his wicket 'never waned', as though he'd hoisted a flag for Trumper above Bradman's head.

Throughout his career, McDonald had no qualms about bowling at the body, thinking it was as legitimate as a bouncer. Frank Woolley insisted McDonald aimed the ball directly at him. After a typical peppering, Woolley began patting down the pitch right next to McDonald's toecaps, to signal his disapproval. 'He looked straight at me and said: "Keep your eyes open." In the next over he hit the peak of my cap,' remembered Woolley.

He was not a solitary target. Another batsman, whom McDonald also unsuccessfully attempted to bruise and intimidate, regarded their confrontation as his first experience of 'leg theory'.

His name was Douglas Jardine.

In his boyhood, Neville Cardus read Pelham Warner's *How We Recovered the Ashes*, an account of the triumphant 1903–04 tour in which the MCC fought Victor Trumper and Monty Noble with the wiles of Bernard Bosanquet, creator of the googly, and also Hirst and Rhodes. Cardus finished the book and told himself that 'some day' he would go there too.

Though not entirely flush with cash, the *Manchester Guardian* was prepared to satisfy his ambition, sending him on the 1932–33 tour of Australia. The plan was to syndicate his writing to partly fund his passage.

Cardus claimed that he turned down the proposal because, like some crystal-ball clairvoyant, he bleakly predicted an 'unfriendly atmosphere' ahead. 'I knew that trouble was brewing,' he said. In fact, Cardus had become so infatuated with Barbe Ede that he asked her to go with him. She refused, aware of the scandal it would create. Cardus, who found the rebuff heart-wrenching, didn't want to spend six months without her, writing and receiving long letters that would take a month or more to cross continents. He stayed at home to court her further.

Cardus was still able to offer an assessment of the genesis of Bodyline, which was markedly different from anyone else's.

The sequence of events traditionally unrolls this way. Douglas Jardine calls Donald Bradman 'the little bastard', a backhanded compliment after watching him incinerate England's bowling in that

Douglas Jardine, the inventor of Bodyline. He would knock a man down and be compassionate about it afterwards, said Cardus.

1930 series. As soon as he is appointed as captain for the 1932–33 tour, he commits himself to a sole purpose: the hope of wreaking some terrible revenge. He forensically examines the Bradman Problem, treating it like a code to be cracked. He studies wagonwheel diagrams of where Bradman scores his runs. He seeks advice from bowlers – from those who had claimed Bradman's wicket and those who had been slaughtered by him. He taps into the intelligence network of his friend Percy Fender, who has contacts in Australia. Jardine is watching reel-to-reel film of Bradman when, at last, a weakness becomes apparent. Bradman recoils and then flinches as Harold Larwood bowls at his leg stump, thumping a rising ball against his unprotected chest. What Jardine says in response to the sight of it is cricket's equivalent of a scientist acclaiming some unparalleled breakthrough in the laboratory: 'I've got it,' announces Jardine. 'He's yellow.'

The rest is familiar. Jardine meets Larwood in the Grill Room of the Piccadilly Hotel. He explains his plan to combat Bradman. He preaches a policy of 'competitive hate' against him. He makes it clear that Larwood will act as his executioner in Australia.

Cardus had a different story.

He thought an obscure South African, Herbie Taylor, was the catalyst for Jardine's ingenious approach. He thought this occurred during a conversation during the Test trial at Cardiff in July 1932. And he thought Bill Voce, Larwood's left-arm partner at Notts, was originally 'cast to play the principal part' in what notoriously became known as Bodyline. Caught in sheet upon sheet of rain, Cardiff was a near-washout. 'Little cricket was seen,' remembered Cardus, who almost 'expired from boredom'. The bad weather 'imprisoned everyone in their hotel'. He and others 'wandered from room to room . . . like lost souls'. The miserable scene reminded him of a Chekhov play. 'At any moment, I expected someone to come up to me saying, "Take this revolver my friend, and shoot; for I am not happy."'

Cardus said that 'in desperation' – and presumably because all other topics had been exhausted – 'we even talked cricket' to pass the time. The Ashes unsurprisingly took centre stage. Taylor was there on holiday. He'd faced Australia less than six months earlier, and spoke of how uncomfortable Bradman appeared against the left-arm medium-quick Neville Quinn, who had taken four for 42 in the first innings of the Melbourne Test by pressurising the leg stump. 'Taylor, of course, did not suggest Bodyline. I don't think he even dreamed of it as an organised system,' said Cardus, who was nonetheless certain that his 'description of Quinn's attack, and the success of it . . . fell on fruitful ground'.

'Jardine listened attentively,' said Cardus, equally convinced that Quinn made him think about Voce, capable of whipping the ball into a batsman's ribs like a thrust knife, becoming England's chief weapon. Less than four weeks later, Cardus witnessed a Bodyline rehearsal. He wasn't covering the match, between Lancashire and Notts, but slipped into Old Trafford inquisitively after returning early from the Salzburg Music Festival. Rain had fallen during the early morning, delaying the start. When play began, Voce had four short legs in an unmistakable statement of intent, but found the pitch too soft and sent two of them into the slips. Larwood, after one uninspiring and unsuccessful spell, returned 'like a lion, fiercer after meat', according to the *Manchester Guardian*. He pushed three men close on the leg side and directed two more to fine long leg, predatorily waiting for the loose hook. His deliveries were wickedly short, and Lancashire's batsmen fended him off 'like men in a hailstorm', added the newspaper's unnamed correspondent. Larwood blasted the ball at leg stump, expecting to be slogged but not caring, because he was honing his technique for Australia. Had the surface been stone-hard, Larwood could have sent someone to the infirmary. Two of his three wickets were clean-bowled – and on each occasion it was the leg stump that went cartwheeling. In Lancashire's second innings, he also sent a bouncer into someone's face.

Jardine unprecedentedly took four fast bowlers to Australia, adding Bill Bowes and Gubby Allen as back-up to Larwood and Voce. The news of Bowes's late selection was made immediately after he had badly roughed up Jack Hobbs in a Championship match in which Jardine had played.

Cardus spent the English winter reviewing concerts. As England won twice in Sydney, once in Brisbane and also in the infamous Third Test at Adelaide, where the deployment of Bodyline and the crack that Bert Oldfield took on the skull almost led to a riot-cum-lynching, Cardus listened to sweeter sounds than the cacophonous roar of aggrieved Australians: Grieg's Piano Concerto, the pastoral notes of Vaughan Williams and, rather more appropriately, Wagner's *The Valkyrie*, which could conceivably have been the menacing backing track to the entire, tempestuous tour.

His Majesty's Press were not well represented in Australia. None of the premier correspondents – or at least those capable of writing intelligently and with clout – were there. E. W. Swanton, suffering the lingering ire of his sports editor, was punished retrospectively for failing to telephone news of Percy Holmes and Herbert Sutcliffe's record opening stand of 555 at Leyton before the *Evening Standard*'s last edition. The ground had only one telephone. Swanton was still in the queue waiting to use it when the presses rolled. The *Standard* sent Jack Hobbs instead. His ghosted columns were politely wishy-washy.

Cardus found himself writing about matches he'd never seen in a country he'd never visited. From half a world away, he didn't appreciate the enmity between Jardine and the tour manager, Pelham Warner, or Allen's refusal to bowl Bodyline – even if such a stance obliged him to board the next ship home. Cardus heard 'the old gentlemen' harrumphing in an asthmatic wheeze in the National Liberal Club, scoffing at Australia's 'squealing' and at Bradman's distress. 'Good God, what's a bat for?' they'd say, before staggering 'to the fireplace and picking up the poker', demonstrating the shots 'they would play' against Larwood. Cardus was no better informed. For his own newspaper, as well as for *The Observer*, he cobbled together facts and formed opinions from agency reports, from other newspapers in England and Australia, or from short reels of film nearly six weeks out of date.

Of Bodyline, he said that 'the firing of the first cannon-ball in the history of warfare did not cause as much consternation.' He condemned it. 'I hope we have heard the last of leg-theory violence,' he wrote in one of his earliest pieces. In another, during the Adelaide Test, he called it 'brutal' and added: 'Frankly, it does not seem cricket to me.' Since Cardus was swimming against the tide of public opinion, he received in return the type of letter best left unread. 'I got awful abuse,' he said, clearly hurt about it.

He questioned 'the morality' of the Bodyline tactics, but some of his fundamental objections were based as much on aesthetic concerns. 'The point is whether any crowd . . . will put up with the spectacle of four fast balls an over flying over the heads of the batsmen,' he wrote. The ploy would suit the taste and palate only of those who wanted matches to be attritional, shot-free, colourless. 'I would not cross the street to see leg-theory exploited over after over . . . if this is how Tests are to be played, we'd be better off without them.'

His dislike of Warner spilled into his pieces. If Larwood and Voce were not bowling Bodyline, he wondered why 'we have not received an emphatic denial of these accusations by somebody in responsibility on the spot'. That 'somebody', though unnamed, was a direct reference to Warner.

He still slapped down the Australian Board of Control for the poorly phrased and intemperate cables it dispatched to the MCC in protest. Cardus believed the tart reply Lord's sent back was justified because, 'as they say in the vulgar tongue', the ABC was 'asking for it'. He claimed to admire Jardine 'beyond words', but made it seem as though in him there was a bit of the bullying Wackford Squeers, the villain of Dickens's *Nicholas Nickleby*. He disliked his approach to cricket, thinking he'd be better suited as a 'leader of armies' standing four-square against 'the raging winds of the mob'. Jardine was 'the dour exponent of realpolitik' in cricket, which meant knocking 'the man down first and being compassionate afterwards'. Cardus felt Australia, led by the more gentlemanly Bill Woodfull, needed someone who possessed the sheer bloody-mindedness of Warwick Armstrong, who would have countered the onslaught with one of his own. He gave succour to Bradman, who had still managed to make nearly 400 runs at 56.57. And, somewhat contradicting his dislike of Bodyline, he called for Larwood to be honoured. 'There are several ancient monuments in London which are not presentable to the public gaze. I suggest that one of them be taken down forthwith, and a statue of Larwood erected in its place. He is today one of the nation's heroes.'

Cardus said that his motto was 'anything for a quiet life', which is why he was glad to have stayed at home for a series that he called 'a tragicomedy'. He was 'anxious' that his first sight of Australia 'should be pleasant'.

It was.

The next tour, then three and a half years away, became one of the pivotal points of his life.

9

WRITE UNTIL YOUR FINGERS BREAK

ONLY AS HE left Australia, the 1936–37 tour over, did Neville Cardus realise how much the sunburnt country meant to him. Or, indeed, how much he had changed because of his experiences there.

Cardus admitted that his workload over the prevous six months had left him 'close' to the second nervous breakdown of his life. In the beginning he'd also suffered acutely from homesickness. He'd felt shipwrecked – 'so far away from the world,' miserable and 'out of joint'. He went as far as to hunt down copies of the *Manchester Guardian*, wrapping himself in them like a comfort blanket. Those he found were weeks out of date. He read them twice over, including the classified advertisements.

Cardus had gone to Australia without a second, love-lorn thought, his romance with Barbe Ede long over now. She had been unfaithful to him – and cruelly so too. Barbe had used Ebury Street to conduct another affair. That fact makes you wonder whether the ten shillings she originally took from him really was an unsubtle ruse, the money borrowed simply to create an excuse to return it and so ensnare someone easily seduced. Cardus, while giving up the flat, was unwilling to lose her completely. He showed a tolerance that even now seems perplexing and desperate. Cardus forgave her, frankly making himself look like a mug. He wanted to remain friends, the hurt of being without Barbe evidently more difficult to take than the hurt of her betrayal. Cardus got what he sought, which was far less than he originally had.

After arriving in Australia, he still missed what he had left behind – his cosy rooms at the National Liberal Club, the Green Bank at Lord's, the music of the Hallé, Barbe's companionship. He counted 'the leaves on the calendar, wishing the days by'. His friend William Pollock, also seeing the country for the first time, reassured him that all would be well. 'He at once made a tremendous hit, as I knew he would,' said Pollock.

Cardus had not appreciated how regularly his articles in the *Manchester Guardian* had been reprinted, whole or partly, in newspapers there. He'd been widely quoted and his books had been widely reviewed. Australia felt it knew the man before meeting him. As early as 1922, *The Argus* in Melbourne was heralding him as 'one of the most interesting writers on cricket of this or perhaps any other generation'. The *West Australian* rated his reports as 'the best' in 'the English Press'. *The Referee* thought him 'one of the most graceful writers' the game 'has ever known'. The *Sydney Morning Herald* stressed he was 'not only a delightful author but just as discerning a critic'. Whatever Cardus wrote about – the Roses matches, Bodyline, the flux and flow of a Championship summer – the Australians generally got to read it. Some of his London broadcasts were even heard on radio there.

No cricket correspondent, before or since, became so feted in Australia. Cardus came to feel a little like Charles Dickens in America, embraced by readers who thought he and his work belonged to them. 'Everyone' was 'so kind', he said.

Australia began to astonish Cardus slowly, like a flower opening.

In letters home, he was soon writing gleefully about his reception, the scattering of capital letters emphasising initially his surprise and then his childlike swell of pride. In one, he said: 'My work is a COLOSSAL success. I am a celebrity with FAN mail.' In another, Cardus announced he was as well known as Bradman or Noël Coward. In a third, he exclaimed: 'VERY FAMOUS HERE.' You get the feeling that Cardus knows he ought to be a little more self-effacing, but cannot contain himself. He tried rather unconvincingly to pretend that the ballyhoo, which he described as 'all this nonsense', was only 'amusing' and 'good fun up to a point'.

Cardus was interviewed for the newsreels. The public 'recognise me and applaud', he said. 'The Australians are cricket mad, and – dare I say it? – they are Cardus mad.' When suffering a dose of flu, which was widely reported, he received a bunch of flowers from the Prime Minister, Joseph Lyons, and the Attorney General, a future Prime Minister, Robert Menzies. 'Oh, <u>what</u> a country!' he concluded, the exclamation mark and the quick dash of underlining uncharacteristic for someone who used such embellishments rarely.

He reciprocated tenfold what Australia felt for him. He began to recognise it as a 'strange' and 'raw' and 'beautiful' place, a 'happy land' that was 'still in the making'. He dismissed his early complaints as 'a provincial Englishman's exaggerations' and the reservations of 'the innocent abroad'.

The Ashes served up consistently high drama. The series was seen by almost one million spectators, a total still unsurpassed anywhere. But the Tests – as he made clear – were 'not the whole of the adventure' for him, but merely the catalyst for a much wider, deeper one.

So, as Cardus stood alone, leaning on the rail of the ship taking him back to England, he confessed: 'My heart suddenly ached.' With the coastline slipping away, he saw a 'quick vision' of sights that had come to mean so much to him. The 'red night-signs' of Sydney. The ferry lights of Manly. The sliver of new moon above the Harbour Bridge 'as though on guard over everything'. There was also the 'falling of Brisbane's mantle of twilight' and the '*bourgeois* geniality' of Melbourne, a city he called 'Australia with its top hat on'. There was a car ride to Perth's King's Park and the Swan River, 'glistening like a silver chain'. There were the hills and 'cosy intimacy' of Adelaide, where he and

Donald Bradman turned respectful acquaintance into solid friendship after Cardus became a witness to – and shared unexpectedly in – a very personal grief.

Cardus sank into melancholy: 'When an ambition of a lifetime is fulfilled ... something has gone from one's life,' he said. 'I can never again cross the seas to Australia for the first time, never again tread for the first time an Australian cricket field and say: "Here it is – here's the place I've dreamed on, and seen in sunshine, far away under the earth, under my bed, on cold winter nights, in England."'

In the next two decades, Australia would become a refuge for Cardus. He'd go to 're-create' himself there. He'd describe 'Australia and Australians' as 'my inspirations'. In old age he would even claim that, given the chance, he'd unhesitatingly live again 'every day' of the Australian years of his life.

That 1936–37 series tends to be overlooked, swallowed up by the shadow Bodyline casts. It was nonetheless an epic. There were big scores and big wins. Two of the Tests were unquestionably classics. Rain sometimes arrived in torrents, changing the course of a match and the direction of a series wildly tumultuous. The high-ups at Lord's wanted – and still got – a contest that cemented 'the sacred bonds of Empire', a phrase Pelham Warner had drilled in to the point of indoctrination before dispatching the team under the captaincy of the Bodyline refusenik, Gubby Allen.

Change was overdue. Under Bob Wyatt, former deputy to Douglas Jardine, England had lost the 1934 home series to Australia, as well as two others, to the West Indies and South Africa. Allen hadn't played a Test for nearly two years before reappearing in conveniently straightforward contests against India, who were flattened. Time and again, as though on a diplomatic mission, Allen stressed that he was on 'a tour of peace'. He reassured sceptical Australians that he'd brought a 'charming lot of chaps' with him.

The core of these 'chaps' were Neville Cardus's friends: Walter Hammond, Hedley Verity, Maurice Leyland, the two wicketkeepers, George Duckworth and Les Ames, and Bill Voce. Allen particularly wanted Voce, persuading him to go through charm and tact. He didn't want Harold Larwood, left behind despite finishing top of the national averages with 119 wickets – 38 more than Allen. Voce was prepared to give assurances to the MCC about his conduct and behaviour. Larwood was not. You could have locked him in the stocks and pelted him with bricks; Larwood, who had only 'obeyed captain's orders', still would not have compromised his principles.

The rest of the side were referred to as 'triers and great enthusiasts', which explains why Allen had to constantly defend them against what he dismissed as attacks from 'pessimists in the country'. Wyatt was chosen, late and reluctantly, for the tour only because Surrey's Errol Holmes withdrew. Herbert Sutcliffe, at 41, was considered too old. Len Hutton, at 20, was dismissed as too young. Each had scored more than 1,200 runs. The selections of some, such as Copson, Worthington, Sims and Fagg, inspired no renditions of the Hallelujah Chorus, despite fairly impressive averages. The vice-captain was the all-rounder Walter Robins, a selection so weird that it only makes any sense when you know he and Allen were matey and both Cambridge blues. Robins hadn't toured Australia before. He'd taken fewer wickets – 82 – the previous summer than the likes of Harold Larwood, Bill Bowes (123) and Alf Gover (200). He hadn't figured among the highest run-scorers. His face fitted, however.

The modern England cricket expedition, which starts at Heathrow airport, is about jet flights and superfast wireless broadband and slick technology. As well as the players, the party includes the management, the coach and his assistant, the specialist coaches, the masseurs, the doctors, the psychologists, the fitness trainers and dieticians, the geeks who shoot or analyse film and sift the statistics, and the kit-men-cum-gofers. The media arrives in battalions. The whole shebang is like the migration of a small town. The 1936–37 tour seems to us now like a village club going on a summer outing. Cardus walked up the gang-plank of the *Orion* at Southampton docks for what he termed four 'pleasant but monotonous' weeks at sea. The MCC took 17 players, a manager and a baggage-man-scorer. There were only eight pressmen.

Cardus began to keep a diary, abandoning it for the simple reason that 'on a ship nothing often happens'. The team merged with the rest of the passengers until Cardus 'scarcely knew . . . which was which'. In the Red Sea, the weather was so hot that he dressed for dinner at his peril; his winged collar became a rag, the sweat waterfalling off his face. He said there was hardly 'an English man or woman' who 'would not cheerfully give pounds and pounds sterling for one hour of Manchester's wettest rain and coldest cold' to ease the torture of the heat. There were deck games, such as quoits, and board games, such as chess. You swam in the pool or you talked all day. At night you drank and talked some more. Duckworth danced 'with a nice understanding of what, socially, he was doing'. Ames entered the fancy-dress contest as Hitler, saluting as he strutted around the ballroom. Leyland smoked his pipe incessantly. Verity read T. E. Lawrence's *Seven Pillars of Wisdom*. Wyatt holed up in his cabin with a wind-up gramophone, which he'd lugged with him to play 78s – everything from Mozart to Beethoven to the popular crooners. Hammond, eager for shore, remarked to Cardus: 'She's a lovely ship, but I wish she bloody well had wings.'

Every morning, Cardus walked seven times around the deck and sought out C. B. Fry, always holding court, a striped deckchair his substitute for the soapbox of Speakers' Corner. 'He talked all the way to Australia and all the way across Australia and all the way back home,' said Cardus. Every evening, he sat in the 'Tavern' with Pollock or Arthur Mailey, the former Australian leg-spinner so modest about his abilities that he'd say: 'If ever I bowled a maiden over, it wasn't my fault but the batsman's.' Mailey was a cartoonist and a landscape artist, once staging a private exhibition of his work in a London gallery. Queen Mary, who attended the opening, approved of all but one of his paintings. 'I don't think, Mr Mailey, you have painted the sun quite convincingly in this picture,' she told him. Mailey paused. 'Perhaps not, Your Majesty ... but in this country I have to paint the sun from memory.'

When talk between Fry, Pollock, Mailey and Cardus turned to the Tests, there was one topic of debate. Cardus described it succinctly:

'Bradman, Bradman, Bradman.'

Cricket lends itself to intense and sometimes obsessive introspection because cricketers themselves are that way inclined. Everything is gone over, reconsidered, thought through umpteen times – often to the point of head-banging insanity.

Neville Cardus used to provide two examples of that. Every time Lancashire boarded the train to face Gloucestershire, A. N. Hornby would gather his fellow amateurs together in a private carriage to discuss the 'ways and means' of 'getting W. G. Grace out for less than a hundred runs'. It was always the same, said Cardus. 'Pencil and paper were utilised. The ground plan and specifications of "W. G.'s" ability were considered'. Hornby completely ruled out even the faint 'possibility of bowling him', insisting it was 'not practical'. The discussion would meander on. On the platform at Bristol, Hornby would have to concede defeat. There was no new plan, no fresh insight into how to better Grace. 'It was usually decided unanimously that we'd better try to "diddle" him out,' said Hornby, which was a hope held together with string and sealing wax.

Cardus also witnessed an extraordinarily eccentric performance from C. B. Fry, still preoccupied with how to conquer the spin of Albert Trott even though neither had faced the other since Edward VII was King. Cardus and Fry were sitting in a hotel lounge. Fry was stretched out in an easy chair, passing his monocle from hand to hand. He fell into flashback, reliving not only the second day of a long-ago game, but also a specific ball. 'I was not out 80 or so, and next morning it was our policy to get runs quickly as some rain had fallen in the night,' said Fry. 'I reached my century and then ... Albert Trott clean bowled me. Yes, clean bowled me with an off-break.' Fry shot up from his chair, as if the pain of that memory had compelled his body to move and relive what his mind saw clearly. The delivery and his response to it. 'His eyes were looking across the distance of three decades,' said Cardus. Fry went through the motions of a batsman playing an off-break. 'I can't think what I was doing,' he said. Something everyone else had forgotten still consumed Fry like a personal torture. As Cardus remarked: 'Thirty years after the event he was still seeing Trott's off-break as a problem to be solved.'

Like Hornby discussing Grace or Fry fretting about Trott, so England travelled in dizzying circles, one inconclusive conversation about Bradman leading to another.

England had lost the 1934 Ashes 2–1, the consequence of a colossal beating in the final Test at The Oval. Cardus initially thought Bradman seemed that summer to 'rebel against his own mastery'. His play was too 'hectic'. On a gluepot pitch at Lord's, Hedley Verity claimed him cheaply twice. He took match figures of 15 for 104, a performance Cardus said was all about 'grace concealing his deadliness'. Bradman had 'hit wildly' against him.

He didn't get past 50 in a Test until the penultimate one, at Headingley, which finished as a draw. At the end of the first day, Bradman cancelled a dinner engagement with Cardus and went to bed early, telling him: 'I must make 200 tomorrow *at least*.' He made 304. That score propelled him to The Oval, where he made 244 in the first innings and 77 in the second. England collapsed, going down by 562 runs.

Douglas Jardine had at least gone to Australia with a plan. Gubby Allen had no plan whatsoever. Silent prayer and crossed fingers were the MCC's strategy. Bradman was now both captain and selector. Allen questioned whether the dual responsibility would be too onerous, weighing him down catastrophically.

At last, Neville Cardus met his best Australian friend.

In 1926, aged 18, the journalist and opening batsman Jack Fingleton had discovered 'Cricketer's articles in the *Manchester Guardian*, copies of which were stored in the file room of the *Sydney Guardian*, where he worked as a cadet reporter. He 'devoured every word' and then sneaked into the library later to surreptitiously razor out the articles from the bound volumes, a crime mercifully undiscovered. He finally wrote to Cardus, who promptly wrote back. The two of them became pen pals, finally shaking hands in Perth when *Orion* docked there.

Fingleton regarded Cardus as 'The Victor Trumper of Cricket Writing', arguing that he 'knew the game intimately', and had 'a love and a "feel" for it'. He 'adored' him and thought being in his company was 'bliss'. Cardus found that Fingleton in person was the same as Fingleton on the page. 'You're on my wavelength,' he told him. He also envied the inside track Fingleton had: 'You know what it is like to be out there in the middle of a Test taking first ball.'

Fingleton had played both with and under Donald Bradman, respecting him as a 'hero' batsman but not as a person. As Cardus said: 'No man is loveable who is invincible.' To Fingleton, a practising Catholic, Bradman was untrustworthy, deceitful and guilty of

*Jack Fingleton. The Australian batsman and future journalist
became Cardus's pen pal and then his friend.*

sectarianism. He claimed even those who knew Bradman well weren't sure 'whether to like or dislike him'. Fingleton was not similarly conflicted; his dislike was intense. Bradman was 'a little churlish man', who had a 'jealous streak' and 'all his life' pursued 'a vendetta' against him.

Bradman ridiculed Fingleton after discovering his bat had been sprinkled with holy water. When passing him on his way to the wicket – Fingleton had been out quickly – he couldn't resist a sarcastic dig.

'We'll see what a dry bat will do out there,' he said, before scoring a century. During Bodyline, Fingleton covered his torso and arms in ribbed padding hidden beneath his shirt. He looked like a prototype for the Michelin Man. He maintained, both then and afterwards, that Bradman rather than Harold Larwood was responsible for the worst bruise inflicted on him. As a newspaperman privy to dressing-room secrets, Fingleton got the blame for leaking Bill Woodfull's famously pithy rebuke to Pelham Warner: 'There are two teams out there. One is trying to play cricket and the other is not.' The real culprit was Bradman, who never owned up to it. Fingleton thought he was also instrumental in blackballing him for the tour to England in 1934.

These were not the rancorous ravings of a lone voice. Some thought a blade of ice ran through Bradman. In the book *With the 1930 Australians*, Geoffrey Tebbutt wrote with a candidness unusual for the period. 'Bradman's immense popularity with the public was not echoed by his team mates.' There was an 'occasional coldness' between them. Bradman was 'rather less than human in the way he took success', hiding in his hotel room to listen to his records and answer his correspondence. One of the Australians told Tebbutt: 'He's not one of us.'

Cardus said that he found Bradman 'difficult as a man but not – as Doctor Johnson might say – impossible'. He accepted that 'he didn't easily make friends, and appeared not to go out of his way to retain those who were proud to call him a friend.' Bradman was 'a bad mixer' and unsociably aloof, he added.

Cardus ploughed a neutral furrow between the enemies. 'Neville had a deep admiration for Bradman,' said Fingleton, who was understanding rather than resentful about it.

While Cardus and Bradman belonged to different generations, the two of them shared classical music as a common interest. An affinity grew out of it. Bradman had been a boy soprano. He could tinkle out a tune on the piano by ear, a talent inherited from his mother. A focal point of every house he ever lived in, the piano was also Bradman's way of relaxing. He listened to Elgar, who reminded him of the English countryside, and Brahms, Mendelssohn, Mozart and particularly Chopin. In 1930, during that first tour of England, he even went into a recording studio to cut a 78 rpm record of his piano-playing.

Cardus regarded him then as 'a socially uninstructed youth'. Bradman asked for a list of books to develop his mind and enlarge his conversation. Cardus suggested a number of titles and Bradman dutifully wrote them down. 'A year or two later he had got through them all – and he had assimilated much,' said Cardus, alarmed afterwards to discover Bradman contradicting his account. It was as though Bradman believed that asking for advice implied some intellectual weakness on his part.

Bradman could seldom take a holiday from the world. He quickly became bound up in the way Australia saw itself, his identity indivisible from his country's. His appearances on the field counted as an event. Whatever he said or did was reported. 'If he cut himself shaving,' said one Australian newspaper, 'it would be front-page news.' That early deal with Sykes of Horbury was soon slim pickings beside other commercial interests – sponsorship deals, broadcasting and journalism, songs written and recorded, plum appointments. 'He easily aroused the most common failing of our kind – jealousy,' said Cardus.

Bradman considered Cardus to be an 'eccentric genius'. He was 'a great admirer' of his writing and 'proud' to consider him as 'a friend'. He needed him sorely at the end of October, almost six weeks before the Test series began. Bradman was at home in Adelaide, due to captain South Australia against the MCC. His wife, Jessie, was in hospital, recovering after the birth of their first child. Congratulatory cards and telegrams began to pile up. Only the Bradmans and the hospital staff knew the baby boy was critically ill, unlikely to survive. That evening, unable to speak about his son's worsening health and suffering 'my torments in silence', Bradman could have called on a dozen or more people for solace. He chose Cardus's company, arriving unannounced at his hotel at seven o'clock and taking him home for dinner.

The exchanges were all about cricket and the tactics for the Ashes. 'He told me of his plans to win the rubber,' said Cardus. Four hours later, as the two of them were still talking, the telephone rang. Bradman was summoned to the hospital. Most fathers, aware of the grim news awaiting them, would have made an excuse, booking a taxi for the guest. Instead, Bradman asked Cardus to go with him. Only then did Cardus realise why his host hadn't wanted to be alone that evening. 'I had no idea what was wrong,' he said. 'He did not once let me feel any gloom, but entertained me.' Cardus sat in the car outside the hospital. The sky was 'a great beauty' of stars. He watched Bradman run up the steps into the main entrance and waited for his return. 'After a short while he came back, took the wheel and said: "I'm afraid the poor little chap isn't going to get through."'

The baby died before dawn.

The grief-stricken Bradman asked Cardus not to tell anyone until the news broke. Cardus wrote about it five months later only to give 'an idea' of Bradman's character. He was 'tired' of hearing him portrayed as a bloodless run-making machine and a 'hard Australian'. The piece was so sensitively written that Bradman saved it and pasted the cutting into a scrapbook.

Cardus saw him very differently now. 'He is not an automaton, but a human and sensitive being.'

In *Farewell to Cricket*, published 14 years after his son's death, Donald Bradman gave only the bare detail of his mourning. 'In the lives of young parents,' he wrote, 'there can scarcely be a sadder moment.' He alluded to the tender care Jessie needed afterwards. 'The hopes and ambitions of a father for his son, fine and noble though they may be, are as nought alongside the natural love of a mother.'

Bradman took a fortnight's break, returning in mid-November to make 192 against Victoria in the Sheffield Shield at Melbourne and 63 for an Australian XI against the MCC at Sydney. By his own gold standards, he went into the first Test at Brisbane and the second at Sydney out of sorts and distracted, as if the series had been rendered inconsequential.

In State games the MCC had been dismal, squeaking a win over South Australia, drawing against Victoria and losing in New South Wales.

At Brisbane, where England shed a wicket first ball and tumbled to 20 for three, Maurice Leyland rescued them with a century. Bill Voce took six for 41 in the first innings and four for 16 in the second. Australia were bowled out for 58, their lowest home score of the century; the MCC, performing when it mattered, improbably won by 322 runs.

Neville Cardus rated Walter Hammond as the 'magnificent Rolls Royce' of batting. He could close his eyes, he said, 'and all the bloom and power' of his stroke-making came flooding into his mind. Sydney belonged to Hammond. He made an unbeaten 231 in a total of 426. Australia were humiliated again – scuttled for 80 and forced to follow on, the bell tolling on an innings defeat.

After arriving in Australia, Cardus had looked wide-eyed at the pavement-hard pitch of Perth, the sun beating down on it like a giant bully. 'If the Nelson monument had stood at one end ... I should have thought I was walking down the Strand,' he said. 'I would rather sweep the streets than bowl in this country.' But Cardus did bowl. He put on whites and a pair of borrowed boots, turning his arm for the first time since an impromptu performance almost a decade before in Manchester's Midland Hotel, where he sent an apple repeatedly down a corridor after a rowdy dinner hosted by K. S. Ranjitsinhji. His rustiness showed. Cardus's first ball in Australia slipped out of his hand and landed on top of the neighbouring net, where Jack Fingleton was practising. He sharpened up after that mistake. In Melbourne he even bowled for two hours, giving up only when his toes began to bleed. The experience gave him a 'little insight' into what it felt like to play in extreme heat, palms perspiring, and run on soil that was like concrete against his spikes.

So he had sympathised with Australia in Brisbane when the ball began to 'rear geometrically' after rain produced a 'sticky', and again in Sydney, where the pitch was originally so brown and arid that Cardus said: 'I thought [it] had been brought in a packing case from the middle of the desert.' It changed after a deluge and Australia got the worst of it. As Cardus remarked: 'Wherever' the MCC travelled 'the team broke droughts on sight'.

Cardus the cricketer. The writer becomes the spin bowler in Melbourne during the 1936–37 Ashes tour. Cardus is alongside William Pollock (left) *and Hector Donahoo, who organised the friendly match.*

At Christmas, Cardus stood on the Gap, staring at the Tasman Sea. He followed the drag of a ship across the horizon, thought of the MCC being 2–0 up and asked himself: 'Shall we really take the Ashes?'

Within another week, the third Test at Melbourne – 'a cruel match,' he said – gave him his answer.

The *Manchester Guardian* had offset the cost of sending Neville Cardus to Australia by leasing him to Sir Keith Murdoch's stable of evening newspapers. Cardus wrote 1,600 to 1,800 words in running instalments on every day's play for the Murdoch chain, before composing his considered piece – a further 1,500 words.

William Pollock said Cardus had been 'bothered' by the task of tailoring himself to an 'afternoon audience' and needed reassurance. 'Don't change yourself a bit,' said Pollock. 'You have been brought out thirteen thousand miles to do Neville Cardus stuff, and for goodness sake do it.'

In retrospect, Cardus thought the agreement with Murdoch had been 'badly and loosely made'. If so, this was entirely his own fault. His ineptitude in all matters related to business poked through his all-too-hasty acceptance of the deal. He hadn't bothered to ask whether the remuneration of 'five hundred' stipulated in his contract was being paid in Australian dollars or British pounds (it was pounds). He didn't know when he'd receive the sum (he'd already received half without realising it). He then became paranoid that Australia's tax authorities were going to fleece him of his earnings (they didn't).

Cardus hadn't considered how onerous or time-consuming the commitment to Murdoch would be. As someone who liked to turn up at his leisure and roam around a ground at will, Cardus found it tedious to be stuck to his seat, forced to watch every ball intently. And, since he still considered typewriters to be wicked instruments, he was scribbling out his reports by hand. Chekhov said that writers should 'write, write, write until your fingers break'. Cardus's almost did. He even took on the odd assignment for the *Evening Standard*, adding commentary to C. B. Fry's match reports. Cardus had also agreed to write a book on the tour, which he knitted together at the end of a marathon day or during the 8,000 miles he covered on rocking sleeper trains. These he condemned as 'AWFUL'. He wrote: 'To climb into an upper berth, a man feels he is performing on a trapeze ... Sleep was seldom easy until exhaustion set in.'

Cardus further complicated matters through his insistence on always writing down the punctuation in his pieces – 'semi-colon, comma, dash and so on,' he said – because of his mistrust of sub-editors, some of whom he considered stupid. He liked to quote a mistake from one of his own concert reviews. He'd said of a soloist: 'In spite of the difficulty of this music, she was quite eloquent.' Next morning the second half of that sentence appeared as 'she was a white elephant'. If a sub-editor couldn't spot an obvious error, Cardus feared his semi-colons might perish with a careless slash of the blue pencil, ruining the rhythm of his writing.

The *Manchester Guardian* allowed Cardus this eccentricity, adding significantly to the cost of telegraphing. The *Evening Standard* and Murdoch's stable were not so indulgent.

'Somebody in the *Evening Standard* office protested that I was being too extravagant with the cable allowance,' he said indignantly. 'They suggested they could attend at *their* end to my punctuation.' Saddling up his high horse, Cardus cabled back without delay: 'My punctuation most important, so if my detailed use of it too extravagant for cabling, I suggest cutting out words used between punctuation, leaving punctuation intact. Then fill in yourself.'

Cardus also discovered that one of the Murdoch newspapers 'never used a semi-colon', which horrified him. The conversation between him and the chief sub-editor demonstrates how protective he could be.

CHIEF SUB-EDITOR: We don't use semi-colons.

CARDUS: What do you mean?

CHIEF SUB-EDITOR: What I said – we just don't use semi-colons.

CARDUS: Do you mean, that you don't use them on principle, or because you haven't got any semi-colons in stock? Because, in that case I'll send a cable to London ordering a shipment of semi-colons labelled 'This side up' – you can't be too careful handling semi-colons.

By January, taking pills to help him sleep, he was 'nearly at breaking point'. He thought Murdoch's editors had treated him 'like a galley slave . . . I am part of a press gang, hurried to death over every sentence.' He also complained: 'Never was a butterfly so broken on the wheel.' Cardus moaned to Edith, who wrote to the *Manchester Guardian* in distress about the 'strain' her husband was under.

Far too much of it was self-inflicted.

Relishing the attention and loving the flattery, Cardus couldn't say no to requests to speak or appear at a lunch or a dinner. He estimated that he was making a dozen speeches a week, discussing everyone from 'Clarrie Grimmett' to 'Beethoven' and everything from the 'future of cricket' to the 'music in Australia'.

The Men of the Hill Association invited him to come on to that barracking mound of grass in Sydney, where the barracker-in-chief, Yabba, had once catcalled Douglas Jardine, seen fanning flies away from his face during Bodyline. 'Hey, Jardine,' Yabba yelled. 'Leave our flies alone. They're the only friends you've got here.' He also told one off-form batsman fumbling with his box: 'They're the only balls you've touched all day,' and shouted at another: 'I wish you was a statue and I was a pigeon.' Cardus sat among the Hillites, telling stories about Roses matches and Jack Hobbs. The Men of the Hill wrote a letter to a newspaper thanking him. Cardus agreed with Maurice Leyland, who thought the grinders' stand at Sheffield was more barbed and biting. 'Compared to them,' said Leyland, 'this Sydney lot is as harmonious as Huddersfield Choral Society.'

Cardus was a celebrity. The more he wrote and spoke, the more mail arrived for him.

On the page, Cardus said, he was 'in form'. One crazily cracked pitch looked to him 'like a Roman pavement discovered by antiquarians'. On another 'the ball behaved preposterously', going 'here, there, everywhere, spitting, darting, fizzing'. Hedley Verity was a bowler as 'secret and self-contained as an oyster', who doused an attack against him as though putting 'another shovel of damp coal' on a fire. He saw Bill O'Reilly 'wrinkle the brow' of Walter Hammond with his guile. He described a shot Hammond made – a late chop with bent knees – as 'a Tower Hill stroke . . . You could almost see the axe and the block.'

When two wickets once fell in one over, Cardus said he 'could not believe my spectacles'. When Bert Oldfield heaved across a potential full toss with a cross bat, he saw 'visions of rustic England, the old tithe barn, the spreading chestnut tree, and the village blacksmith'. And when the rain 'played jokes', starting and stopping so that the players and umpires didn't know what to do, he observed them wandering 'to and fro from the pavilion's direction like people lost in the Hampton Court maze'. Chuck Fleetwood-Smith bowled with 'the incalculable properties of genius'. Stan McCabe compiled runs with 'a courtliness that even the toiling bowlers must appreciate'. Offering proof that friendship guaranteed no one preferential treatment, Cardus was waspish about a slack shot from Jack Fingleton. 'This was self-destruction as clear and as unmistakable as any occurrence in a gas oven with a passionate farewell letter left on the mantelpiece.'

He saved some of his finest polish for the National Hero.

*   *   *

The third Test at Melbourne spun the series around on its axis. When it began, Donald Bradman's captaincy was under scrutiny. When it ended, the matter of Gubby Allen's competence was more relevant, so comprehensively and embarrassingly was he outmanoeuvred.

On the first day, nearly 90,000 flocked into what Neville Cardus called 'the great amphitheatre'. Being part of such an enormous crowd 'dwarfed the sense of personal identity', he said. The press benches rose, steeply banked, in the heart of the stand, and Cardus could barely think in the cacophony around them. When Bradman came to the crease, he did so, according to Cardus, 'amid a roar which told not only of hero-worship, but almost of supplication', a vote of confidence measured in decibels.

The build-up had been all about Bradman. His tactics and his leadership. His relatively dismal performances. His shaky relationship with other players. His mental state after the death of his son, the effect of which Cardus believed had 'not been given enough importance' in discussions about his form. His first four scores were 38, 0, 0, 82, and he'd batted as 'though riddled with fallibility', said Cardus. He'd made one golden duck and also got out – as if some imposter had taken his place – swishing at a Hedley Verity long-hop. It was a shot 'not fit for public view', explained Cardus, who saw a succession of 'unreal, inexplicable strokes' from him.

The MCC's 'monstrous' good fortune most concerned Cardus. The night before the Test began, he urged Gubby Allen: 'For heaven's sake clinch the rubber at once. Bradman cannot go on like this much longer.' Allen promptly changed his call from heads to tails, thinking Lady Luck wouldn't be generous to him on a third successive occasion. That was Allen's first bad decision.

On what Cardus called 'an island of green in the sunshine', Bradman made 13 before Verity's arm ball claimed him. Australia slipped to 181 for six. Cardus felt the 'spirit of defeatism' had taken hold of them, the series now over. From the old lags of the Ashes, he'd repeatedly heard stories about the 'sprightly terrors' of a Melbourne sticky, far more treacherous than any other. He assumed this was a grisly fable, greatly exaggerated.

Then he witnessed one for himself.

Raindrops the size of halfpennies smacked into the turf, ending the first day prematurely. Next morning, the ball became as elusive as a jumping flea. Sometimes it rose high. Sometimes it shot low, grazing bootstraps. Sometimes it took off at an oblique angle. Sometimes it stuck on the pitch and half-hopped forward. 'Never before had I, or anyone else, seen a wicket so spiteful and eccentric,' said Cardus. Bradman described it as 'the worst I ever saw in my life'.

Knowing it was now or never, Bradman declared the innings closed on 200 for nine. An Australian onslaught began.

Maurice Leyland used his body as well as his bat to cling on for 40 minutes, his flesh spotted with livid yellow bruising. He made 17. On technique alone, Walter Hammond survived twice as long, reaching 32. Each fell to glorious short-leg catches, the hand taking them as 'swift as a bird of prey', said Cardus. The MCC went spectacularly downhill. Les Ames lost his cap to one ball and fumbled for 22 others. 'He did not get his bat within a foot of one of them,' explained Cardus. The last seven batsmen accrued only nine runs between them. 'There was no ignominy in the collapse,' insisted Cardus. There was, however, ignominy for Allen.

With Hammond gone and all resistance spent, he ought to have declared as Bradman had done, allowing him to create mayhem of his own. Forecasts for Sunday – the rest day – predicted hot, dry weather. The pitch would lose its venom. Even if the MCC fell well behind, there would still be a chance of chasing down a target.

Allen, lacking the gambler's instinct and nerve, pressed on. Bradman, sensing wickets were coming 'too quickly' for Australia, now told his bowlers to hold back and bowl wide of the stumps. Close catchers were sent into the outfield too. A cricketing dolt could have worked out that Bradman didn't want to bat again that evening. 'I was afraid that Allen would see through my tactics,' he said.

Allen wasn't so astute. He could be prickly, a superbly obnoxious man capable of undermining those he thought were beneath him and also reluctant to take advice. He listened to no one else, overcomplicating Bradman's battle plan and convincing himself that it was an elaborate ruse. He feared Australia would declare again, forcing the MCC back in immediately on a pitch now so deteriorated that Cardus thought no batsman would last 'ten minutes' on it. The MCC were 76 for nine before Allen waved them in. This was his second bad decision.

It was like playing chess on a constantly tilting board; Bradman robbed pieces from Allen everywhere, always outflanking him with gamesmanship and original thinking. He first pretended not to know whether Allen had declared, dispatching the umpires to confirm it. This ate up more precious minutes. He then sent his tail-enders in first, protecting himself and the top order. Chuck Fleetwood-Smith handled a bat like a piece of complicated machinery, never sure which end was up. He was so flaky that 'going in at number ten was an adventure'. He thought he'd misheard when Bradman ordered him to open. 'Why?' he asked, uncomprehendingly. 'The only way you can get out on this wicket is to hit the ball,' replied Bradman. 'You can't hit on a good one, so you've got no chance on this.' Australia batted for only 18 balls before bad light sent them back to the pavilion.

Sunday and Monday's sun warmed the pitch, becalming it slowly. Australia were 221 ahead when Bradman came in at number seven. It was 'the game's point of crisis', announced Cardus. 'Everything depended on Bradman, and he knew it.' Despite battling a cold that turned into flu, he eliminated all risk to grind out 270 in a total of 564. Australia cantered home, winners by 365 runs.

In a strangely pessimistic statement, like the chronicle of a defeat foretold, Allen had made a prediction before the Test. If the MCC didn't win it, he felt 'we'll lose the rubber,' which was hardly the stuff of Henry V at Agincourt. Here was the commander who demoralised his own troops, first with his words and then with his actions.

With momentum lost and the initiative surrendered, so the MCC's self-belief shrivelled. Allen's authority dipped and then became significantly diminished as soon as Bradman gradually showed him up as a strategically timid, vacillating and unimaginative captain. There was a lot of arrogance, bombast, entitlement and control-freakery in Allen's approach. Bradman broke through the thick shell of it, revealing a dodgy heart beneath. Psychologically, the MCC were wrecked.

Three weeks later, at Adelaide, Australia crushed the MCC again – winning by 148 runs – to draw level. Bradman made 212 in 437 minutes. Cardus said of that innings: 'The journey was long for Bradman, but he travelled by Pullman, plush cushions and all. The precision of his cricket was so unfaltering that I began to wonder whether he could get himself out, even by trying hard. I thought of a short story I have never yet been able to find time to write, about a girl trapeze artist who, disappointed in love, decides one night to crash in front of the crowded audience and break her neck, but cannot crash because she is enslaved to a perfect technique.' Cardus was aghast that Allen ringed the picket fence with fielders in a thick-headed attempt to block boundaries. 'Bradman,' he said, 'has so many strokes that he can score at a run a minute without once taking a risk.' He made Allen look a chump.

There were sights in Australia that Cardus would never forget. He collected them like picture postcards.

On the way out of Perth, after his train stopped to take on water, he saw a cricket pitch built out of railway sleepers placed on sand. 'A few tin sheds explained the presence of the wooden cricket pitch: a sad, lonely tribute to the game's hold over Australia.' In Sydney, he loved 'the great blue curves of the bays', the hard brilliance of the sky and the sun like a smoulder of gold. In Adelaide, where shimmering heat blurred the hard lines of distant hills, the 'steeples of the cathedral were given the outline of an old-time stage setting.' And back in Melbourne, for the fifth and final Test, the entire city seemed to be going to the match. 'A bird's eye view would have shown the population being sucked into the round space of the cricket ground like water down the hole of a bath.' He thought of H. M. Bateman and a missed opportunity for one of his 'The man who . . .' cartoons. Had Bateman been there, explained Cardus, he would have drawn a picture of someone 'who, on a Test match occasion, asked a policeman the nearest way to the Art Gallery'.

Australia beat the MCC, of course, making Bradman the first captain to win a five-match series after overcoming a 2–0 deficit. And, of course, he again contributed most to it. His 169 showed, said Cardus, 'complete control, with technique not a servant of the mind but the outward and swift manifestation of the mind itself'. Bradman was murderous. If wood could talk, his 2 lb 4 oz bat would have screamed because of the amount of punishment inflicted on the blade. When the Tests began, one of the subplots had been whether Bradman or Hammond would emerge as the greater batsman. Cardus explained the easy superiority of one over the other. 'The difference between Bradman and Hammond can be stated in a few words. Hammond can be kept quiet, Bradman never.'

The MCC lost by an innings and 200 runs.

Afterwards Cardus heard Allen make his concession speech, announcing himself 'a sad and disappointed man'. He was incandescent. In what amounts to the closest Cardus ever came to a foot-stomping rant, he condemned the MCC's defeat as 'a failure as much of character as of technique'. The team's 'falling away' had 'sickened' him, he said.

He would have sickened further if he'd known how Allen, full of miseries, had derided his own players in letters home – some of them to 'Dear Plummie'. The team did not have 'a great deal of cricket brain'. Bill Voce was 'a fat pig'. His bowling partner, Ken Farnes, was 'always seen asleep both on and off the field'. Walter Robins was 'a disappointment' as vice-captain. As a whole, the side was 'rotten'; Allen couldn't 'think how we ever won a single match'.

Cardus clung to one mighty consolation from the tour. He had achieved what Allen hadn't. He had conquered Australia.

If imitation truly is the ultimate flattery, then he was able to luxuriate in it. A correspondent on the *Brisbane Courier* wrote: 'Since Neville Cardus came to Australia, I have noticed a remarkable change in cricket writing generally. It is difficult now for me to follow the Grand Old Game without a book of words and phrases and a classical dictionary. The elegance and charm of Mr Cardus's cricket writing have not been lost upon cricket writers in Australia.'

Cardus's ego was now the size of a battleship. He left the tour triumphant, his goodbye to Australia a long one. Farewell lunches were arranged wherever his ship docked.

The monologue-raconteur was eager to claim that he had 'heaps to tell' any pair of ears prepared to listen to him back home. These stories would be about himself.

With a sigh, and supposedly tired of all the clamouring attention he had received in Australia, he claimed nonetheless: 'It will be a relief to drop back into the obscurity of England.' He looked forward to seeing the daffodils and the daisies and a squall of good rain on a gusty afternoon. He said he was 'thoroughly exhausted' and didn't care 'to see another cricket match for years'. He hoped the *Manchester Guardian* wouldn't want 'too much cricket' from him until he had refreshed his 'bankrupt mind'.

In case anyone thought he really meant the previous three statements, Cardus helpfully added a fourth: 'No doubt the May breeze of Old Trafford . . . will revive the failing spirit.'

He was wrong. Cardus was about to learn that sometimes it is better to travel hopefully than to arrive.

10

THE SPECTRE OF
HIMSELF REPEATED

NEVILLE CARDUS SAID it was easy to 'nostalgically glorify by memory', dwelling on the past and so becoming caustic and gloomy about the perceived inadequacies of the present. 'The Golden Age is *always* well behind us,' he said. 'We catch sight of it with young eyes, when we see what we want to see.'

Cardus sometimes still gave the impression that he wished time had stopped, trapping him to live for ever in the early 1900s, when R. H. Spooner, A. C. MacLaren and Victor Trumper swept across every hot, high summer that was memorable to him.

His favourite cricket photograph – in later life John Arlott presented him with a copy as a surprise gift – preserves Trumper at the point of furious, gorgeous grace. Jack Fingleton thought the picture so exquisite that 'all the dressing rooms of the world' should hang it prominently. For Cardus, it froze his boyhood in a 10 x 8 frame. In remembering Trumper, he saw himself as a ragamuffin again, eagerly queuing outside Old Trafford or searching for the scoreboards in the morning newspapers.

Cardus said that Trumper was 'supreme in every stroke' and had made him 'fall in love with Australia'. His patriotism became conflicted during the Ashes Tests in which he played. He wanted England to win. He also wanted Trumper to get a hundred. 'I realised it would be unreasonable to expect God to do for me these two things at one and the same time,' admitted Cardus, settling on a carefully worded prayer of compromise: 'Please God. Let Victor Trumper score a century today for Australia against England – out of a total of 137 all out.' Cardus was in thrall to the 'artist-cricketer' and 'master batsman'.

Trumper never fell into 'the miserable philosophy of Safety First', said Cardus. He preferred to live 'dangerously' instead, which made him 'compelling'. The ball, whether good, bad or something indifferently in between, was there to be clouted, hard and far. Some of Trumper's biggest hits were made without apparent effort.

The photograph that George Beldam took of Trumper was published in 1905 as Plate XXVII in *Great Batsmen: Their Methods at a Glance*. The caption read: 'Jumping out for a straight drive.' The description is prosaic for something that shocks the eye with beauty, conveying the daring of the cavalier. You look at it and know what Cardus meant when he said Trumper was 'dramatic and lyrical at the same time'. The backdrop is The Oval. Smoggy south London is seen in the middle distance, a ghostly smudge of pale grey. The crowd, gathered in shallow rows on the boundary edge, are a much darker smudge, their faces and bodies indistinct. You imagine them, however, watching avidly and perhaps a little bewilderedly too, as Beldam sets up and positions himself and his Videx camera, and Trumper then goes through his array of strokes with no fieldsmen, no bowler, no ball.

Familiarity never diminishes what Beldam caught in a phosphorous flash and a little fist of smoke. You can stare at the photograph and never tire of it. Come across it unexpectedly, either as a plate in a book or on the wall of a pavilion, and you become conscious again – as if seeing it for the first time – of the energy in this single shot. The slim bat, as dark as a blacksmith's hammer, is held high and gripped at the top of the handle. The right boot is planted a yard outside the crease. The left, outstretched, is raised six inches above the grass. The side-on image is compositionally perfect. The toe of the bat and the toe of that left boot are aligned as though Beldam had calculated the angle to a

Neville Cardus's favourite cricket photograph. George Beldam
immortalises Victor Trumper in classic pose at The Oval.

quarter-inch. Trumper's long stride is like an extravagant dance step. His noble profile – the solid head, the line of his slim face – is fit for the prow of a ship. Seldom do you look at anything static and instinctively see it moving. Alight on this and the mind brings him alive. Everything suggests motion now and motion to come. The athletic, leaping attack. The bend of the knees and the position of the legs. The equipoise of the arms in their backswing. The rippled folds of the marble-white shirt, the sleeves rolled above his bony wrists. You also see what logically must have come next – the powerful pendulum arc of the bat as it came down and the heave of his upper body through the drive. And so Trumper remains immortal in our imagination, a monochrome symbol of the Golden Age. He holds for ever the pose he took that day, during those few seconds when the focal-plane shutter opened and closed on him.

Cardus understood this: it is difficult to convince one generation about the merits of a world to which it hadn't borne witness. Cardus sensed that Trumper, dead from Bright's disease in 1915 at only 37, seemed even in the mid-1930s to belong to antiquity – at least to those who hadn't watched him bat. 'I have no patience with the man who is constantly saying that cricket is not what it used to be,' Cardus insisted.

He was once stopped in the Long Room at Lord's by 'a modern cricketer' – identified only as a 'Test match aspirant' – who was staring at a great gallery of the game's forebears, most of whom Beldam had photographed. 'I suppose you saw all these men, Mr Cardus?' he asked. 'Were they really any good? Were they as scientific as players are today? They look old-fashioned in technique to me. Look at that photo of Trumper half-way down the wicket. He'd be stumped if he tried that game on nowadays.'

Another conversation, also at Lord's but much earlier, found Cardus standing near the Green Bank, 'contemplating the sunlit field'. An elderly, gnarled vicar approached him. He wanted to know where the scorecards were sold, telling Cardus: 'It's really necessary nowadays to obtain a programme in order to pick out one player from another. They are all alike. When I was a young man every cricketer had a distinct personality.' Cardus tried to humour him. 'Ah yes, there are no MacLarens, Tom Haywards, or Lockwoods knocking about any more,' he agreed, expecting a polite nod to signify mutual understanding. The vicar gave him a slightly appalled look: 'MacLaren? Hayward? Good heavens, sir, the game was going downhill long before then.' He went off in a huff, leaving Cardus to stress wryly: 'At the match in question ... the following cricketers were on view: Hobbs, Woolley, Hammond ... Bradman.'

Not so far into the future, Cardus imagined a scenario in which the same exchange took place on the same spot. The question then would be: 'Was Bradman any good?'

Knowing all this, the irony is that Cardus, packing his bag in 1937 for his 19th season, began both to pine for the Golden Age, Trumper still flaring 'like a comet', and to whine about the 'Efficient Age', of which Bradman was the chief beneficiary.

Neville Cardus began his summer on home territory. 'It will be good to go to Old Trafford today,' he said, 'and to hear the oldest inhabitants of the pavilion comparing their winter rheumatisms.' Australia and 'the lidless eye of the sun' now seemed 'far distant', he added. The *Manchester Guardian* responded sympathetically, as if demonstrating a duty of care, to his pre-season plea about rationing his commitments. He seldom went to Old Trafford again; or, indeed, anywhere else. He barely covered more than a dozen matches from May to mid-September. Most of these were at Lord's, marking its 150th anniversary. Cardus continued to claim he was 'a man of the north' while seldom going there. He saw the Players beat the Gentlemen; Oxford beat Cambridge; the South beat the North; the MCC's Australian Touring Team beat the Rest.

He found the cricket uneventful and even a mite dull. The Tests against New Zealand scarcely made the blood gallop. The Championship was a drawn-out formality and emphatically Yorkshire's, already guaranteed the crown before mauling their nearest and almost only rivals, Middlesex, in the final week. 'Yorkshire toyed' with 'the remains' of Middlesex, said Cardus, as though witnessing the former, present and future Champions eviscerate the opposition like a butcher dealing with a carcass. He concluded: 'And so the season died, mourned by a good crowd which went home reluctantly with nothing to do until next summer but watch football and work.'

Cardus didn't mourn. There was ire in his ink now. Out went tranquil objectivity. In came diatribes. He described himself as 'Diogenes', carrying a 'sceptical lamp' to illuminate everything bad in the English game. Cardus had periodically grumbled about the state of it. He thought matches lacked 'gusto' and 'variety', becoming 'unattractive' and 'mechanical'. He complained about 'the dearth of really good young players'. He griped that England, long since lacking the pace of Harold Larwood, didn't possess 'a single great fast bowler'. He protested that the Championship had become 'all about winning' rather than entertainment, which was contrary to the 'amateur spirit of old'.

The sort of spirit, amateur or otherwise, that Cardus wanted to see became evident in his curious preview of the Roses match at Bramall Lane. It was unmistakably prelapsarian in tone – some Housman-like land of lost content. He included the scorecard from the 1905 fixture at Old Trafford. 'I could not watch for sheer fright,' he remembered, constantly twitchy about Spooner losing his wicket. Spooner was dismissed only after a briskly brilliant 109 – an innings Cardus subsequently described as 'all gold and silver' – and then Lancashire continued to flay and tan Yorkshire's bowling without him, amassing 399 in three sessions.

In comparison, his report on the present-day Roses match, also at Old Trafford, read like the choleric chuntering of a disgruntled old man. He lamented the loss of 'the glorious years', summoning again Makepeace and Hallows, Wilfred Rhodes and – of course – Emmott Robinson. 'The Lancashire and Yorkshire match has obviously gone to the dogs,' he said, appalled that no one appealed when the ball was thrown in and accidentally struck the pad. The 'old Emmott' would have indulged in this 'honoured custom' with 'an involuntary, if half-suppressed "How's that?"' added Cardus, unimpressed by 'small cricket' played by cricketers who were 'of small stature' compared with their predecessors. 'Nobody glares down the wicket nowadays as George Macaulay always did whenever an umpire said "Not Out" ... This match has lost its character.'

'Character' was the word Cardus frequently reached for. He preached that 'a game is exactly what is made of it by the character of the men playing it.' He was adamant that the 'charm of character' gave it 'greatness far above competitive and statistical estimation'. And, falling into the same trap as that 'gnarled' vicar at Lord's, he doubted that contemporary cricket was as 'rich in character' as it had been when the 'masters of the Golden Age' were centre stage.

Wheeling out the heavy artillery, Cardus took aim and then fired at everything, never caring where the shrapnel flew. 'There is nothing wrong with cricket in England except the players,' he declared. The Championship needed 'wholesale overhauling'. There was a surfeit of 'dull workmen' in it. 'Anybody not blind or cross-eyed can stay at the wicket for hours ... at the present time it is possible for all sorts of second-raters to score a thousand runs in a season or take a hundred wickets.'

Wishing the past back, he longed for cricket to become 'an expression of personality' again. 'Today too many performances are judged on figures alone. That is like judging the worth of a poem by Shelley simply on how many lines it contains.' Cardus thought one of Victor Trumper's finest innings came in the 1909 Test at Old Trafford, a cameo of eloquent flourishes. 'He made only 48 ... but I've never forgotten it,' he said. 'If you can remember a short innings ... then that batsman did something, *had* something, quite remarkable. I can see Trumper now, making those 48 runs with a grace and ease that has seldom been excelled.'

His tip to aspiring journalists was always 'Try to avoid writing when you're in a bad mood.' He didn't heed his own advice. Cardus was fatigued, which made him grumpy. The travel to and from and around Australia had been draining, and a constant diet of matches since 1919 had soured the taste of them for him.

He believed cricket held a 'mirror up to English nature'. In the 1920s, when runs poured out of Hobbs and Woolley, it reflected 'the atmosphere of the period' – mostly relief that the Great War was over, but also carefree optimism. In the late 1930s, after recession and depression and with the looming prospect of another war to come, Cardus saw disillusion and disquiet accruing steadily, the way sand piles up in an hourglass. His exuberant anticipation of seeing England again had evaporated almost as soon as he set eyes on it. He thought of it as 'more and more unfriendly and shut up in itself'.

Australia had spoilt him. 'When an experience has been lived through, reflection has sieved the irritants away. I do not think now of the mosquitoes, the humid weather ... the scarcity of theatres, music and good talk.' Australia made him look at England anew and judgementally, nit-picking and finding fault. Whereas the English 'lived in pens or hovels', the Australians had 'beautiful' homes. The thick forest of factories and mills and red-tiled roofs in England's provincial cities contrasted with 'the great emptiness' of Australia. England seemed drably grey to him beside Australia's blast of primary colours. Everything on its shiny plains was washed in 'perpetual sunshine'. He missed the sight of the palm trees, the flower shops and the taxis in mother-of-pearl livery. The stars of the night sky, 'never seen' at home, were 'piercing' in Australia – the points of each visible, 'as in a child's picture'.

Cardus swore he could live on Sydney's South Head peninsula, in Vaucluse or Watson's Bay, and 'be happy, given a gramophone and Test matches only once every four years'. He proclaimed his good fortune too. 'I had the luck to find in time Australia's secret. This is the land of the sun, the land in which to release oneself from sickly introspection.'

His words were heartfelt, but also strangely prophetic. Only nine months after leaving Australia, Cardus sailed back there, the palliative cure for a sink of despair so severe that articulating it was almost impossible for him.

Some of the pain stayed with him for the rest of his life.

In late autumn 1937, Neville Cardus sent a letter to a friend: 'I have been rather ill. I'm taking a few months leave.' He did not go into details.

That well-worn line from Dante's *Divine Comedy* – 'in the middle of our life's journey, I found myself astray in a dark wood' – summed up his state of mind. He suffered what he subsequently described as another 'bad breakdown'. His own 'dark wood' was full of griefs.

In a short letter to W. P. Crozier, written in mid-January from the ship, Cardus confessed: 'Apparently I've been through a sort of crisis.' The rest of his letter hovers between confession and concealment. Cardus doesn't plunge into an explicit explanation or go into the specific causes of his overwhelming gloom, because Crozier did not need them spelt out to him. Cardus does make clear – lucidly, but with typical self-containment – that his 'sort of crisis' was profound enough to force him to re-examine his life. This was no mild midlife malady, which could be casually overcome. 'We begin when we are young with certain ideals and ambitions,' said Cardus. 'Then we find that the ideals are either unobtainable or stupid, and the ambitions we outlive. Our problem now is to find another way of life, based on the knowledge (and the ameliorating cynicism) we have achieved.' He reassured Crozier somewhat unconvincingly: 'I am already cured.' He was 'feeling like a new man' and 'aching for work', optimistic again. 'I've found, I think, the bridge-passage which most of us need at middle-age.' Cardus also asked Crozier to 'forgive this outburst'.

The requirement to construct that 'other way of life' stemmed from reasons both professional and personal. Cardus would later admit that, as the 1930s wore on, he became concerned about his status as a writer.

He had 'no serious book' to his name on music. There were only collections of cricket articles, which he began to dismiss as shavings from the workbench. It displeased him that he was 'better known' for his contributions to 'the literature of *a* game' than for his music criticism. That frustration boiled into an irrational resentment of cricket, which he said 'appealed less and less to me each year'.

The once contented routine had become a chore. The man who had proclaimed that 'there can be no summer in the country without cricket' now didn't care whether or not he saw any.

Cardus also believed that 'every journalist is haunted by the spectre of Himself Repeated.' He succumbed to it. Since the fanfare for *A Cricketer's Book*, he had published another four: *Days in the Sun*, *The Summer Game*, *Cricket* and *Good Days*. A fifth, *Australian Summer*, his account of the 1936–37 tour, was about to appear. As though spinning endlessly on the same carousel, unable to jump off, Cardus had been everywhere and seen everybody so many times that he felt there was little original left to say. The daffodils of Oxfordshire and the blossom of Gloucestershire held no allure for him now. Long train rides across familiar countryside were tedious. The facilities at grounds appalled him too. Many 'had no cover for rain', he groused. The press boxes were 'inadequate not to say inhumane' and often positioned at an odd angle to the pitch, which made it difficult to judge individual performances. He sympathised with 'the tortured souls' who attempted to make a truthful record of a game 'which ought really to be forgotten at once'. He was also fed up with hotels where the wardrobes opened stiffly. Where the commode had a tin clasp. Where the dressing table bore the scars of stubbed-out cigarettes. Next morning he'd find in the breakfast room exactly what he'd encountered before – 'the same cloistered dyspeptic gloom, and fried eggs like baleful yellow eyes'.

What had once been paradisiacal was now purgatory. For him cynicism became the norm. He even began to rebel against what he called his own 'romanticism', insisting that 'more cant is written and spoken about cricket than any other game in the world.' He perversely became 'vastly amused' when a stylist such as Walter Hammond occasionally 'fell off his pedestal and struck a ball with the oil-hole of his bat, or received a blow from a fast ball on his toe'.

The business of covering so many miles and writing so many words had physically worn him away. He felt stale and restless, claiming to spend 'whole days' at Lord's and scarcely see 'half a dozen consecutive overs bowled from noon to evening'. Most matches were a battle against boredom. Cardus candidly explained that he 'often felt a sense of dejection' during them, unable to see why even bothering was worth it. 'There were days when I was to be seen walking alone round and round the edge of a cricket field, careworn of visage, with eyes glazed with abstract thought. I occasionally found my daily task as heavy as that of Sisyphus,' he said, as though operating on procedural memory alone.

Cardus once made the mistake of reviewing a piano recital he had not waited – or not wanted – to hear. Unbeknown to him, the pianist had decided not to play the piece billed in the programme. The pianist wrote to complain to the *Manchester Guardian* and criticised him for failing to recognise 'the G minor Ballade of Chopin'. The newspaper published the letter and told Cardus to write an explanatory footnote. He navigated himself out of trouble. 'From where I was sitting the music sounded like the Ballade in A flat,' he said. As far back as 1929, he had also ducked out of the last day of a Test between England and South Africa at Headingley. South Africa led by a paltry 24 runs with just three wickets left. With only the formalities to be tidied up, Cardus assumed he could put together a short piece by cannibalising copy from one of the evening newspapers. He left Leeds and next day, which was 'bright with sunshine', went on a country ramble. Arriving back at teatime, he saw a news-vendor's bill:

SOUTH AFRICA'S GREAT RECOVERY

Tuppy Owen-Smith, a leg-spinning all-rounder, had hit 129. England, left 184 to win, had been 13 for two and 110 for five before an unbeaten 95 from Frank Woolley rescued them. Cardus rescued himself from what he described as 'a nice mess'. He wrote his report – about 1,500 words – from knowledge gleaned through his earlier close observation of the series and the players in it. The piece began: 'History has been made at cricket today in the burning heat of mid-summer.' The second line is the crucial one, a delicious joke at his own expense. 'The South Africans kicked back from a position so hopeless that few of us even took the trouble to be present at Leeds.' No reader guessed that Cardus hadn't seen Owen-Smith's 'very mobile footwork' or Woolley's 'sweet but strong command'. A fortnight later, during the following Test, South Africa's captain Nummy Deane congratulated him on his description. 'You must have had the glasses on Owen-Smith all the time,' he said. Since Cardus hardly went into a press box, even some of his colleagues supposed he had seen Owen-Smith from elsewhere on the ground and then filed from his hotel. Cardus had both escaped his predicament and pulled the wool with bravado.

Nowadays he didn't even pretend. Occasionally he would arrive late or abandon games for an hour or two, leaving Beau Vincent or William Pollock to fill in the gaps for him afterwards. But his tipping point, which came in mid-September, had nothing to do with cricket at all.

Often it is the things we don't see coming that shape our lives most dramatically. So it proved for Cardus. Barbe Ede, aged only 44, died of acute asthma and bronchitis. The death of a loved one creates a heightened sense of mortality in the living; it also leads to self-examination. Cardus, looking at his own life, found himself thrown badly off balance.

He and Barbe had remained friends, speaking on the telephone only the day before she died. He found her 'full of life and laughter'. He had planned to send her proofs of *Australian Summer* for checking, underlining his literary trust in her and the closeness between them. The news of Barbe's death was relayed to him at the National Liberal Club. Barbe's eldest daughter, who was 19, rang Cardus from a telephone box. Her 13-year-old sister, who accompanied her, was told to say nothing about the call to their father. Rupert Hart-Davis, despite being almost twenty years younger than Cardus, had become a sounding post of sorts. His ebullience and actorly magnificence – he had trained for the stage before going into publishing – chimed with Cardus's own personality. The two of them had something else in common. Hart-Davis had doubts about the identity of his father too, convinced he was the child of one of his mother's lovers, a Yorkshire baronet. He appreciated the hole Barbe's loss would leave in Cardus's life. He wrote to console him, saying she had been 'so affectionate and sympathetic and attractive'.

Barbe's respectful single-column obituary, published in her local newspaper, the *Kent Messenger*, explained that she had recently not 'enjoyed the best of health'. She had nonetheless written about cricket, covering the women's Test matches for the *Manchester Guardian* and becoming a frequent contributor to the *Messenger* as well. She had 'a delightful style', it announced. One name stands out in the long list of those who had sent wreaths: 'Mr Neville Cardus.' Flowers were the only respects he could pay. There was no question of attending the service. His presence would not have been decent or socially acceptable then. Elton Ede was warden of the Gravesend church where the funeral took place. Cardus was bound by another convention. He couldn't write a tribute to her either; for that would have embarrassed Ede and Edith too.

A week after Barbe's death, scribbling a note from the offices of the *Manchester Guardian*, Cardus told Crozier that 'empty days in Manchester' were unendurable to him, which was hardly a testimony to Edith's company. After deciding to return to Australia for what he coyly termed his 'rest cure', he conspicuously booked only one berth. Mrs Cardus was left home alone again, waiting for telegrams and airmail letters.

In pieces for his Australian audience, Cardus claimed the idea for the trip had come from a doctor who suggested that he needed a 'change of air' and a break from writing. 'As soon as he spoke those words a map of Australia appeared on the screen of my mind like a film,' he said. Friends, he added, 'unanimously declared that I was mad' and suggested the South of France as an alternative. Proclaiming his admiration for the country, and wanting it reciprocated, Cardus boasted: 'I had the choice of the world . . . but I chose Australia.'

He did so as a desperate means of escape, as if putting mere distance between himself and England would make his miseries there disappear. How considerable these had become as a consequence of Barbe's death – and how confused and lonely Cardus felt – is encapsulated in one line he wrote to Crozier.

'I must have been in a dreadful state – to have envisaged the voyage at all.'

Neville Cardus had a plan.

He would relax, writing only rarely, and promote *Australian Summer* before sailing back with Donald Bradman and the rest of the tourists for the 1938 Ashes series.

He spent time batting and bowling under the unlikely tutelage of the 70-year-old Hugh Trumble, who had twice captained Australia in 1901–02 and had twice taken hat-tricks in Tests. In his youth, Trumble had sported a black moustache that must have taken half a tub of wax every morning to hold immovable its regal, upward curve. In his retirement, the moustache was grey and clipped slightly, the points not quite as sharply prominent as before. His 6 ft 4 in frame had no such slouch about it. The bespectacled Trumble arrived in the nets wearing his suit and an immense sombrero. He proceeded, according to Cardus, to stand still and spin the ball with fingers that seemed 'almost illegally long'. Trumble's three deliveries each pitched on a perfect length. 'Temporarily I became years younger,' said Cardus of his seven-week stay in Sydney and Melbourne.

The Australians left for England in late March amid a parade of coloured streamers, waved handkerchiefs and torn-up shards of news-paper – a substitute for ticker tape – that fell like dirty snow. It was as if an army were being sent off to fight a war. The crowd wanted Bradman. As though suddenly monumentally shy, he preferred to linger discreetly in the background. Cardus attempted to coax him into taking a bow. 'I tried to lift him into sight,' he said. 'I might as well have tried to lift one of the Pillars of Hercules. Bradman is, for his size, tough in thew and sinew.'

It was almost the only occasion on which Bradman didn't take the spotlight in the next six months.

Cardus found the Australian side rather 'austere' and 'Cromwellian in intent and aspect'. The selectors hadn't chosen Clarrie Grimmett, which he considered a mistake. Grimmett could still tie a batsman in his crease as if staking him to the earth with invisible thread.

Once he returned to England, Cardus remained impatient with games that didn't entertain him. During the Roses match at Bradford, he lambasted Lancashire for crawling to 232 in six laborious hours against 'mediocre' Yorkshire bowling. Giving the first of forty lashes to that performance, he dismissed it as a 'public nuisance and a bore'. In future the contest between the counties 'should be played in camera, with the players the only spectators.' He didn't want to be there to write about it. 'If the good fairies granted me one wish I should ask for freedom to stay away from all Lancashire and Yorkshire matches for the remainder of my days.'

The Test series, however, produced two masterpieces of batting. At Trent Bridge, Stan McCabe made 232, so transfixing Bradman that he urged his team-mates, playing cards in the darkness of the dressing room, to pile on to the pavilion balcony with two shouted sentences: 'Come look at this. You may never see its like again.' Cardus watched as McCabe 'smashed the bowling', inheriting the 'sword and cloak' of Victor Trumper. He cut and drove and lifted a six over deep square leg.

With 'consummate judgment', he also constantly retained the strike. Cardus said McCabe's partners were 'almost as much a spectator as I was.' He called his innings 'one of the greatest ... ever seen anywhere in any period of the game's history'.

Only 12 days later he saw another. Wally Hammond was known as 'a funny bugger', oddly peculiar rather than humorous. Cardus endorsed that view of him, doing so more diplomatically: 'He could be changeable of mood as a man.' Bitterly truculent, uncommunicative, saturnine and prolifically promiscuous, Hammond juggled mistresses the way a circus performer juggles plates. In the mid-1920s, during a

Walter Hammond, who had one of the most beautiful techniques in the history of English cricket.

tour to the West Indies, he had contracted an illness that was probably syphilis. Doses of mercury, used to treat the condition, triggered a change in his personality. Cardus thought cricket was Hammond's 'only way to self-realisation'. With the emergence of Bradman, who had replaced him as batting's top dog, his esteem took a kidney-punch. When envy consumed him, Hammond would describe the foe he disliked as 'That ***** Bradman'. So his 240 against Australia at Lord's was a jewel of one-upmanship. 'The greatest innings I ever saw. The one innings I'd like most of all to see again,' said Cardus. For 'sheer classical elegance' he compared it to 'the Elgin Marbles', refusing to 'retract a single word' after some pedant carped about the incongruity of the simile.

The sun was so hot that spectators made two-cornered hats from newspapers, a dainty piece of origami, or wore knotted handkerchiefs over their head. This was the first Test ever shown on television, the BBC clogging Lord's with cables as thick as rolled carpet and enormous, fixed cameras and tall metal poles on which microphones were placed. Cardus felt as if he'd 'wandered into a drawing by Heath Robinson'. For those actually there, and for those at home watching on black-and-white screens barely the size of a sheet of A4 paper, Hammond demonstrated batsmanship that Cardus announced as 'fit for the throne room'. He added: 'Using all the proportion I can muster, I declare that Hammond ... batted with an ease and style beyond anything he has ever done before.' England were sinking on 31 for three. He doused the panic 'much as a mild outbreak of fire is drowned by an honest bucket of water', said Cardus. His late cuts seemed to be 'an optical illusion' because of 'the leisurely poise' of the stroke. Hammond was simply 'a joy' to Cardus. At one point, five fielders were scattered against the ropes, a despairing tactic that signalled, like a surrender, the failure of every other that Bradman had attempted. Cardus's last salute to Hammond was this: 'It was the easiest thing in the world to write about that great innings; it was as easy as making love to a beautiful woman.'

He was thinking about Barbe Ede.

The summer of 1938 is still primarily remembered for a number: 364. Australia had won at Headingley, regarding Yorkshire as a home away from home, its clay soil under their flag. Donald Bradman scored another century there, one of his 13 that season. But what Len Hutton did, during the last Test on The Oval's hard, dry pitch, defined his whole career as well as levelling the series 1–1. He batted for three bone-aching days and three hours – a total of 797 minutes. He hit 35 fours, 15 threes, 18 twos and 143 singles, each run pitilessly scored in a world-record innings. On 41 he gave a solitary chance, a stumping, which was fumbled. Poor Chuck Fleetwood-Smith; his figures were

Tea is served at Headingley in a very civilised
fashion during the Ashes Test of 1938.

87–11–298–1. Poor Bradman; he lost his Ashes record – never regaining it – and sprained his ankle while bowling, forcing him out of the match. And poor, poor Australia, their attack severely depleted beforehand and not so much defeated as steamrollered by an innings and 579 runs.

Hutton batted on remorselessly, revealing concentration of such frozen seriousness that he could have been under hypnosis. Denis Compton, predisposed to a flutter, bet Eddie Paynter one pound that 'when it's our turn we won't score ten between us, old chum'. Exhausted through waiting so long to bat, Compton won his wager. In England's 903 for seven declared, he made a single. Paynter was bowled for a duck.

Neville Cardus was lukewarm about Hutton's feat. He criticised the Test as a 'calculated monstrosity' and a 'libel', finding it yawningly dour. After Hutton scaled 200, he wrote a line crackling with sarcasm: 'Then, like a proper Test match batsman, he proceeded to play himself thoroughly in and did nothing perceptible for half an hour.' As Hutton approached the 334 Bradman had scored at Headingley in 1930 – and the 336 Hammond had made against New Zealand in 1933 – Cardus put aside his own misgivings to acknowledge the anticipation and tension. It was as if he and the rest of The Oval were witnessing a long tightrope walk into history. Some could barely look at the field in case some rotten roll of luck caused Hutton to fall.

'Everybody ached for Hutton's sake,' he said. 'We trembled to think that on the verge of achievement he might fail, get run out, or die, or something.' Cardus said that the 'grand late cut' – off the beleaguered Fleetwood-Smith – that took Hutton past Bradman led to a 'scene which ... moved even the hardened critics', by which he meant himself. Predating the Barmy Army by half a century, someone with a cornet began to play 'For He's a Jolly Good Fellow', the tune picked up and sung in an evangelical tone. 'The voices and the cornet did not

*Len Hutton, who broke batting records and Australian
hearts during the 1938 Ashes Test at The Oval.*

keep together,' remarked Cardus, 'but in the circumstances I admit
that to say so is a piece of pedantic musical criticism.' He was more
touched by Hutton's 'charming modesty' in response to the acclaim.
'He raised his cap . . . and bent his head. But what a moment for him
– the moment of his life.'

Neville Cardus would always remember a quite different moment,
near the end of that same summer, when newspapers were preoccupied with Germany and the conflict between Japan and China.

The conversation meant nothing to anyone except the friends who
shared it, exchanging a snatched few words in the café at Lord's.

Cardus was sitting with Beau Vincent. He was smoking his pipe and sipping his coffee, watching the sun 'warming all the world'. The ground was filling up slowly, early arrivals claiming the prime seats in the pavilion.

'Has it occurred to you that we are paid to do this?' Cardus casually asked Vincent.

'Yes, it has occurred to me,' said Vincent. 'And it's too good to be true, isn't it?'

Cardus's reply comprised only three words, but it suggests already a counting of the days and the realisation that normality – the simple act of filling a summer's day with some cricket – was about to end. You imagine him sighing portentously, his face falling into a solemnly grave expression.

'It can't last,' said Cardus, aware no elaboration was necessary.

Only a few weeks later Chamberlain flew to Munich, saw Hitler and returned with a piece of paper that bent and fluttered in the wind as he held it aloft.

II

SPEAK, MEMORY

ONE OF THE most poignant accounts of the last day of cricket, before the Second World War rearranged the fixture list, belongs to J. M. Kilburn of the *Yorkshire Post*. Poignant because he captures so well the fear amid the confusion, doing so almost obliquely, and also because of Hedley Verity, that gentlest of souls, who would die of the wounds he received during the Allied invasion of Sicily in 1943.

'The final matches of the 1939 season were the acme of unreality,' wrote Kilburn, accompanying Yorkshire to Hove. On the third and final morning, Verity took seven wickets for nine runs to skittle out Sussex for 33, crowning a seventh County Championship title in nine years.

Kilburn wrote about the newspapers, every column full of the war. About the fact telephones and telegraphs were 'so heavily engaged' that cricket scores couldn't be filed. About the cancellation of trains, forcing Yorkshire to hire a bus. About the long, silent and moody ride northwards from the south coast, the wheels jolting on bumpy roads. About blackouts along the way, the towns vanishing under a gown of darkness. And about Yorkshire's arrival home. 'Finally came journey's end in City Square, Leeds,' said Kilburn, 'and then departed their several ways one of the finest county teams in all the history of cricket. It never assembled again.'

Neville Cardus's last match report is infused with the same sense of loss and longing. An enterprising sub-editor gave it the ironic, but fitting, headline:

A DAY OF PEACE AT OLD TRAFFORD

The plain ordinariness of Lancashire against Surrey – Cardus saw no Verity-like performance to subsequently send it into the history books – made a memory for him that tugged at his heart. The 'pleasant monotony' of some of the play. The 'grand sound of a strong drive'. The ball which 'undoubtedly turned'. The autograph hunters, clustered around the pavilion gate to gather signatures of men who would soon be soldiers. What had been would never be again, he said. 'Each grain that fell in the hour-glass was counted and seen as pure gold,' wrote Cardus of that day, which brought him 'the unexpected boon of some fleeting hours of cricket in warm, mellow sunshine'.

Absorbed in the match, you could fool yourself for a minute or two into believing that beyond Old Trafford everything was in order – greenly calm and imperturbable. But then the truth, the very incongruity of the moment, would dawn on you again. 'In the pavilion old gentlemen watched philosophically and now and again they discussed Hitler,' said Cardus. Watching Surrey bat, he realised 'how happy we have lived in the past'.

You appreciate most something you have taken for granted only when you are about to lose it. So it was with 'Cricket in England', which was restored in Cardus's eyes as 'the greatest of games'. He squeezed from a wet summer as much pleasure as he could get. He saw Len Hutton score a classic hundred in the Roses match at Headingley – 'I have seldom seen a day of grander cricket' – and also one unforgettably fine shot from Wally Hammond that 'nobody since Hercules' could have made. Hammond's blistering hit for Gloucestershire against Middlesex was so hard that Cardus recalled it 'crashed against the palings . . . and came so far back into the middle of the field that cover point was saved the trouble of fetching the ball'. In a losing cause he saw George Headley, 'noble in his isolation', score powerful Test hundreds in each innings for the West Indies at Lord's. Cardus witnessed what he called Headley's 'accession to the kingly place he now owns with Bradman'. And in what would be the final Test of his career, still a month short of his 38th birthday, Learie Constantine captivated Cardus with his 'beautiful and savage powers' at The Oval. Even Constantine's 'mis-hits possessed a curious rightness, as though he were turning upside down the accepted ideas of cricket geometry'. In a cameo of 79, Constantine was out to a cleaving shot that went higher than a bird of prey and which the wicketkeeper, Arthur Wood, caught at third man. 'After the catch was safely taken,' wrote Cardus, 'Wood needed only to take a few steps to the right to fall exhausted into the first seat he could find in the dressing room.'

Neither Lancashire nor Surrey mustered anything like that. The first day, which is all he watched, petered out but was still consoling to him.

'And as the sunshine of the evening fell on the field most of us felt that the world had somehow grown a little less stupid than at breakfast when the barrage of the newspapers challenged our nerve and philosophy. A day on a cricket field can be extremely sanative.'

Cardus finished his report, walked down the press box steps and then away from Old Trafford. He would not go back there for another eight years.

His Golden Age was over.

At the beginning of 1940, Neville Cardus walked past Lord's in the foggy dark, finding the ground 'blind, vacant, lost to the world'. He said to himself: 'We shall perhaps never see cricket again.' He then fell over a sandbag into a filthy heap of melted snow.

Less than three months later, he was sitting in the sunshine of the Sydney Cricket Ground, beneath a 'fantastically blue' sky which appeared to him to 'reach to eternity'. In a game between the Rest and New South Wales, Bill O'Reilly was bowling to Donald Bradman. He was 'rolling over the earth, arms like a windmill', allowing him to disguise his quicker ball with no discernible change to his action. He looped a tweaked delivery one moment and arrowed it in flatter the next. Bradman groped and prodded, often fooled. So it was that Cardus saw 'the best bowler now living beat the best batsman now qualifying for immortality'. The contest was both duel and duet to him. He said the sight of it 'moved me profoundly' and 'felt for a while unreal – even a little unfair'.

In Australia there were neon lights instead of blackouts, the sun instead of sleet, and sailing boats in the harbour instead of battle-ready ships on the Thames. In bars he found that drinkers 'talked of Bradman' rather than of Hitler, the war then only 'an abstract idea' to a country holding at bay for as long as possible the inevitability of its coming.

It seemed to Cardus he'd 'come up the Beanstalk' and found himself in 'fairyland'. He thought getting there constituted a personal 'miracle'.

The miracle happened like this. Shortly after war was declared, Cardus had gone to London to retrieve his belongings and move out of the National Liberal Club. He strolled around St James's Park, which he found 'a picture of English peacefulness'. He walked across the bridge, looked into the so-still lake and took in the pale 'heaped up' buildings of Whitehall. An air-raid siren screeched. He watched as people got up from benches and passers-by turned abruptly on pathways to head underground 'with far less haste and determination ... than is shown during the rush hour'. He went back to Manchester to live with Edith, enduring the longest period he and his wife would spend hemmed in together. What followed was the phony war, which every night brought the fearful expectation of being bombed. Cardus searched for things to occupy him and became 'terribly depressed' and 'suffered acute unhappiness' when so little turned up. With no cricket and almost no music to write about, he regarded himself as 'amongst the unemployed' and added: 'I was imprisoned in Manchester, useless to anybody.'

Rescue came in a telegram. Sir Keith Murdoch asked him to cover Sir Thomas Beecham's forthcoming concert tour of Australia for the *Melbourne Herald*. He secured a 'leave of absence' from the *Manchester Guardian*, holding out both hands to accept the offer. Conveniently forgotten now was how Murdoch's newspapers had exploited him like a 'galley slave' under the whip in 1936–37. He would have walked to Australia to work for his new benefactor.

Cardus subsequently insisted that his original plan was to stay there for only 'three months'. The claim isn't credible. He swiftly abandoned Melbourne, swapping it for Sydney and that city's *Morning Herald*. Before the year was out, Cardus's hour-long programme, *Enjoyment of Music*, began broadcasting weekly and became compulsive listening for an appreciative audience, the circle of which constantly widened. In the beginning, Cardus acted like a highbrow professor dispatched to enlighten and educate the desperately ignorant locals.

Cardus had followed one rule when dealing with either a cricketer or a musician: 'not to allow friendship ... to have influence on my criticisms of him'. He added: 'In fact, I have made it the test of friend-ship – if so-and-so likes me and wants to see me after he has read my report today, very well: we shall then be greater friends than ever. If he doesn't want to speak to me again – well, "that's just too bad".'

He was far more caustic with musicians than cricketers. He took a blowtorch to substandard performances in Australia. He was wither-ingly patronising in the process, patting the Australian public on the head while simultaneously mocking it as musically primitive. 'I became notorious,' he admitted. 'I was the one-eared man in the land of the musically half-deaf.'

A cartoon, printed in a rival newspaper, skewered his highfalutin' tastes. It depicted two mangy street buskers. The first urged the second: 'Look out, Bill, and tune-up.'Ere's Neville Cardus coming.' Taxi drivers, taking him to concerts, would ask: 'Are you giving them hell again tonight?' He received abusive letters for his intemperate reviews. One incensed senator asked parliament: 'How much longer are the people of Australia to be pestered with Neville Cardus?' He finally accepted that 'culturally brash' Sydney was not London – or even Manchester. He couldn't expect his adopted city to match either for quality of musical performance and so he sanded off the sharper edges of his criticisms. He thought highly of himself nonetheless. 'I don't think that any music critic has written in any city with the influence I wreaked in Sydney,' said Cardus, unable to resist that boast. 'I enjoyed myself vastly.'

There were exceptions, however. A disapproving, but by no means damning, four-paragraph review Cardus wrote about a pianist who had given a recital at the Forum Club precipitated a clandestine inves-tigation by Military Police Intelligence. In retribution – his perfor-mance had been criticised for 'woolliness of tone' – Archy Rosenthal alleged Cardus had made 'subversive utterances' at a party. Rosenthal was conveniently the lone witness to this. He was also anxious to tell the MPI that Cardus carried 'so much weight' that he could do him 'a very great amount of damage' if details of the accusation leaked. The MPI must look into Cardus covertly, he demanded.

Cardus had supposedly praised Hitler – 'the greatest force for good in the world today' – and described Nazism as the 'only hope'. Rosenthal claimed Cardus had also met Hitler (untrue); believed Britain was 'finished'; and detested Australia and despised Australians (not true either). The MPI interviewed Cardus's landlord-cum-care-taker, who described him as a 'very quiet man' who did not 'give any cause for complaint'. Further enquiries failed entirely to corroborate one sentence of Rosenthal's claims. As the accuser's attitude towards

Cardus softened considerably during subsequent interviews, the MPI concluded that: 'There seems to be no doubt that the reason for airing the complaint was born of the unfavourable criticism after the recital.' Knowing little of this, Cardus offered support to Rosenthal and continued to invite him to social occasions – other concerts and cocktail parties – around which his own world had shrunk.

How Cardus was perceived at home proved more troublesome for him. When W. H. Auden had left England to write his poetry in America instead, Evelyn Waugh disparaged him as craven: 'He departed at the first squeak of an air-raid warning.' Cardus was too naive to think that anyone would regard him as similarly fey and yellow-bellied. He was wrong. Resentments were stored up against him, logged and catalogued like bad debts. Cardus, careless and flippant, stoked trouble for himself too. Explaining in old age why he had retreated, he said: 'I thought Australia soon might be needed as another sort of Noah's Ark for the preservation of remaining European culture.' However much Cardus meant it tongue-in-cheek, the sentence is frivolous enough not only to demean him but also to evidence to the hilt the airy attitude he took to Australia. He carried it over his shoulder like a bundle tied to a stick.

In the early 1940s, Cardus made luncheon and after-dinner speeches celebrating the British bulldog's spirit, courage and adaptability. He shared the contents of one telegram from London which had assured him that everyone was 'safe' and 'unperturbed'. The running commentary he gave on the home front from abroad increasingly struck those who were actually in Britain as smug and insulting. As news from the war worsened – Dunkirk, the occupation of the Channel Islands, the start of the Battle of Britain – his reaction to it did not travel well across 12,000 miles. There were some – even on the *Manchester Guardian* – who under their breath branded him as a coward for forsaking the country and loathed him for it.

Cardus would have been useless to the war effort. He was too old to enlist. He had no previous experience of armed-forces discipline. His eyesight and his record of depression and debilitating digestive problems made him unfit for anything except the lightest voluntary work. He was the least practical and most passive of men. In the Home Guard, he'd have been a cross between two members of the *Dad's Army* cast: Sergeant Wilson, 'terribly sorry' for the inconvenience of everything, and Private Godfrey, always asking to be excused. Cardus would have been of value, especially in the early years of the conflict, only if the Luftwaffe had bombed cities with gramophone records of Wagner.

None of this made Cardus sanguine about being in Australia when Europe began to burn. He was just typically good at hiding it, the face worn publicly betraying neither gnawing concerns nor sorry isolation. On the page, it was a different matter. In the letters Cardus sent, like a foreign correspondent's dispatches, his apprehensions tumbled out.

Edith, still in Manchester, confided in W. P. Crozier. She told him that her husband was 'sad' and 'troubled'. She wondered, too, whether 'as an artist' he 'should experience our troubles here' and write about them. The trusted, ever patient Crozier soon found himself counsellor to Cardus, who occasionally thought that 'in exile' he was 'missing a page in history'. He likened it to 'being in France, but not Paris, when the revolution was on'. In England, he had seen himself as 'superfluous'. In Australia, he was 'afraid' of seeming 'irrelevant and banal – out of touch with reality'. He moaned to Crozier: 'You might imagine that I am lucky to be here just now – well, there are different sorts of trials to one's fortitude in his world, and helpless suspense and anxiety is pretty awful.'

Another matter bothered him greatly, and he sought Crozier's reassurance about it. 'If I don't return now, I'll "lose my public" irretrievably.' Raising the issue from Australia merely emphasised that he hadn't contemplated it properly – if at all – before he got there. It's another reminder that Cardus was a political dunce, never considering how his escape from the deprivations of war would be viewed. You can scarcely credit that someone so intelligent could be so stupid.

Cardus had rented a one-bedroom, third-floor flat on Crick Avenue, which was only two letters shy of the perfect address for him. The flat was in King's Cross, 'a sort of Soho' close to two bays – Rushcutter's and Rose. He hired a cleaner to dust and to iron his shirts and could be seen wandering up the road with a packet of cornflakes to a café that supplied the milk for them at breakfast.

Cardus longed for some familiar companionship. He made the strangest request to Crozier. It was as though his own powers of persuasion would not be enough to get what he wanted. 'Would you compel Mrs Cardus to come to Australia, even if you have to use physical force about it?' he asked. Mrs Cardus arrived at the end of 1941, picking up the threads of their odd-couple relationship. She took a separate flat, a mile from his own, and embedded herself into the artistic community. He visited her daily and the two of them dined together twice a week. Edith was nonetheless required to give 'decent warning' of *any* visit to Crick Avenue. Her husband didn't want to share the flat with anyone. 'Only the privileged few entered,' he admitted.

Vanity has always been the vice of men who flatter themselves about their attraction to women and exaggerate absurdly their successes with them. It is one of the thousands of lies we tell ourselves. Cardus was particularly prone to this. 'The girls of Sydney could plunge into bed even as they could plunge into the Pacific surf,' he insisted, a nudge and a wink suggesting first-hand experience.

Edith had still to arrive in Australia when Cardus said he began a relationship with a woman who seduced him with the question 'Would you recommend the Tausig or the Busoni edition of the Bach Toccata and Fugue in D minor?' If so, it is a chat-up line heard neither before nor since. A month later, the woman telephoned him to say she was pregnant. Cardus feared another 'bastard' in the family would not have 'signified a warm welcome' to his wife. The pregnancy turned out to be a false alarm.

One Australian friend said Cardus's courtship of women never amounted to much. Another suggested he'd indulged in the fantasy of wishful thinking. But unquestionably Edith had to be stoic again about her husband's social activities, which went on without her. When Cardus was spotted in Sydney's Prince's Restaurant, courting 'an attractive blonde', a gossip columnist wrote a snide piece to enquire whether Mrs Cardus was aware of it. Edith reached for her handbag and swung it lustily. She wrote to the newspaper: 'Your gossip columnist appears to be limited, not to say short-sighted, in his muck-raking researches. If he would direct his investigations further, and to the Normandie Restaurant in particular, he would find my husband frequently there with an equally attractive brunette.'

The women he courted tended to have 'high cheekbones' which reminded him of Barbe Ede's.

Cardus, writing mostly about men, much preferred the company of women. An exception was Keith Miller, who for a while lived in the same block of flats. No cavalier had such dash about him. He smothered brilliantine into his hair, making him look as though he had just swept a wet comb through it. Miller looked stupendous even when doing nothing. Cardus described him like this: 'Handsome in a sun and windswept way . . . at first sight he suggests the typical Australian who "couldn't care less".' Miller played as he lived – ebulliently, extravagantly and with a 'dance the midnight hour through' mentality. No party invitation was ever rejected. No drink was ever refused. Conformity was death to Miller. He could carouse until dawn began blinking and arrive to bat or bowl still in his tuxedo after a black-tie ball. He came out of the pavilion whistling 'a Beethoven piano concerto', with his hands stuffed inside his pockets. He then gave the sort of rousing performance that was like watching a box of rockets explode. Physical effort was his art. As a bowler, the 'right foot prances on to the crease'. As a batsman, the 'wrists and superb forearms whip the ball to the boundary'. To Cardus, he was another Trumper, another MacLaren, another Jessop. Miller's subsequent service in the Royal Australian Air Force put cricket into perspective for him – particularly in regard

*Keith Miller, who had film-star appeal. No cavalier
had such dash about him, according to Cardus.*

to pressure on the field. Asked how he coped with it, Miller gave a scoffing response that sums up the inconsequentiality of sport. 'Pressure is a Messerschmitt up your arse. Playing cricket is not,' he said.

A man such as Miller, his glass always half full – literally as well as metaphorically – wouldn't at first sight have struck you as someone who would choose Beethoven's 'Emperor' Concerto as a desert-island disc. But Miller adored classical music and he and Cardus would listen and talk about it for hours and go to concerts together. If Miller saw Cardus coming towards him, he'd begin whistling whatever record he'd last heard. Cardus would be challenged to identify it. 'He would also come up to my room and ask if I would play the gramophone for him. Always he would ask for a piano concerto,' said Cardus. 'Sometimes I would say: "Why not a symphony this time?" No; it had to be a piano concerto. I imagine that he has scored hundreds of his runs and taken many wickets to the accompaniment, supplied mentally by himself, of the *Emperor*. The right music to go with his cricket at its greatest.'

There were nonetheless days – despite Miller, despite Edith, despite his assortment of 'little girls' – when Cardus said he felt 'isolated from a world far away'.

In a piece for the *Manchester Guardian*, he went into a swoon of dreamy surrender about Lord's, thinking about the ground empty and asleep. 'On many a summer afternoon nobody will be there – nobody in the pavilion, outside the Tavern or on the high stand under the trees.' He went over some of the innings he'd seen there, including Bradman in 1934, and then asked unanswerable questions: 'Am I ever again going to walk into the Long Room on a hot day, escaping from the sun? Am I ever again going to feel the shadiness and dignity of the Long Room as I see around me all the pictures and relics of the game's history? Am I ever again going to look through the windows and look at the cricketers in the burning daylight, the scene all suddenly suspended and held in Time, breathless and silent?' He took solace

The Long Room, Lord's.

from a stranger, met in the dying days of that August before the war. An old man – 'one of the game's ripest preserves' – had approached him on the practice grounds. 'I won't be here to see the next match that takes place at Lord's,' he told Cardus, 'but Lord's will be here and there will be a next match and lots of them.'

A letter from home, arriving as surprisingly as the cable which had taken him to Australia, also came as a comfort to Cardus. It was a sign that someone hadn't forgotten him or his contribution to cricket.

In March 1941, Len Hutton was doing routine gym work in the army. He slipped on the wooden floor, falling on his left forearm. He fractured the radius and dislocated the base of the ulna in his wrist. The plaster cast stretched from his fingertips to his shoulder. Even after a series of bone grafts, his left arm was 'some two inches' shorter than his right. He lay in a military hospital, afraid he would never play again. During his convalescence, Hutton, a copious collector of cricket books, read Cardus's *Days in the Sun*, wallowing in its evocations of Bramall Lane and Old Trafford, J. W. H. T. Douglas and J. T. Tyldesley. Hutton felt compelled to write to Cardus and thank him for such an inspiring book. He wasn't to know how timely his words would be. 'That letter gave *me* consolation,' reflected Cardus, taken back to 'the pleasant past'.

He was about to look back and pull that past towards him.

Neville Cardus called Crick Avenue 'my ivory tower', which for six years he seldom left until twilight.

The decor was predominantly brown. The walls were untouched by the sun, the whole place retaining the coolness of a cellar even on the hottest days. It was as if Cardus had transported to Sydney the frugal room he'd occupied at the National Liberal Club and unpacked it there. He had a divan bed, a table, a chair or two, a radio-gramophone and a bookshelf. There was also a writing desk; Cardus calculated that he produced 'nearly a million words' on it. On some days, from 10 a.m. until 5 p.m., he scribbled away in frowning concentration; sometimes he was still wearing his pyjamas late into the afternoon. On others, he walked about the living room 'in aching despair', incapable of producing a sentence.

Here at last Cardus was able to write a learned study of music. His essay collection *Ten Composers* included assessments of Schubert and Brahms, Elgar and Delius. The more important work was his memoir, which Cardus claimed he went to Australia always intending to produce, because it would remind him of home. In fact, the idea belonged to the publisher William Collins, who wrote to ask whether he would consider writing 'a sort of autobiographical book'. The inducement was money. The advance was £900 – well over £100,000 today.

Neville Cardus thought wistfully of places such as Canterbury during his war-time exile to Australia (left). The rather austere 'West End' on Sydney's Crick Avenue, where he made a temporary home and wrote Autobiography.

Cardus first had to extricate himself from his current publishers, Jonathan Cape. The divorce was long and not altogether pain-free. As though flexing his memory in preparation, he also began a syndicated newspaper series about 'the most interesting matches and personalities' of his cricket-writing career while crafting the genuine autobiography in private.

Cardus had stories that he could deep-mine and the literary tools with which to haul them elegantly to the surface. Several cricket scrapbooks, jammed in tea chests before leaving England, were source material. He split his book into three parts: his early life, his cricketing life and his music life. He gave it a Dickens-like flavour and also a Dickens-like cast. In that hidebound and less enlightened age, Cardus confessed things that other writers would not whisper about. He shouted them aloud, thinking both his reputation and his social position were so fixed and firmly tethered that whatever he said wouldn't loosen them.

Most of us go into our past on tiptoe, afraid to disturb it and kick up dust. Cardus went at full pelt. As his memory spoke to him, he wrote about his illegitimacy and the father he never met. He wrote about his mother Ada and his aunt Beatrice, outing each of them as prostitutes. He said Beatrice 'walked into the book and threatened to play everybody else off the stage' for a while. Her ebullience began overshadowing even Cardus, the book in danger of becoming predominantly about her life instead of his own. 'I had to kill her,' he said. He also wrote about the small rooms of Summer Place and the hardscrabble existence within them. About his ignorance and then his self-education. And about that mazy path to the *Manchester Guardian*. He dressed the cricketers he'd seen – especially MacLaren and Spooner, of course – in the white-flannelled splendour of their youth and his own.

John Constable once said that a painter paints 'his own places best'. So it is with Cardus. You see what he once saw, everything rendered both minutely and expansively. Manchester sits beneath a canopy of smoke. There are handcarts and horses, cobbles and gas lamps, high chimneys and hulking factories. The shrillness of hooters call or release workers into streets that reek of coal and are spotted with smuts that fall like black confetti.

For this ripping yarn, he chose the blandest possible title: *Autobiography*.

In 1782 Rousseau published *Les Confessions*, commonly recognised as the first modern memoir. He began: 'This is what I have done and this is what has been done to me. If on occasions, I have added some innocent embellishment, it has been only to fill the odd defect of character. Sometimes I may have taken for a fact what was no more than a probability, but I have never put down what I knew to be false.'

The same cannot be said of the whole of *Autobiography*.

It has to be stressed that Cardus's grip of numbers – dates especially

– was always appallingly loose enough to suggest he suffered some sort of neurological blindness towards figures. Read his match reports and you'll notice that usually only the barest statistics buttress his descriptions of play. Read his complete works and you'll find that he stumbles regularly over the chronology of events personal to him, as though he can't precisely mark the map of his life with an X. He is always confusing one year with another, as though unable to separate them. He gets days and dates mixed up too. In *Autobiography* he even misidentifies his first senior coach at Shrewsbury School, Walter Attewell, as his cousin, William Attewell. These are honest and benign errors of memory, an obdurate and fickle beast. The dazzle of the writing in the book was nonetheless intended to blind the reader to some of the evasions, the omissions, the false trails and the obfuscations. Sometimes a writer omits things because he does not know them; Cardus omitted things because he didn't want us to know them. He behaved in print the way he behaved in person.

He tells us how Beatrice married, had a child and then died. He doesn't reveal that her death from tuberculosis came as early as the summer of 1918. Nor does he say whether, already established on the *Manchester Guardian*, he attended her funeral. He doesn't explain why his mother Ada is marginalised. The lady vanishes, never to be seen again, and he demonstrates not one pinch of guilt about her disappearance then or later. Only those closest to him knew Ada was alive and living in Manchester when *Autobiography* appeared. How estranged the two of them had become, and how little he cared about it, is contained in this admission, made decades later: 'As soon as my wife joined me in Sydney ... I had no personal anxieties concerning what happened in England.'

His treatment of Edith in *Autobiography* is extraordinary too. She appears only as a shadow. The first part of the book is dedicated to Edith, but she is subsequently never mentioned by name in 288 pages.

Instead, she is just 'the good companion'. For this reason, she doesn't even make it into the index.

On the morning of his wedding in 1921, Cardus claimed he went to Old Trafford to watch Lancashire's Makepeace and Hallows, the openers who sound like a music-hall double act. He hailed a taxi from there to the registry office, where the formalities of the ceremony were hurried through. He makes the occasion sound unimportant and nondescript. It's as if, rather than completing what Cardus described as 'the most responsible and irrevocable act in mortal man's life', he and Edith had nipped out to a department store to choose a gas cooker. Since there was no honeymoon – he was due at Lord's the next day – Cardus said he travelled back to Old Trafford, glancing at the scoreboard to discover Lancashire hadn't been riotously busy during his brief absence. Seventeen runs had been added: Makepeace had scored five of them. Hallows had made eleven. There was one leg-bye. The pinpoint specificity of the leg-bye gives the surface appearance of authenticity. The scorebook, which could be checked straightforwardly even back then, does not. Makepeace and Hallows weren't opening on the day of Cardus's marriage; Makepeace, injured earlier in the summer, wasn't even in the team.

His account has consequently been dismissed as a deliberate concoction, a little embellishment that proved irresistible to him. Cardus didn't cover the match and so he couldn't consult his scrapbooks, but the purpose of the story he tells is to cover another. The comic passage is cleverly done, enabling Cardus to record his wedding without elaborating on it or his bride. You're through the paragraph and reading the next, still thinking of slow scoring, before you realise Cardus has got away with a trick. He's told you nothing at all about either Edith or the relationship, which was the point all along. It was typical Cardus: he gave the impression of telling you everything while, in reality, holding back.

Autobiography consumed him. He escaped inside it, forgetting the war.

It still almost didn't reach the public eye. Somerset Maugham laid down a rule which Cardus followed: put a book away in a drawer for six months and then read it again. He did so and got a fit of the collywobbles. 'I tremble to this day when I think of it,' said Cardus, who slid his manuscript out of a drawer and then went over it. 'I thought what I had written was a complete flop, a miscarriage.' He went to the building's incinerator, intending to give the flames a present. 'Then a voice spoke to me,' he claimed. 'If anyone is going to reject this manuscript, don't you reject it.'

He then feared it had been lost in the post. A cable to William Collins's office in London read: 'manuscript sent three weeks ago. anxious.'

The publisher, describing Cardus enigmatically as 'a creature of moods', soon received a lot more correspondence. He began selling the book to them. 'I am satisfied that it is a BIG BOOK!' he wrote. Then he went further: 'Here is a book that I think at times is genius and at other times . . . well, I'll let you find out for yourself.' He promised William Collins it was 'a remarkable thing – of extraordinary range and variety because my life has been like that'. It was 'full of comedy, some tragedy'. Finally, he urged them to 'hurry' to get it into print, afraid 'one or two characters in it' would die before publication.

The book that was almost burnt became a bestseller.

The second anniversary of VE Day had already passed before Neville Cardus – 'dying with nostalgia' for the old country – arrived back in England. It was late June 1947 – that feast of a summer for cricket when the sun boiled the pitches, turning them dust-dry, and Denis Compton and Bill Edrich boiled the bowlers, making over 7,000 runs between them. *Wisden* would say it bore 'favourable comparison with any year within living memory'.

Cardus dubbed himself 'the native returned'. With publication of *Autobiography* set for early autumn, he 'hungrily descended' on London, finding the 'quiet dignity' it demonstrated 'brought a lump to my throat every day'. On a rambling odyssey of rediscovery, he walked 'for miles' and saw the wounds of war pathetically visible around every corner. The business of clearing debris and rubble, and then of levelling bomb craters, went on with a ponderous slowness, the air full of flakes of plaster and concrete and grit. What remained of bombed-out buildings was covered in willowherb, rosebay and fireweed. He saw, too, the wan, undernourished faces of men and women in drab, worn clothes and the roads almost deserted of traffic. Rationing of food and clothes and fuel had made it so. Cardus thought he had wandered into some provincial outpost of an England he only faintly recognised. He couldn't reconcile the post-war London he saw with the pre-war London he remembered. It felt to him as if he was visiting a friend in 'reduced circumstances'. The city had contracted. 'The place is shabby and, curiously enough, it seems to me that the buildings are not as tall, or the squares as spacious,' he said. The statue of Eros was still absent from Piccadilly Circus. Nelson looked thin and diminished on top of his column. The pavement artists, once ubiquitous, had no chalk with which to colour their pictures. Speakers' Corner had all but lost its voice. Cardus looked for and found some consolations. The flash of a red bus . . . the trees of Green Park in full, heavy leaf . . . the ducks in St James's Park . . . the band in Embankment Gardens playing the slow movement of Elgar's 'Enigma Variations'.

As if, for some unknowably perverse reason, Mother Nature had wanted to punish the victors, the country had suffered a winter of brutal cold, a throwback to an icier age. For week after frozen week the snow had come relentlessly, piling so high and so thickly that in

*The native came home from Australia and saw the
consequences war had inflicted on London.*

places, where scything winds sculpted curved drifts of 50 feet or more,
it was impossible to distinguish what lay beneath it. The sea froze at
Whitstable. The Thames froze in Oxford, where a motorist drove his
Austin Seven across it. The geography of the earth was simply made
invisible. You could walk across the tops of hedges, but not along the
cut-off roads. And then, after the snow melted, the flooding began
and the banks of rivers broke and the land beside them drowned. A
wet, soggy spring came next. No one expected the fantastic burst of
the summer, a warm July and a hot August, the thermometer touching
93 degrees.

Like everything else, the cricket grounds were dilapidated shells.
Seating, if it existed, was rough wood. The rest of the facilities were
crude and unpainted. None of it mattered in the heat. Cricket, as it
had been when Cardus first reported on it, became a way of

forgetting loss and deprivation. That season Yorkshire alone attracted a total of 300,000 people to watch them. For the match that effectively decided the Championship – Middlesex beating Gloucestershire at the Cheltenham Festival – a crowd of 14,000 was banked behind the boundary on the first day. Even more came for the second. At Lord's, as Compton became what Cardus called 'the hero of every small boy and every grown up man', there were gates of 30,000. As Cardus observed: 'In the beneficent warmth they are restoring themselves.'

Cardus admired Edrich, believing him to be someone 'direct and masculine of expression ... a very human cricketer' who 'drives to the on as though prepared not to feel shame even if by some slight miscalculation the ball should go into the air'. But it was Compton, blood brother to their mutual friend Keith Miller, who made Cardus glad to be home and glad to be watching cricket in a season that passed 'with a poignant swiftness' for him. 'His cricket in 1947 gave a nation-wide pleasure which was somehow symbolical,' he said. 'In a world tired, disillusioned and threadbare ... thousands of us ran his runs with him. Here at any rate was something unrationed.' Like Miller, he was handsome. Like Miller, he was an optimist, capable of seeing 'the bright lining of a cloud'. And, also like Miller, he had a social hinterland, a body-clock that never stopped ticking loudly whatever the disgracefully early hour. Sleep was a waste of valuable hours to him.

Compton was the Entertainer, a modern George Gunn – eccentric and original. What Cardus liked was 'the ease and loveliness of his strokes', played with glorious pliancy of the wrists.

He said of him: 'He disguises his power and antagonism so well that a bowler might easily suffer the hollow delusion of thinking that this bright bird is going to be comparatively easy game.' That summer a bowler could slog out his guts and get only blisters in return and barely make eye contact with the ball once it left Compton's bat. The nimbleness of his footwork enabled him to change shot even when he had misjudged the flight or length of a ball. He could make 'a superb stroke with his feet in the wrong place', said Cardus, who remembered an 'unplayable' spinning pitch at Lord's on which Compton scored 168 against Kent. He saw 'whenever I close my eyes' one shot from that innings as though it were being spooled on film in front of him. Compton had danced out to drive with the spin, anticipating a leg-break. What he got was a consummately disguised googly, whipping into him viciously. 'Compton had to readjust his entire physical shape and position at the last split second,' said Cardus. 'As a consequence he fell to the earth flat on his chest; but he found time to sweep to the leg-boundary the fizzing spin from the off. It was a case of delayed science.' Compton frequently appeared 'to be playing to a law of his own, and making it up as he went along'. And Cardus thought the crowds were so adoring in their response because 'in him they saw the cricketer they themselves would have wished to be'.

A season later, Compton would meet his drinking buddy Miller at a murky Trent Bridge and take the match to him. At a point of crisis, he made 184 disciplined runs in almost seven hours. Cardus regarded it as a 'classic' performance of 'easy unselfconscious batting'. But nothing Compton had done before 1947, and nothing he would do later – even repelling Miller's hostility in the half-light – resonated with Cardus as much as the summer of his own homecoming; a summer 'all aglow', which had 'revived' the game and allowed everyone to 'absent themselves from austerity awhile'.

Watching Compton at Lord's was a strangely emotional experience for Cardus. 'Never have I been so deeply touched on a cricket ground as I was in this heavenly summer, when I went to Lord's to see a pale-faced crowd, existing on rations, the rocket bomb still in the ears

Denis Compton was the epitome of easy unselfconscious batting, lighting up any match he dominated.

of most folk – see this worn, dowdy crowd watching Compton,' he said. 'The strain of long years of anxiety and affliction passed from all hearts and shoulders at the sight of Compton in full sail, sending the ball here, there and everywhere, each stroke a flick of delight.'

Cardus was touched by the 'humane togetherness' of those who had been through the war's 'darkness and despair and hell' and were able now to sit pleasurably in the sun at Lord's. But he considered himself separate and even isolated from them. 'I felt out of it,' he said, believing his 'exile in Australia' disqualified him from sharing completely in their relief, their joy and their sense of triumphant collaboration. He didn't quite belong.

Cardus got to know that feeling all too well.

12

THE BIRTHDAY PARTY

O N HIS FIRST full day in London, back from Australia and unable to resist the pull of Lord's, Neville Cardus stood again near the Green Bank and stared at the trees beyond the Nursery End. They were 'as gracious as of old', he said. No plot of turf had ever looked greener to him.

Cardus had spent seven years thinking, dreaming and writing about Lord's, a loving recreation in his mind's eye of the way it had looked. The match – who was playing and why – didn't matter to him. It was enough to be there and find the pavilion intact, the flags flying. Cardus became conscious of 'the great place shrouded in ghosts' and felt that 'no other game is played to a background of the past, so continuous, so like a moving pageant.' It was true for him. He thought of going to Lord's in the 1920s and his initial nervousness there. He drifted into memories of the players of his own Golden Age, never to be seen again: Hobbs and Woolley, Verity and Larwood, the old Emmott and Rhodes.

Cardus craved then one thing above all in cricket. It was membership of the MCC.

Some of his press-box colleagues were members, able to wander in and out of the Long Room without being chaperoned as a guest. Beau Vincent had been elected as far back as 1919; R. C. Robertson-Glasgow in 1924; Alec Waugh in 1932; E. W. Swanton in 1939.

Cardus didn't only want membership but also felt entitled to it. His repeated claim not to care one jot was just a case of protesting too much.

With conspicuous flattery, the *Punch* cartoonist Bernard Hollowood once put into perspective Cardus's lofty status among cricket-watchers. Hollowood, a fan of the game and an admirer of Cardus's too, drew two boys standing in front of a set of stumps chalked on a brick wall. One of the boys, clearly the lean, sporty type, is holding a cricket bat. The other is slightly geeky. He wears a hooped school cap, a blazer and a pair of dark-framed glasses. He has a book tucked under his arm. The caption reads: 'No, you be Len Hutton and I'll be Neville Cardus.'

At the war's end, Cardus had made the firm resolution to largely abandon cricket and concentrate on music. The new editor of the *Manchester Guardian* – W. P. Crozier had died in 1944 – was A. P. Wadsworth, who had arrived in Cross Street in the same year as Cardus. As early as December 1945, Cardus confessed in a letter to Wadsworth that his 'main intention in the future' was to write books.

"No, you be Len Hutton and I'll be Neville Cardus."

As if Wadsworth would not believe him without the emphasis of capitals, he wrote: 'NOW is the time to break for ever from routine cricket-journalism.' He would 'never again go through the press box grind', because only a 'big match' would attract him. Sounding high and mighty, Cardus proclaimed that he was – and always had been – 'a student of music primarily'. Rather than dwell on *Autobiography*, Cardus wished to 'stand or fall as the writer of *Ten Composers* and be the best-equipped music critic of the day' in regard to 'experience' and 'range of knowledge'.

But *Autobiography* was so successful that the Book of the Month Club promoted it on the recommendation of J. B. Priestley. Sales took off and the reviews were laudatory. In six months it went through four printings to meet demand, each of 30,000 copies. The publishers even began advertising a sequel. Reviewing *Autobiography*, *The Listener* described Cardus as 'the poor boy who made good' and a 'butterfly [who] had to escape a variety of hampering nets' before becoming successful. The *Times Literary Supplement* thought he was born with a 'talent worth more to any child than a round dozen of silver spoons'. *The Observer* called it a 'very, very good book'. A year later, the BBC broadcast excerpts on the radio, hiring actors to dramatise the characters in it. *The Observer*'s radio critic, though broadly appreciative, made a point about the book's content that his literary colleague either hadn't registered or had deliberately ignored. 'Its candour,' he said of *Autobiography*, 'may have brought a prim flush of disapproval to many cheeks.' He was referring to the night-time gallivanting of Cardus's mother and his aunt.

The war had not liberated prudish attitudes towards sex. The Lord Chamberlain's blue pencil still threatened theatre scripts, poised to redact anything failing to maintain 'a decent level of propriety'. The titles of revues such as *Soldiers in Skirts* or plays, including *Pick-Up Girl*, were guaranteed to provoke. But even a Christmas pantomime

– *Aladdin*, staged in Salford at the back end of the 1940s – brought prosecutions because the dialogue contained unlicensed material considered to be a smidgen unsuitable.

Cardus, who hadn't wanted to produce a 'modest or uninhibited' book, failed to consider the consequences of revealing Ada and Beatrice's alternative careers. Some of those he most wanted to impress were not broad-minded and backed away from such frankness. He was mooted as a candidate for MCC membership in 1949. Rupert Hart-Davis gently lobbied a member of the committee: George Lyttelton, a fellow gentleman of letters, with whom he would eventually share a voluminous correspondence. Lyttelton was a former master at Eton, and had covered Eton–Harrow matches with scrupulous impartiality for *The Times*. Before discovering a willing penfriend in Hart-Davis, he had tried to recruit Cardus to the role. For a short while Cardus wrote to him regularly before losing interest. The jilted Lyttelton didn't hold a grudge. On the contrary. He strongly supported Cardus's candidacy for the MCC: 'No other writer on the game can hold a candle to him. At his best – and how rarely is he not at his best – he is alone and supreme.' Lyttelton thought there was 'something like genius' in Cardus and balked at his imitators, who were 'too numerous' and 'nauseating'. Lyttelton warned Hart-Davis about the obstacles he faced, however. He said one of them amounted to 'odd streaks of jealousy and exclusiveness' and also 'snobbery' among his committee colleagues. How well he judged the temperature of the room.

Lyttelton had been a friend of Sir Pelham Warner for 30 years. They corresponded often and sat together at matches and functions. Lyttelton even composed a 32-line poem celebrating Warner, circulating it among fellow admirers. The work owed more to William McGonagall than to William Wordsworth. Warner was wholly immersed in the minutiae of the MCC – particularly in the matter of who could and could not gain admission, the old boys' network stretched like a cat's cradle of privilege around the pavilion. Alec Waugh, for example, admitted that 'the backing' Warner gave shoved his own application along. As cricketing aristocracy, Warner could decide who deserved to be draped in ermine too.

Lyttelton quickly reported back, regretfully telling Hart-Davis that a formal proposal would have 'no chance of going through'. He had witnessed the 'pursed lip and the raised eyebrow' of pompous condemnation of Cardus whenever *Autobiography* was mentioned. The MCC's blue bloods showed contempt for someone who was a self-confessed graduate of Manchester's municipal libraries rather than the product of a public school and an Oxbridge education. He was looked down on as mere 'trade', as though he was the sort of man who would sup his tea from a saucer. 'Some of them admit that N. C. has written well about the game, but they say he has been very well paid for it, and that is adequate recognition,' said Lyttelton, who did not name names. Another reason, he added, was 'precedent . . . you can only jump the queue if you are a distinguished cricketer or a great servant of the state.' Feeble excuses did not disguise the main reason for Cardus's exclusion. Others had opposed him on moral grounds. *Autobiography* had appalled those on the MCC committee who were as censoriously Victorian in outlook and sensibility as the College of Cardinals. 'There is some feeling against him as a man,' said Lyttelton, 'because he said . . . that his aunt (or even his mother) was a harlot.' The admission was considered a sin by association.

Cardus committed another without knowing it. In 1946, he wrote a glowing foreword to the book *Cricket Crisis*, in which his friend Jack Fingleton turned over and poked the still-hot coals of Bodyline. *Cricket Crisis* is a mirror image of its author: uncompromising, pugnacious and practical. Fingleton asked pertinent questions of Warner's role as MCC manager. Still sensitive about the series, Warner didn't

Jack Fingleton's book Cricket Crisis *dug up the 1932–33
Bodyline conflict and replayed the series all over again.*

want his own version of things held up to the light. With Warner, it
was sensible to pay less attention to what he said and more to what he
did. During the war, while he was working as the MCC's deputy
secretary, crucial documents relating to the 1932–33 series were
misplaced, conveniently never to be seen again. While Warner was
'friendly' with him post-Bodyline, Fingleton suspected he had
attempted to obstruct publication of *Cricket Crisis* lobbying the
publishers against it. Warner had agreed to write the foreword for Ray

Robinson's *Between Wickets*, published in the same summer. It devoted almost 30 pages to Bodyline without mentioning the MCC's manager. Seldom above personal pique, Warner had also not forgotten that pre-war spat with Cardus over the selection of the Test team and his criticism of Gubby Allen. Cardus had shown him up, making Warner's counterclaims seem mere squirts of ink beside the eloquence – and the facts – of his original argument.

The MCC was open to 7,500 members. There were technically 112 vacancies to fill when Lyttelton floated Cardus's name before the committee and saw him blackballed without a vote. No wonder Cardus felt slighted. Among the 92 members elected, there were men who ought to have been distantly behind him in the queue: six army majors, seven captains, one brigadier, four lieutenant colonels and two colonels. The list was at least balanced by a clutch of former players, including S. F. Barnes, Wilfred Rhodes and Tich Freeman. That Cardus, the laureate of game, wasn't deemed suitable to join them was unfathomable to those who knew him. To them, the snub could only be deliberate and spitefully motivated too. His contribution to cricket's literature was then unparalleled, which ought to have been qualification enough.

The private wound is always the deepest. Among the MCC committee who heard Lyttelton's plea on Cardus's behalf was R. H. Spooner, the hero of his boyhood.

Living well is the best revenge, but the success of *Autobiography* didn't bring Neville Cardus comfort or contentment. This was entirely his own fault.

Cardus settled easily into the National Liberal Club again, taking residence as though merely back from a fortnight's holiday on the south coast. The hall porter, who had not seen him since 1940, said: 'Good evening, sir,' and then told him: 'Some letters waiting for you

Pelham Warner, dressed for the Eton–Harrow game of 1952, was a Lord's toff from the tip of his top hat to the toe of his shiny shoes.

here . . .' The club satisfied what he called his occasional 'selfish craving for the delights of solitude'. He needed the sanctuary of his tiny room because everything outside it was in flux.

In the four years between the publication of *Autobiography* and 1951, a period which ought to have brought about a renaissance for him, Cardus abandoned the *Manchester Guardian* and then went back to it, worked for two other newspapers – each proving to be uneasy, doomed matches – and shuffled back to Australia three times. His health began to suffer under the strain. Added to troublesome digestion were lumbago and sinus pain, which caused insomnia. Every morning, his eyes were half-moons of weariness. At one stage, Cardus confessed to writer's block and an 'inability to get down to any sustained stretch' of work because he had 'run dry'.

The plan to grow rich from music rather than cricket was built on presumption and wild hopes. Cardus said he found it 'increasingly difficult' to be a clubbable Londoner 'on a basic income of £1,200 a year devoting one's time mainly to music'. The average working man, earning £3 18s per week, would have ridiculed that statement. He finally had to accept that cricket was 'a good way of supplementing my income, especially when the Australians are in the news'. As though making some terrible sacrifice, he was 'willing to go through the racket and the tedium' of Test matches whenever a 'large amount of money' could be made from it.

This reluctance to turn towards cricket was not entirely what it seemed. In private, he fretted that the post-war Cardus would not be as lyrical or as perceptive about the game as the pre-war Cardus had been. He thought he had exhausted his imagination in describing seam or flight or a cover drive. Sometimes he read back his old cuttings, once telling John Arlott: 'Afterwards, I'd shake my head and tell myself: "Well, Cardus, you can't write like that nowadays."' Oddly referring to himself in the third person, he also explained the difficulty of living up to the stellar standard he'd set himself: 'I'm afraid the maestro's hand may have lost something.'

The public wanted Cardus to write about Keith Miller rather than Mozart. To do so, he snipped the stitches holding him to the *Manchester Guardian*, briefly flirting with the *Sunday Times*. It had promised him the position of chief music critic in succession to Ernest Newman. His old adversary, unable to stomach the thought of Cardus taking his place, refused to budge – and the editor refused to sack him. Cardus covered the 1948 Ashes series for them. He sharply elbowed aside Elton Ede, forcing him to cover Championship games. The Australians humiliated England, giving them a 4–0 hiding. 'So long as Bradman is there they'd beat us even if lbw was suspended while England batted,' said Cardus.

He moved on, taking the *Evening Standard*'s shilling instead. He soon found the editor there would not give his pieces sufficient space to breathe, eventually resigning in a huff after finding his essays shredded into a single column.

The journalist and broadcaster Malcolm Muggeridge, a former leader writer on the *Manchester Guardian*, found Cardus in a confused and depressed state of mind. 'He seemed downcast,' said Muggeridge, who offered him a cure for his malaise: working again for the *Manchester Guardian*. Muggeridge heard Cardus say 'most unconvincingly' that he preferred to be 'free'. He then admitted to Muggeridge, equally unconvincingly, why returning there was not possible. 'First love cannot be repeated,' he said. Knowing this, he tried to rekindle the romance anyway because the alternatives were so unattractive. He became the *Manchester Guardian*'s London music correspondent, admitting: 'I'm as nervous as a beginner.'

Not everyone at the *Manchester Guardian* was ready to allow Cardus to stroll back along the primrose path. The sports editor, Larry Montague, campaigned against him as though his byline was unclean. Montague was the fourth son of C. E. Montague, which explains how in 1933 he had managed to leave Oxford University and make a direct landing on the newspaper's sports desk, where he wrote predominantly on athletics and rugby. When Cardus asked A. P. Wadsworth whether he could cover the Tests as well as write about music, Montague reacted with such vitriol that his typed letter – headed 'Private and Confidential' – had to be handled with a pair of industrial tongs. Montague said the very suggestion was a 'painful shock to me'. He found Cardus's writing 'almost nauseating' and listed three damning allegations: he 'does not watch the cricket properly'; cricketers find him 'rather a sad joke'; and 'every member' of the *Manchester Guardian*'s sports department 'would be most reluctant to have to work with a man whom they trust in no way either as a journalist or as a private individual'. Wadsworth took soundings of his own, slapping Montague down firmly. 'We can't run a newspaper on the basis of personal likes or dislikes,' he replied, tersely.

Montague spelt out his disproportionately zealous opposition to Cardus. He said it was rooted in his 'actions during the war' and also because of the portrait presented of his mother in *Autobiography*. He referred to her as a 'respected neighbour of mine' and argued that 'she had specifically asked' Cardus to 'put nothing about her in the book'. The credibility of those claims takes a substantial dent when you learn that Montague had previous form in his attitudes towards Cardus. In 1946, well before anyone in England saw *Autobiography*, Montague wrote what Wadsworth described as 'long distance bombardments' to Cardus in Australia. The letter Montague posted to him in Sydney is lost, but Wadsworth's curt rebuke to the contents survives. He called it 'extremely tactless and even a little silly . . . I have had to clear up a pretty mess.' He also told Montague: 'I . . . disowned your personal judgements.'

Only a thin file of correspondence exists between Montague and Wadsworth. The sum total of it nonetheless makes Montague look like a bit of a nuisance and a serial whinger – about Cardus and on other matters. At one stage Wadsworth, tolerant but exasperated, reminds him that the sports department 'is really not a self-contained empire but part of the paper'.

Despite announcing he had escaped his 'obsession' with Lord's and the cricket season, Cardus was always drawn back there. No one – and certainly not Montague – would stop him. The game was changing, of course. In that 1948 series he saw Donald Bradman walk into the 'pale sunshine' of a Saturday in August for his final Test at The Oval. At the top of the stairs, Bradman tugged at the peak of his baggy green to shield his eyes against the glare. He had scored 508 runs in the lopsided series, including an unbeaten 173. England had been bowled out for a pathetic 52 in their first innings. The crowd, afraid Australia wouldn't bat again, roared a goodbye almost loud enough to be heard on the Old Kent Road. The England team, already accepting the hefty defeat to come, huddled around him, each man doffing his cap in respectful salute. Bradman saluted them back, removing his own cap in the crease and nodding his gratitude. Sawdust had been scattered across the bowler's footmarks. There were a few scuffed patches of dark earth on the pitch. Bradman patted these down with the blade of his bat like a gardener using the flat of a spade. Then there was silence. Eric Hollies, bowling around the wicket, lured Bradman back and across with his first delivery and brought him forward to the second. Bradman groped for the ball and discovered it gone. 'A googly,' said Cardus, bowled him off a faint inside edge for 0. Then there was silence again. Poleaxed in astonishment, Bradman turned, tucked his bat beneath his left arm, pulled off his gloves and retraced his steps, his head up and his stride dignified. The slanting sun was so low that his elongated shadow spread across the outfield, a parody of his body. There was one question no one could answer definitively then or later. Was it Hollies's spin or the ovation, fluttering his usually steady heart, that claimed Bradman's wicket?

His friendship with Bradman had spanned 18 years. Cardus still described him as 'an enigma', a man he found 'hard, really, to get to know'. It was also hard to 'get him to realise that you really liked him', he added. Bradman must have known all the same. Whenever he went to Australia, Cardus was guaranteed one invitation. 'A welcome at the Bradman home,' he said.

Rupert Hart-Davis increasingly became an important confidant to Neville Cardus. Not a player in the behind-the-scenes machinations of cricket but a follower of the game, he was the honest broker, able to listen to Cardus and then afterwards offer trusted and intelligent counsel untainted by ulterior motives. He got to know him better than most. Hart-Davis hit the bullseye when he said of Cardus: 'It's difficult to imagine how one could write about cricket year after year without getting bored with the ordinary.'

Cardus managed it because of the Ashes. While insisting that he was 'sick' of Australia through overfamiliarity – 'whatever it was, the spell is broken' – he rushed up the gangplank to go back there, renewing old friendships and creating new ones.

On the MCC's 1950–51 tour, he befriended John Woodcock, then 24 and still to become cricket correspondent of *The Times*, a position he would hold from 1954 to 1987, like the long reign of a much-loved monarch. Cardus looked on him with paternal solicitude. 'People said to me: "He thinks of you as a son,"' remembered Woodcock. 'He certainly treated me like one.'

Woodcock had 'read and re-read many times' Cardus's *Australian Summer*. 'It was a marvellous thing for me that the two of us were going on a tour together.' On the boat, so familiar now with seafaring, Cardus would gesture towards Woodcock after dinner and say: 'Come on, young John. I've booked the deckchairs and ordered the cigars and the glasses of port.' In a quiet spot on a lofty deck, Cardus held court rather than conversed. He summoned his yesterdays for Woodcock, who considered it 'the most congenial cricket education possible'. Only in retrospect did he realise something about Cardus which struck him as 'rather sad, I suppose'. To be a friend of Cardus's you had to be a good listener. Other correspondents were unwilling to comply, having grown jaded of his voice. Cardus believed 'No story is worth telling once, if it is not worth telling twenty times.' He forgot that not everyone was so fond of repetition. Woodcock said: 'The tales had been heard so many times before. No one who'd been on tours before with him wanted to hear them again. That was hard for him because he was the sort of man who *had* to talk. He was lonely and he felt a bit isolated sometimes too. You wouldn't have known that if you'd met him, of course. He was always outwardly cheery and positive.'

Woodcock, 'the new boy and a new audience', found Cardus 'so generous and so entertaining' and became fond of him. 'I was very grateful to him,' he explained.

Also grateful was Harold Larwood, freshly emigrated to Sydney and hired by the *Sunday Express* to provide expert analysis.

As well as those players on either side of the Pennines, Cardus had got to know well the 1920s Nottinghamshire team, which under Arthur Carr won one Championship and ought to have claimed at least one other. He lodged regularly with George Gunn, the batsman who was 'incalculably a law unto himself' and 'the great improvisatory genius', always producing 'some new stroke which beggared description'. Gunn was mercurial, dancing to no tune that he didn't play himself. Leaving together for a match, Cardus heard him ask his wife what time she would arrive at Trent Bridge. About 12.30 p.m., she said. She told her husband she would park the car on the apron of the ground. Gunn, not out overnight, promised: 'I'll look for you about that time and then get out.' Having reached a hundred, Gunn did exactly that – sending a catch to the boundary almost in front of the car's windscreen.

The Notts team, under Arthur Carr, were an eccentric but Championship-winning team. Ben Lilley, the wicketkeeper (left), is in discussion with Harold Larwood and George Gunn (right) at the Trent Bridge nets.

In bold exhibitions of gamesmanship, designed to intimidate, Gunn also often strode yards out of his crease, bat aloft. Cecil Parkin once feigned to bowl, holding on to the ball and running to meet him instead. The two men came together near the middle of the pitch, so close as to be practically nose to nose. 'Was there something you wanted to say to me, George?' asked Parkin, the humour as dry as sand.

Gunn's friendship ensured Cardus got Carr's as well. At Lancashire, the players downed an extra pint swiftly before chucking-out time. At Notts, the players drank on until the wee small hours because Carr, broad and beefy-faced, liked a lock-in. His was a side powered on beer and the Nottingham sandwich – comprising cheese, fags and bitter – even during a match. Cardus was a wine-drinker, preferring Beaujolais to hoppy bitter, but he always stood his round and supped with them. Larwood politely called him 'Mr', before Cardus asked him to drop the formalities. He then became 'Our Nev' to him instead.

Larwood arrived in Australia with grey hair and wearing a pair of horn-rimmed spectacles. No gateman recognised the Bodyline bowler before the first Test, at Brisbane. He drifted from entrance to entrance, unable to gain admission. Impatiently, Cardus took him by the shoulder and thrust him forward like the good chaperone. 'Look here,' said Cardus to the officials. 'This is Harold Larwood. You've heard of him? I should think so. Well, there was a time, I agree, when every precaution might have been taken to keep Harold Larwood out of all Australian cricket grounds. But, look at him now – he's quite harmless.'

Cardus later intervened to stop a minor diplomatic incident between Larwood and a member of the MCC team. Larwood saw the player, whom he knew well, crossing a road with his wife on his arm. He called towards them. He waved. He called again. The player deliberately turned his head away from him. Larwood saw the slight as related somehow to Bodyline and planned a face-to-face confrontation. Cardus defused his anger with an explanation. 'Harold, let me tell you something . . . the woman you saw was not his wife.'

The MCC lost the series 4–1. Cardus's personal highlight came at Sydney, during what he described as 'one rare period when Australia could not get an Englishman out for an hour'. A voice from the Hill yelled: '*Put Neville Cardus on!*'

The Ashes finally 'came home' in the Coronation series of 1953, after what Cardus said was 'years of waiting and hours of anxiety'. He awarded the laurels not to the stylists, such as Len Hutton or Denis Compton, but to the 'remarkable character' Trevor Bailey, the Barnacle. 'He prevailed, conquered and frustrated Australia by sheer will power; he decided at any cost not to get out. When at Lord's he faltered at long last [Bailey made 71 in 257 minutes, salvaging a draw] and lost his wicket to a poor stroke . . . he clutched his brow, swayed as if about to fall, the whole man and body of him the living image of self-disgust, heartbreak, self-flagellation, misery and the vanity of all things.'

A paragraph as good as that one meant that editors, never the most altruistic of breeds, were still willing to pay Cardus for his byline because it carried lustre as well as gravitas, and also because readers stayed loyal to him. Stamping his name on the cover of a magazine shifted copies of it.

He anointed himself as the 'doyen of the press box' by virtue of being the lone newspaper survivor from Warwick Armstrong's tour 32 years before. The description was only half true. In the 1950s, he saw less of any press box than ever before, preferring a seat elsewhere. 'Generally you'd glimpse him only at the beginning and at the end of a day's play,' remembered Woodcock.

Since he'd seen England regain the Ashes, Cardus wanted to watch the MCC retain them also. In 1954–55 he went back to Australia.

He took two 'wives' with him.

The success of *Autobiography* persuaded Rupert Hart-Davis to publish *The Essential Neville Cardus*, a 'greatest hits' collection pressed between hard covers. The most significant thing about the book is the dedication. It read: 'To the Happy Memory of Barbe Ede.' Cardus said the tribute, which was Hart-Davis's idea, 'moved' him. 'How she would have loved it,' he told Hart-Davis. 'God bless her dear ghost.'

Other women had succeeded Barbe without entirely replacing her. The first was Else Mayer-Lismann. In 1938, when she was 24, her family fled Frankfurt and came to England. Mayer-Lismann's mother, a 'distinguished-looking white-haired lady', had lectured at the Salzburg Festival. She became friendly with the extraordinary, opera-obsessed sisters Ida and Mary Louise Cook. The Cooks were responsible for arranging the escape of 29 Jews from the Nazis in what the two of them so self-deprecatingly described as 'our amateur way'. This included posing as harmless English eccentrics, smuggling fur coats and passing off expensive jewellery as paste imitations. The operation was funded by the romantic novels Ida profitably wrote for Mills & Boon. The Mayer-Lismanns were the first people to benefit from the sisters' bravery and ingenuity.

Before the war, Else had attended Frankfurt's Musikhochschule. After it, while lecturing on opera and also teaching opera interpretation, she accompanied Cardus to concerts, festivals and musical sorties. The letters Cardus sent to her are lachrymosely sugar-sweet, each of them a Valentine. 'You are a girl in a thousand . . . I miss you and I love you . . . No one but you enters my heart or is on my wavelength . . . I miss you more than I can say . . . I really don't want to write another word – except a love letter.'

Mayer-Lismann became what Cardus called his 'music wife'. His 'cricket wife' was Margaret Hughes, always called 'Meg'. There was something of the tomboy about Hughes, a mere 5 ft 2 in tall. She nearly always wore trousers, hating skirts.

Her fanaticism for cricket had been formed during her girlhood in Kent, sport dominating the household. 'I have always been led to believe that my father . . . desperately hoped for his own private cricket team of sons,' she said. Hughes, born in 1919, took an advertising job on *The Star* just so she could 'see the cricket scores before the general public'. She saved her money, penny-pinching during the winter so she could spend it travelling to watch cricket in the summer. When war came, she served as a Wren. When it was over, she headed to New York for a while and then returned to work on *The Queen* magazine. Hughes had one ambition: 'To put cricket at the centre of my life.'

She published *All on a Summer's Day* in 1953, establishing herself as a pioneer. As Cardus wrote in the foreword: 'This is the first book on first-class cricket not written by a man.' He highlighted the 'sense of scene and character' in it and also her 'knowledge of the things that technically and tactically matter'. He added: 'Miss Hughes ... sees all her cricket as though for the first time, yet she always brings to her vision a remarkably mature understanding.'

Some – both reactionary and antediluvian – were suspicious of Hughes from the start, her presence enough to provoke harsh whispers about her rights and qualifications to a press seat. The fact she could write and knew cricket backwards was less important than her chromosomes. Others were just pettily jealous that an old coot like Cardus had persuaded the attractively auburn-haired Hughes to be his regular cricket companion. She was in her mid-thirties. He was nearly 70.

He often escorted her to Lord's and The Oval, drawing snide remarks. The gossiping about them increased during the MCC tour of 1954–55 as soon as Edith Cardus arrived in Sydney. Edith was unconcerned about Hughes – she was another of her husband's harmless infatuations – but not everyone knew or understood that, imagining instead a resentment and rivalry which didn't exist.

Hughes had cajoled the Packer newspaper group into hiring her, offering *All on a Summer's Day* as her impressive calling card. She became the first woman to cover an Ashes series. One Packer paper announced her arrival with a headline that makes you think of a circus ringmaster barking at a crowd to 'roll up' and gawk at the bearded lady. 'A Woman Writes on Cricket,' it said, never thinking of the words as patronising. Sad as it seems to us now, this was only to be expected back then. After all, Hughes was attached to an MCC team led by Len Hutton. His opinion of women's cricket was so low as to be almost subterranean. 'Ladies playing cricket? Absurd. Like a man trying to knit,' he said.

Hutton became the first MCC captain since Douglas Jardine to win an Ashes series in Australia, clinching it 3–1. Cardus recognised

*Margaret Hughes, who lived for cricket and became
a successful author because of it.*

his abilities as a captain without relishing them. He was too dour for
him. The MCC won because Frank Tyson whipped in with 28 wickets
– only five fewer than Harold Larwood had claimed in 1932–33.
Tyson, the Typhoon, so scared Australia that those about to face him
went to the wicket like 'the condemned man going to the scaffold',
according to Cardus. Hughes, often beside him in some tucked-away

spot on a ground, surpassed that description with her own. 'The mere sight of Tyson with the new ball,' she wrote, 'was now and forever to cause panic in the Australians.' She saw their batsmen 'flash' at deliveries outside off stump, getting out rather than 'risk permanent injury' against him.

One event during the tour went unrecorded.

During the last Test, the second held in Sydney, at the end of February, Cardus received a telegram sent from his mother's bank. The details were frugal. She had died more than a month earlier. Her funeral had already taken place. She had been living in Withington, a suburb of Manchester. The bank enquired how her estate would be handled. Ada had dropped the surname Cardus, reverting to her mother's maiden name Rawlinson. She'd used it, like a disguise, during earlier periods of her life. Her death notice, a few modest lines in typically small type, appeared in the *Manchester Evening News*. It contained no mention of her illustrious only son.

Cardus shared the contents of the telegram with only two people: his real wife and his 'cricket wife'.

He was leaving the Sydney Cricket Ground with Margaret Hughes when one of the locals buttonholed him, drunkenly and aggressively.

'Neville Cardus,' shouted the man. 'You're an effing English bastard.'

Cardus quickly removed his spectacles, thinking the amount of grog the barracker had consumed might lead to fisticuffs. He decided that agreeing with him was the best way to avoid a punch in the face. With all the decorum he could muster, Cardus replied:

'English, yes.

'Bastard, yes.

'But effing – not at this precise moment, old boy.'

The man was both disarmed by his politeness and too far gone to appreciate the craft of the sentence.

Autobiography made Cardus's illegitimacy public knowledge, but he was never curious to discover more about either his birth or the identity of his father. When John Arlott once asked him whether he had ever gone looking for information, Cardus shook his head and said: 'It does not matter.' He gave the same reply in a letter to Else Mayer-Lismann, who had been gently teasing him about his advancing years. Cardus didn't know his age because he had never sought out his birth certificate. 'I have always been brought up to believe I was born in 1890 – or was it really 1889?' He added the next line in German: *'Es macht nichts – ich bin geliebt'*; (It does not matter. I am beloved).'

In his passport Cardus plumped for 1889. He was wrong. He was born in 1888. It meant that a grand party, held for him in 1959, celebrated the wrong birthday. Everyone there toasted his 70th when he was actually 71.

The party was a strange and ever-so-slightly surreal occasion.

A total of 47 of Cardus's dearest friends, casual acquaintances and the odd hanger-on gathered in the Regatta Restaurant of the Royal Festival Hall.

The Festival Hall was chosen after careful debate among those who considered themselves to be closest to him. His friends regarded it as far more appropriate – and thoroughly more worthy – than Lord's. This was entirely the fault of the MCC. Belatedly, and rather grudgingly, it had granted him associate rather than full membership 12 months earlier. Sir Pelham Warner, then 84, no longer had the clout to stop it. George Lyttelton described Cardus's old foe as 'fearfully

Proof of the passport. Even in ripe old age, Neville Cardus believed he was born in 1889.

fragile and almost transparent'. Cardus still grumbled, rightly surmising that a compromise had been reached. He saw himself as 'a sort of poor relation' of the club. Associate members were not permitted to sit in the pavilion during Test matches, which peeved him.

The Royal Festival Hall was conceived and constructed as a post-war symbol of a vibrantly modern and forward-thinking Britain. Its management was not sniffy about Cardus's background or his lack of schooling. He was treated there as writing royalty. Sometimes he composed his notices late at night in a far corner of the cafeteria, where staff carried cups of tea and biscuits to him. 'It was all done with such reverence,' said a fellow critic.

The Regatta Restaurant put on a decent show for Cardus. Stark white walls, a 50-feet-high ceiling and wide, tall windows made the place look like a cavernous glass box. Eight round tables, as well as the long, rectangular top table, were each decorated with a bloom of Lancastrian red roses, delicately arranged in short, ornate glass vases. The square-patterned carpet was red too, a lovely coincidence that made it seem as though the guest of honour had been in charge of the decor. The early afternoon was cold and bright, and all that glass meant the mannered scene was washed in huge wedges of light. The only problem was that the vastness of the room, which the diners barely half-filled, did not lend itself to cosy intimacy. Odder still, there was no music; no one had thought to arrange any. The soft clatter of knives and forks on porcelain, and the low murmur of small talk, were the only sounds anyone heard, which gave the occasion a strange air of solemnity.

Those who faced the Thames at least had the view to console them: small boats and tugs chugged up and down the river and slanting funnels of wispy steam smudged the sky as trains rattled slowly across the Hungerford Bridge. Those who did not 'might have been in a provincial hotel out of season', complained Rupert Hart-Davis, who sent a contemporaneous account of his experiences to Lyttelton. As his eyes and ears at the event, Hart-Davis dismissed the food as 'eatable rather than memorable' and dwelt on the guest list, most of whom were of Cardus's vintage. The names were fairly prominent then, but are obscure now unless the history of Grub Street, the conductors and composers of classical music and elderly socialites in inherited pearls count as your specialist subject. Hart-Davis made the party sound like a motley collection of characters from the Theatre of the Absurd. With some glee, he reflected on the 'fun' of 'fitting the odd faces to the still odder names, which I have so long passed quickly by in newspapers'. He spoke of a literary critic who was 'even more liberally spread with scurf, cigarette ash and shaving soap than before'. Of a musicologist who had 'black hair growing on the top of his nose'. Of a Baroness-to-be who 'must have strayed in from some other function, since she clearly had no connection with this one'.

Chosen to share Cardus's direct orbit were: Arthur Bliss, Master of the Queen's Music, who sported a white moustache and thick eyebrows, both in need of clipping; Sir Malcolm Sargent, chosen to give the toast; and Baroness Violet Bonham Carter, the daughter of former prime minister Herbert Asquith. She was a prominent voice in Liberal politics and also a close friend of Winston Churchill.

Sargent kept things brief. Cardus's writing, he said, made 'so many people wish they had actually been at a cricket match or actually been at a concert'.

Cardus replied to Sargent with 'some signs of shy diffidence'. If the statement is accurate, it recorded a moment peculiarly out of character. Cardus relished an audience, no music sweeter to him than the sound of his own voice; he always found himself interesting. He announced himself to the room as an 'adagio man', a musical reference to slow composition, and also as a 'one column man', explaining that 'everything' he had ever written came from his desire to be 'moved by the occasion ... [and] to be moved sentimentally'. Cardus added, jokily, that he didn't want to be 'swept away too riotously by his emotions' or he 'might be provoked into saying too many unprofessionally kind things'.

There were no cards and no cake with a thicket of candles. In a ceremony devoid of fuss, Sargent presented Cardus with a red leather book containing handwritten tributes from those whom his career had touched prodigiously.

Out of loyalty to one of its own, the *Manchester Guardian* – four months later the newspaper dropped 'Manchester' from its masthead – dispatched a reporter from its 'London Letter' column. The four paragraphs he filed implied boredom with his task, as if listening to a bunch of old buffers was a punishment. Bonham Carter, whom Cardus kissed twice on her arrival, provided a blunter assessment of the event. Sargent had spoken 'without a bit of distinction', she said. Most of the fellow guests were 'unknown' in her opinion. The lunch itself 'crept slowly by'.

Knowing how much Cardus adored the limelight even when pretending to back away from it, Hart-Davis was more positive. 'I think Neville was delighted with it all,' he told Lyttelton.

Lyttelton still fastened on another aspect of that apparently morose afternoon. It nagged at him. 'Surely the cricket world was poorly represented.' He then asked a direct question in a manner that suggested he already knew the answer: 'Is my feeling correct that he is not altogether *persona grata* there?' Lyttelton had alighted on an uncomfortable truth.

If Cardus wasn't exactly divorced from cricket, he and it were definitely in a state of semi-separation.

His waning relationship with the game had been emphasised in the portentous title of his most recent book, *Close of Play*, and also in the opening sentence of the final chapter: 'As it is possible that this book is my last about cricket ...' Cardus mostly took a long look at the gorgeous past. The book included essays about Herbert Sutcliffe and those tough, taciturn pros of Yorkshire in the 1920s and 1930s. He wrote about Jack Hobbs, Walter Hammond and C. B. Fry, whom he compared with the exotic Ranjitsinhji. Fry 'batted by the book of arithmetic', acquiring runs 'not as a miser his hoard, but as the connoisseur his collection'. Ranjitsinhji 'seemed to toss runs over the field like largesse in silk purses'.

Cardus had always revealed a remarkable generosity of spirit towards cricketers and cricket writers.

With a word discreetly dropped in the right ear, he had arranged for Emmott Robinson to write a column in the northern edition of the *News Chronicle* after his retirement. When J. M. Kilburn was just starting out at the *Yorkshire Post*, he received an unsolicited letter from Cardus – thoughtfully copied to his editor – that told him: 'To my mind yours is the best cricket reporting today.' Shortly after C. L. R.

James arrived in England, a 31-year-old unknown from the West Indies, he discovered that Cardus became almost godfatherly towards him – 'much to my astonishment'. He first urged the *Manchester Guardian* to publish one of James's articles, and then to take him on as a writer. 'Sesame! Presto!' said James. 'I had a job.' In three seasons he wrote over 130 brief reports.

Cardus also acted as mentor or inspiration to other correspondents, such as Dudley Carew, his work slavishly copying Cardus's early work in style.

But the weave of his cricket life had come loose, weakening his friendships in the game. The England team, sent unsuccessfully that winter to Australia, had been home for a week and a half. The start of the County Championship season was more than a month off. There were still no cricketers, past or present, at his birthday party. There were no administrators, current or former, either. Only two men and one woman from the entire cricket community were present: Arlott, John Woodcock and Margaret Hughes.

Cardus wore a cheery mask, displaying his customary warmth to his guests. This is why Hart-Davis reached the wrong conclusion about his mood. He hadn't been 'delighted with it all'. Lyttelton correctly saw what Hart-Davis hadn't. The lack of recognition given to his cricket writing troubled Cardus; specifically his stellar years as 'Cricketer'. He conceded as much in a private note sent afterwards to the *Manchester Guardian*'s deputy editor, Patrick Monkhouse. He received a sympathetic reply, referencing the 'point you touched on'. Monkhouse went on: 'Nothing about "Cricketer" ... I don't think that's right. Music may have been your oyster, but cricket ... was the knife with which you opened it.'

Cardus's confession to Monkhouse adds in hindsight a tinge of melancholy to the party.

It would be a while before he shook it off.

13

LOVE ME, LOVE ME

THERE IS A loop of black-and-white film barely a minute long. Neville Cardus wears a dark polo-neck sweater and a long, baggy grey coat with a thick belt. The collar of the coat is upturned, making the wide lapels look unruly. He pushes open the door of *The Guardian*'s offices on Cross Street and steps into a wintry Manchester day. The camera follows his slender frame along the pavement. In his right hand he carries an ebony walking stick, purely for ornamental purposes. It allows him to pose, showing off a little. He is magnificently straight-backed, his chin slightly raised and his gaze a hundred miles ahead. He strides rather than strolls, moving at a brisk lick and with a springy step. Someone once said his gait was 'as loose and thin as a puppet', a description this small played-out scene shows is accurate.

Old age can caricature the person someone used to be. Not Cardus. He is nearly 80, the age which he considered as 'crossing the Rubicon of mortal life'. No one would have guessed from the film, shot at the end of the 1960s. Cardus could pass for a decade younger – at least.

That era when everything changed convulsingly – the look, the mood and the sound of the country suddenly and simultaneously so different – had proved disorientating at first for a Victorian who dressed conventionally in a double-breasted suit and tie, puffed on a pipe and preferred Brahms to The Beatles, calling their music 'respectable wailings'. He found 'hippies' perplexing and parked his bum on the pavilion seats at Lord's beside retired colonels who thought *The Times* vulgarly modern for putting news, rather than classified advertising, on the front page.

Cardus didn't understand the celebrity bestowed on fashion designers and models, footballers and pop singers, photographers and TV actors. 'When everybody's somebody, then no one's anybody,' he complained. The hedonistic 'anything goes' indulgence confused him too – though only because he couldn't work out what the fuss was about. 'The word permissiveness makes me laugh,' he said, stressing it was not the new invention the newspapers were pretending. Cardus had seen permissiveness walk naked in and out of the parlour of Summer Place, along Manchester's Oxford Street and also backstage in the city's theatres and music halls. '"Immorality" in my youth was taken for granted [and] covered up hypocritically,' he said.

However quizzically Cardus stared at the 1960s, not quite believing some of the upheavals it brought, the decade proved to be a good one for him. He began it with his reputation in need of repair and his position on *The Guardian* insecure. He ended it with a knighthood.

Cardus's fortunes took a favourable turn as soon as the 1960s got under way. It had seemed incongruous that the leading writer on cricket rarely contributed to *The Cricketer*, then the only magazine dedicated to the game. In 39 years he'd written only four articles for it. The last had appeared almost a decade earlier. He preferred to work for the monthly *World Sports*, the magazine of the British Olympic Association, rather than for Sir Pelham Warner, still listed as *The Cricketer*'s editor.* Launched to coincide with the opening of the 1960 season, *Playfair Cricket Monthly* began to rival Warner's rather staid publication. Cardus was signed as a columnist and it became a safe haven for him.

Dudley Carew once took a sly dig at Cardus, telling Alan Ross in a letter: 'Nothing can stop Neville, bless him, going on with stories

* Following Warner's death, in January 1963, Cardus contributed almost 30 articles to *The Cricketer* during what remained of that decade.

about A. C. MacLaren.' *Playfair Cricket Monthly* allowed him to discuss MacLaren again, and also Parkin, Hobbs and Sutcliffe or whomever else he chose. Cricket was revolutionising, shedding the distinction between amateurs and professionals and creating the one-day game too. Cardus sometimes seemed torn apart by nostalgia, the changed world upsetting him, but he always celebrated talent that would have flourished whatever summer it graced. He crafted each of his pieces for *Playfair* with immense industriousness, anxious to prove he wasn't a timepiece capable of recording only the long hours of the past.

In a parade of sweet reminiscences, he accepted that 'several cricketers playing for Lancashire round about 1904–14 would not stand a ghost of a chance of survival' in the 1960s. 'I could get them out personally with off-breaks.' In the same breath, he could sigh and shake his head at 'an England XI that sometimes contains only one Yorkshireman and not a single Lancastrian'. He regretted that the modern pro 'seldom read history' and so didn't know, as comprehensively as a dressing-room school ought to have taught him, about Ranjitsinhji and Grace or Verity and Clarrie Grimmett. (Cardus told John Arlott how Grimmett, aged 53, claimed to have invented a new kind of delivery and resented the intrusion of the Second World War because it deprived him of the chance to bowl it.)

Watching the County Championship, mostly at Lord's or The Oval, Cardus felt that he 'might be hard put to find material' for a column from some of the matches. He had previously liked workmen who knew how to finish a task, always claiming some of the 'most fascinating' cricketers he had ever seen were 'slowish' scorers. He began to change his mind in the late 1950s, recoiling from matches so slow that you could feel the cycles of Nature turning through them. Of one Trevor Bailey innings, he reflected: 'Before he had gathered together 20 runs, a newly-married couple could have left Heathrow and arrived in Lisbon, there to enjoy a honeymoon. By the time Bailey had congealed 50, the happily-wedded pair could easily have settled down in a semi-detached house in Surbiton; and by the time his innings had gone to its close they conceivably might have been divorced.' Bailey, his man of the series during those Coronation Ashes, had been charged with boring him and found guilty.

In another delicious put-down Cardus, as a self-confessed 'conservative of cricket', made plain his disdain for one-day 'slogging'. The games were the equivalent of holding a concert in which the 'laurels of leading musician' went to 'the player of the most semi-quavers in a given time'. He was afraid that 'if limited-over cricket puts real cricket out of fashion ... the literature of the game will dry up.' He feared there would be 'no scope, no material in all the scramble for the writer with a feeling for subtle changes of technique and mood'. It was as though he still loved cricket but could no longer remember exactly what that love had felt like in the beginning.

Cardus only made big gestures in his writing towards players he judged worthy. He liked Garry Sobers, whose 'idea of a cricket ball, as he waited for it bat in hand, was of an object to be removed forcibly and at once, and far into the distance'. He liked Colin Cowdrey, who was 'fit for all the tents and bunting of the Canterbury Festival'. He particularly liked Tom Graveney, without equal 'as a complete, stylish stroke-player'. Every innings from Graveney was alluring because 'some suggestion of good nature and well-bred manners exists within it ... I'd rather see him make 20 than some other batsman make 200.' In contrast, he looked at Geoffrey Boycott and regarded him as a tortured soul in his pursuit of absolute perfection. He was the 'Hamlet of Cricket'. Cardus thought he could have made 'characters' of the Lancashire side which became all-conquering in the Gillette Cup and the John Player League. Harry Pilling, just 5 ft 3 in tall, was another Makepeace. 'Flat' Jack Simmons, carrying his portliness well, was a figure in the Parkin mould. Clive Lloyd, with shot-making of glorious beauty, was a combination of MacLaren, Spooner and Constantine.

He was also particularly fond of Richie Benaud, a feeling reciprocated. Cardus immediately identified him as 'shrewd' and sharply astute, a 'close student of cricket at all hours', whose smart leg-spin 'gripped the earth'. Benaud identified him as a friendly face and a trusted analyst, accurate in his assessment of players. He made the judgement on personal experience. Before the Ashes Test at Lord's in 1956, Benaud, then 25, had taken 41 wickets and scored 572 runs in his 19-Test career. Cardus addressed the likelihood of him being dropped, admitting: 'I doubt if any England player would be trusted by our selection committee so far and for so long with no more practical or viable contribution.' He then went out on a limb to defend him, a case based on his own eyewitness testimony. He wrote of watching Benaud make 97 and take seven for 46 against Yorkshire at Bradford three years earlier. 'It is not possible for mediocrity ever to rise to the level of this kind of mastery. And what a man has done once he can do again.' He also wrote of watching Benaud in the nets at Lord's just the day before – 'defending seriously, scrupulously behind the ball'. He regarded Benaud as 'every inch a cricketer' and 'plainly gifted'. And he forecast: 'It will be no matter for wonder if at any moment he confounds those of his critics who have more or less written him off.' In the second innings at Lord's, Benaud hit 97. Australia won by 185. Benaud rated Cardus's article – and what he did to 'live up to it' – as 'a turning point for me'. We know where that turning point led. That Cardus recognised it well before the event proved how much he knew about the game; he was not simply a prose stylist.

Cardus was both performer and passionate preacher, especially to the converted, and he generously spread himself around. Whenever the Australians toured, he would always put on a one-man show for Jack Fingleton and Keith Miller. He'd pretend a rolled-up umbrella was a bat and then mimic 'Slasher' Mackay's helpless efforts to play Jim Laker on the wickedly turning Old Trafford pitch that brought him 19 wickets in 1956. The imaginary ball went in one direction. Mackay's lunge for it went in the other. He could no more read Laker, said Cardus, 'than he could read a verse in Latin'. Cardus exaggerated every movement and added commentary of his own, mocking Mackay's desperation in bagging a pair. 'He had his stories to tell and demonstrate, and bystanders might as well have been in another country,' said Fingleton. 'Nobody enjoyed his stories more than Cardus himself. He would cup a hand to his mouth and laugh behind it . . . He got such relish in the telling.'

His column in *Playfair* was so popular that a collection of them soon appeared as a book. Donald Bradman wrote the foreword to it, calling Cardus not only 'unique' but also a 'literary genius'.

The Guardian did not necessarily agree.

Asked to write his own obituary, Cardus had said the penultimate line of it would be: 'In spite of all temptations, he remained a *"Manchester Guardian* man".' He called the newspaper 'my dear tyrant' and said: 'If I had been a reasonably wealthy man, I'd have paid to write for it.' He made the mistake of thinking that what he loved would always love him back unconditionally. But, by the early 1960s, he and it seemed romantically incompatible.

Changing Faces is a history of *The Guardian* that essentially starts with the death of A. P. Wadsworth and the appointment of his successor, Alastair Hetherington, in 1956. The author Geoffrey Taylor agrees that 'in his prime' Cardus was 'one of the most important reasons for reading' the newspaper. After this compliment comes the criticism. Taylor adds that Hetherington, not quite 37 when he became editor, regarded Cardus as 'too stodgy to be borne'. His relationship with the newspaper warped because of it. There were small spats, most of which Cardus lost because he came across as pernickety and resistant to all change. In truth, he was afraid for his future but couldn't bring himself to confess it. He wrote to Hetherington to complain about the niggling cuts and sometimes the butchered slashing of his copy. As he saw it, the sub-editors' department was becoming an 'abattoir' and 'upsetting me more than a little'. That line was polite compared with the next. 'I have known no experience as disheartening in all my 40 years on the *M. G.*' Late in life he once sent a review comprising nothing but the title and venue of a concert and also his name beneath it. At the foot of this otherwise blank sheet, he wrote sarcastically: 'Please do not cut.'

Cardus disputed – and railed against – the opinion of his fellow music critics on the newspaper too. He moaned that some of his music criticism wasn't being published in the paper's northern editions. He expressed anguish at the number of misprints littering the text. Even a letter of congratulations could be accompanied with a tetchy PS expressing a minor grievance. Cardus didn't like the new design Hetherington had introduced. He thought dropping 'Manchester' from the masthead was a mistake. He believed the newspaper's move to London was a betrayal of C. P. Scott's legacy. When, eventually, *The Guardian* abandoned Cross Street completely, Cardus was aghast, thinking it akin to 'the Pope leaving the Vatican'.

Amid the irritations and vexations, what pokes sharply through the correspondence is Cardus's vulnerability. He is a living piece of the newspaper's history and does not want to leave. But he also knows he doesn't quite fit in, without ever understanding why his new boss isn't benevolently bountiful towards him. While working at the *Glasgow Herald*, Hetherington had read *Autobiography* and 'loved' both his description of the *Manchester Guardian*'s ethos and its 'care for words'. The irony is this: it was Cardus's evocation of the newsroom that Hetherington said 'reinforced my wish . . . to become a member of its staff'.

Small fires continued to burn between them. At one point Cardus's expenses at the Edinburgh Festival were questioned. A needling internal memo, alluding to Else Mayer-Lismann without naming her, theorised that his claims were high because *The Guardian* was 'paying for two people ... he usually takes his girlfriend around with him.' Cardus, despite feeling victimised, promised to watch how much he spent in future. In the exchanges between him and the newspaper, as well as in letters to friends, Cardus continues to come across like a servant slightly nervous of the sack, his former influence dwindling and his very usefulness questioned.

The relationship shifted in 1967, the short tap of the Queen's sword on Cardus's shoulders changing everything.

Like most honours lists, it was an odd rattle-bag of names. Most were male, the bulk unrecognisable to the general public. The headline recipient was Alf Ramsey, his personal prize for steering England to the World Cup the previous summer. Others were sufficiently unknown as faces to be guaranteed anonymity in a railway carriage. There were the respective chairmen of the White Fish Authority, the British Railways Board and the Dairy Council. There was a cement manufacturer, the head of a further education institution and a Government bureaucrat. There was also one name Cardus knew well. Rupert Hart-Davis became 'Sir' too, a reward for his literary work.

Cardus's knighthood was awarded for services to 'cricket and music'. The order of the citation ought to have been reversed. The influential voices in music, rather than the panjandrums of the MCC, had been responsible for the recommendation and pestering the honours committee about it. Len Hutton, knighted a decade earlier, said that his title always meant at least 'ten shillings on the bill', the minimum tip any 'Sir' was supposed to leave a waiter. Far more recently, the playwright Alan Bennett said he refused a knighthood because it would have felt too much 'like wearing a suit every day'. Cardus – who *did* wear a suit every day – accepted without hesitation. He explained why in *The Times*. His 'humble self' was 'pretty certain that I'd enjoy being a knight'. He also added it was 'not for the likes of me to go counter to the pleasure of Her Majesty and (to adapt the language of Doctor Johnson) indirectly "bandy civilities with my Sovereign"'.

John Arlott said Cardus showed a 'slightly surprised gratitude' at the honour. He tried to be modest about it too, asking friends not to use the title; he was 'still Neville'. He admitted more quietly to Arlott: 'It's so useful. It gets me a table at The Savoy.'

It was also 'useful' in fending off, like a protective shield, anyone at *The Guardian* who thought of him as a pampered relic who ought to be got rid of. As Sir Neville, he was unsackable now. Not long afterwards, the newspaper was hiring a car to collect his copy and take it to the office.

As a boy, Neville Cardus didn't believe he would 'ever grow old', but instead become 'the first of mortals never to die'. The discovery of what became his 'favourite poem' changed his mind. In the first stanza, from Act IV, Scene 2 of *Cymbeline*, Shakespeare's unflinching focus is on death.

> *Fear no more the heat o' the sun,*
> *Nor the furious winter's rages;*
> *Thou thy worldly task hast done,*
> *Home art gone, and ta'en thy wages;*
> *Golden lads and girls all must,*
> *As chimney-sweepers, come to dust.*

Cardus stood at the midpoint between agnosticism and belief. He didn't think often about why life turns out as it does. He did, however, learn something else to sit alongside Shakespeare's speech. 'The essence of real beauty is that it is fugitive,' he said. 'But of course it is not beauty that is passing; you yourself are passing. When I was young I felt a saddening poignancy when I realised I couldn't hold on to beauty. As I got older I came to see that Mozart isn't going. Love isn't going. The spring isn't going . . . No, it is you and I who are going.'

Some had already gone, leaving him in lonely eminence. His youth and his early professional life began to pass before him, like a shadow eating up the light.

Cecil Parkin died of cancer in 1943, aged only 57. All men have their moody sides – clowns more than most – and within him deep currents swirled. He could be sulky and curmudgeonly. He'd become one of those publicans over-fond of his own product. His daughter wrote to Cardus in Australia, beginning an on-off correspondence lasting almost 30 years. She revealed how her mother had placed two red roses at each end of the Old Trafford pitch before Parkin's ashes were scattered across the ground. For years afterwards, Lancashire's bowlers would take the ball, lick their fingers before gripping or wrapping them around the seam and say with black humour: 'Old Cec doesn't taste too good today.'

A year later A. C. MacLaren also died of cancer, a fortnight shy of reaching 73. His last significant public appearance was on the cinema screen rather than the cricket pitch. He got a walk-on part as a Crimean War veteran in the film *The Four Feathers*, an Alexander Korda masterpiece. MacLaren's monocle and moustache made him the perfect candidate for typecasting.

Loss begat loss. The war was in its final year when William Pollock, working in public relations for the RAF, died after a short illness. He was 62.

Kidney failure claimed C. B. Fry in 1956. Cardus celebrated him as 'one of the last of the English traditional amateurs, the connoisseur and, in the most delightful sense of the word, the dilettante'. At 67, just after the 1958 cricket season had ended, Beau Vincent died too. Noting his dislike of ever leaving the Home Counties, *The Times* said of him: 'It was one of his foibles to pretend that he was quite unable to reach any northern point, such as Manchester or Leeds, on his own.' R. H. Spooner, approaching 81, died in a Lincolnshire nursing home in 1961. R. C. Robertson-Glasgow succumbed in 1965 to his depression, taking an overdose of barbiturates. The ambulance, called for quickly, might have saved him if it had not been slowed on roads thick with snow. He was only 63. And in 1969 Emmott Robinson was taken ill on his 86th birthday and died the following day. As a fledgling umpire, Robinson had once appealed for lbw before the bowler did and instantly answered his own call, giving the batsman out. The story sounds apocryphal – and possibly it is – but with Robinson you can never be certain. Cardus wrote three long obituaries of his friend, building a tomb of fine phrases around him.

No death left such a cold space in his life as Edith's. She died of a heart attack in 1968. Husband and wife still lived apart – she in Bickenhall Mansions, he at the National Liberal Club – but the two of them spoke daily on the telephone. Each bolstered the other. In the short time she basked in his knighthood, Edith liked to shop in the food hall of Fortnum & Mason purely so she could order a delivery and tell the cashier in broad Lancastrian: 'I'm *Lady* Cardus, tha knows.' After she died, the undertakers tried to charge Cardus twice for her funeral. He enquired whether the second bill was 'for Resurrection charges', the sort of composed reply he thought Edith 'would have loved'.

Cardus described her then as he had done decades earlier. She was still no more than his cherished 'good companion'. Her death, however, released him to write at last and at length about the woman he had loved most of all.

* * *

Neville Cardus considered himself to be 'one of the worst pianists ever'. He still composed a 'Kitsch' waltz, the lyrics about broken hearts, unspoken vows and the hope all will be well in the end. The title was 'Love Me, Love Me', which both summarises his longing for affection and acknowledges the fact he never found it – at least to his own satisfaction. Where Cardus was concerned, you get the idea that the saddest words from mouth or pen truly were 'what might have been . . .'

Barbe Ede used to chide him about his dedication to work. 'If I were to be knocked down by a taxi and brought into this room dead on a shutter, you'd go on with your writing just the same.' Barbe had been dead for nearly twenty years when she appeared to him in a dream so vividly that he was 'terribly moved' afterwards. 'She was walking with me as of old, in her grey-flannel suit, green scarf and a little hat which fitted the shape of her head.' She laughed as he awoke. 'O God,' he said. 'It was as though she knew I was being taken out of the dream and she being left in it . . . She seemed in spite of this knowledge to go on laughing and walking so that I saw her vanish, leaving me.'

All of us cling to hours we wish to live again. For Cardus, it was an autumn morning of 'ripe sunshine' between the wars. A day in Windsor, an outing to a town where no one knew or would recognise them. He stopped to stare into the window of a bookshop. Barbe strolled a few paces ahead of him. When Cardus turned again, he looked at her 'as though anew'. He remembered: 'I flew to her, embraced her, kissed her.' The memory of that moment decades earlier, there and gone again, was real and alive to him, as if it had just occurred.

You read this and think about what Keats said about his love for Fanny Brawne: 'Everything . . . that reminds me of her goes through me like a spear.' You also realise that Cardus had accepted Barbe's death without ever getting over it. She remained exactly as he'd last seen her. Still with rose-red lips. Still with coiled hair. Still flaunting those high cheekbones. Still walking with a hip-sway in her step.

Cardus wrote about Barbe in a book of reminiscences, a tidying-up of his life called *Full Score*. The eight-page chapter about her is entitled 'Milady'. She is not named in it. Her identity is as mysterious to the reader as Shakespeare's Dark Lady. Even *The Guardian*, publishing an extract early in 1969, illustrated the page with an uncaptioned photograph of a demure-looking woman, her eyes bowed over a book held in upturned hands. This is Barbe. The photograph, which *The Guardian* enlarged and reversed, was used in the *Kent Messenger* after her death. One reason alone made Cardus and *The Guardian* coy about identifying her. Elton Ede was still alive. He died six months later, his two-line obituary in the following year's *Wisden* merely recording that 'for some years' he had 'reported on cricket for the *Sunday Times*'.

Cardus's admission about the 'beautiful woman' was revelatory to those who only read his writing and knew nothing of his personal life. His friends were pestered to reveal Barbe's name. As a friend and fellow music writer wrote in the *Yorkshire Post*: 'He had the whole nation guessing.' The writer 'rebuffed' attempts to get him to whisper who she was; confidentiality between critics was sacrosanct, he argued.

The closing lines of 'Milady' include these two sentences: 'Life in her was too abundant and self-consuming. It couldn't last.' Cardus's most poignant tribute to her was still something only Rupert Hart-Davis read. In a letter to him, Cardus returned to the loan of that ten-shilling note . . .

What a God's blessing to me it was that, after my first meeting, and somehow she didn't spellbind me, she wrote that letter next day saying: 'I really did leave my purse at home'. To think I might have missed her, never had her so endearingly, so beautifully in my life.

*   *   *

Barbe Ede.

Elton Ede.

Cardus described her as the most beautiful woman he ever knew.
Her early death devastated him. Barbe Ede's photograph sits beside
her obituary in her local newspaper, the Kent Messenger.

The writer Nikolai Gogol, who never lived to see old age, declared it was 'terrible and remorseless', a time which 'gives back nothing, nothing'. It nonetheless gave Neville Cardus one last platonic 'romance'.

Elizabeth Grice was a 26-year-old journalist on the *East Anglian Daily Times*. After watching Cardus in conversation with John Arlott on the BBC, she wrote a fan letter and received an invitation to call on him. She did so only four days later. Cardus had moved out of the National Liberal Club and into the Bickenhall Mansions flat, vacant after Edith's death. He was waiting for Grice on the front steps, smoking a cigarette and watching her park a mustard-coloured Mini. 'I somehow fancied I'd be able to identify you at sight,' he said.

Green was the predominant colour in the flat. The carpet was light green, like a cricket field bleached in the sun. The furniture was upholstered in dark green velvet. The curtains were a startling contrast – a red more richly ruby even than the rose on a Lancashire cap. The living room contained a baby grand piano beneath the window and a low white bookcase in which the authors he had read as he grew up – Dickens, Shaw, Donne – took prominence on three shelves.

Grice was Cardus's sort of woman: attractive, inquisitive, intelligent. He began introducing her as 'my young journalist friend from Ipswich'. At least once a month – he called them 'visitation days' – Grice went to London, bringing Gorgonzola cheese and digestive biscuits with her. He supplied claret and music. Letters were exchanged between them on 'most days'.

Cardus became her 'correspondence course tutor', explained Grice. He would ask her to review a piece of music and then critique it. Sometimes the two of them would go to Regent's Park, taking bread to feed the ducks. He took her to Lord's too. She finally persuaded him to travel to Ipswich, which was like embarking on a Grand Tour for someone who now so seldom left the London flat. Aware of his passion for Dickens, she booked him into the Great White Horse, a hotel which had appeared in *The Pickwick Papers*. He toured the offices of the *East Anglian Daily Times*, where the sports staff and the music critic greeted him as reverentially as a monarch. He spoke ambitiously to her afterwards about a much bigger adventure to Vienna.

Cardus once said that 'extreme loneliness' was the burden of the writer. Grice recognised it in him. 'If it were not for your presence in my life,' he wrote to her, 'I think I would take the next plane to Sydney.'

At the end of the 1960s, as physically fit as could be expected, he complained that his doctor charged him five guineas for 'nothing'. At the beginning of the 1970s, bedevilled by numerous aches and pains, his now bony body had begun to tell him where his limits lay. He suffered from peripheral neuropathy, numbing the soles of his feet and making walking difficult. 'The tragedy of what is called old age,' he said, 'is that the body gets older and the mind gets younger. I want to go for an eight-mile walk. My mind *goes* for an eight-mile walk. My damn legs won't go.'

He passed a lot of his time putting on and taking off 'gramophone records' of Brahms's *Alto Rhapsody* or Elgar's Cello Concerto. From the 1940s, when her career began, Cardus had developed a harmless crush on Kathleen Ferrier, a 'Lancashire lass' considered among the greatest singers in the history of classical music. Cardus heard her sing Mahler's *Das Lied von der Erde* at the Edinburgh Festival in 1947, heading to the dressing room immediately after the performance to worship at the hem of her gown. 'I had never met her before in my life, but I felt as though we were meeting for the hundredth time,' he said. Cancer silenced Ferrier's voice, aged 41, in 1953. She lived on in Bickenhall Mansions, singing *Das Lied von der Erde* so repeatedly that the vinyl was worn almost as thin as a communion wafer.

Cardus had appeared on *Desert Island Discs*, choosing it as one of the recordings to take with him. As his luxury, he had wanted an Airedale terrier for company. Told that only inanimate objects were allowed, he picked a watercolour set instead, reminding him of his boyhood as a pavement artist. The most revealing part of the programme was this: asked how he would cope as a castaway, sitting alone beneath a palm tree, Cardus replied: 'not very well'; he would have to put his 'trust in Nature', he explained.

This was more or less his strategy for survival in Bickenhall Mansions. In her comic novel *The Provincial Lady in Wartime*, E. M. Delafield writes of a woman called Lady B, who possesses no domestic skills whatsoever. She tells guests that she would like to offer them a glass of water, but it is the servants' night off and she doesn't know where they keep it. Cardus and Lady B had much in common.

Cups of tea or coffee and the odd slice of toast were the only things made in the galley kitchen of his flat. He took his meals in the London Steak House on Baker Street, a three-minute walk from his front door. He sat, back to the wall, at table seven, which was permanently reserved for him. The Steak House was furnished in dark wood and brass. It was a long, narrow and rather dowdy restaurant. Each table, worn at the edges, was set with an amber-coloured ashtray and place mats depicting country-house scenes. He always ended his meagre dinners with a Bendicks mint chocolate, removing the bright gold wrapper and rolling it into a ball. This was placed in a jacket pocket.

On some days, going to and from the Steak House constituted Cardus's sole contact with the outside world.

He sent his shirts to be laundered. He bought bottles of Mouton Cadet and Chablis, but drank only rarely. He masked the smell of pipe and cigarette smoke with generous splashes of Eau Sauvage. The day-to-day struggles of housework and personal grooming were minor compared with his financial difficulties. He knew well Mr Micawber's definition of economic happiness and misery, making light of them as 'these paltry economics'. Poets are rarely rich. When the Inland Revenue looked into the tax affairs of W. B. Yeats in the

1920s – he had recently won the Nobel Prize – investigators were astonished that someone of such renown earned so little. Yeats almost made church mice seem semi-affluent. The same could be said of Cardus. Above his mantelpiece hung an early L. S. Lowry sketch that depicted neither a working-class landscape nor stick figures (people milled about in front of a country house). In the bank his savings had dwindled to near nothing, the royalties from *Full Score* soon whittled away.

Cardus was never as wealthy as he ought to have been. 'I am not a man of business,' he admitted to Rupert Hart-Davis, a statement that staggeringly underplays his uselessness in all things financial. He had for years lived above his means, feeding Edith's prodigality with cheque after cheque.

Unlike Arlott, who advertised tobacco and Brylcreem, Cardus never had an agent. He never took much notice of contracts or publishers' statements either – especially the windy legalese condensed into six point. He never owned property. He never invested his cash. Edith's will bequeathed him only £300 worth of Defence Bonds and a 'large diamond ring', which she instructed him to sell. Most damagingly of all, Cardus had never contributed to *The Guardian*'s pension scheme, assuming the wages department were handling the matter for him. An internal memo confirmed the newspaper did not regard him 'as a member of staff in any way'. He was a contributor, responsible for his own insurance stamp.

J. B. Priestley wondered why Cardus 'didn't fight harder to keep his books in print'. He didn't know that Arlott had taken on the task without success, informing Hart-Davis of his efforts. In one of his tetchiest moments, Cardus said Arlott could be 'a prime pompous ass' and lacked even 'a glimmer of humour', an allegation as untrue as it was ungrateful. No one did more, quietly and unrewarded, to promote and sustain him than Arlott. He and other friends on *The Guardian* tried to persuade the newspaper to provide Cardus with a pension or honorarium in recognition of his long service and contribution to sales. The plea was ignored. It paid him an annual retainer, a sum barely £400 more than the £1,000-plus salary he had received from them in 1930.

The Guardian does not emerge gallantly from its treatment of Cardus. In 1966, a little prematurely, the Hallé Orchestra marked his golden anniversary on the newspaper with concerts in Manchester and London. In Manchester, the conductor Sir John Barbirolli was asked to make a presentation to Cardus on *The Guardian*'s behalf. It was insulting enough that the newspaper delegated the task rather than send someone senior to the Free Trade Hall. A far deeper insult was contained inside the envelope handed to Cardus. He found a cheque for £100 – £2 for every year he had worked for them. 'I thought of sending it back,' he said, his sourness at such a stingy amount understandable. He was not alone in his animosity towards the newspaper. Alistair Cooke, whose weekly *Letter from America* was already a BBC institution, had become a correspondent for the *Manchester Guardian* in 1947. He was similarly bitter with them, even refusing to write further articles, because he had never received 'a penny' in pension. Cooke was born in Salford and became a Lancashire cricket fan, modelling his own bowling action on Cecil Parkin, his sporting hero. One of his other heroes was Cardus. He collected his autograph during a match at Blackpool. When the two distinguished writers finally met, dining at the London Steak House, Cooke discovered the newspaper 'had been no more generous to Cardus than it had been' to him.

Cardus was desperate for money. He continued to read the poetry of Francis Thompson, but worried he would end up exactly like him, thrown into sorry destitution. Thompson once had to turn down an MCC invitation to Lord's; he had no socks to wear. In spring 1974,

Cardus wrote what he described as 'almost a begging letter' to Alastair Hetherington, asking for a pay rise. Back came a negative reply, which upset him deeply. He confided to Grice: 'How I wish I could break free from *The Guardian*. And never did I think I would live to say this; for I have devoted my life, at some financial loss, to the paper.' *The Guardian*, he added, was 'breaking my heart'.

As only a 'contributor', Cardus was free to peddle words where he liked. He became friendly with Harold Evans, editor of the *Sunday Times*, who commissioned him to write a one-off article about music. The £75 fee relieved an 'awful income tax drain', he said. The piece proved so successful that Evans offered him £1,800 a year to write for him.

Cardus had already confessed to friends: 'I've calculated that if I live another 12 months, I'll be bankrupt.' His only assets were the Lowry and the piano. He held various insurance policies, each of which could only be cashed in after his death. So he wrote to accept Evans's offer and then wrote again, nervous that his original answer had gone astray because it had not received an immediate reply. He was too ill to post the second letter. Never sent, it was found among his belongings after his death.

In late February 1975, Neville Cardus collapsed in his bedroom at Bickenhall Mansions. Margaret Hughes found Cardus and called the ambulance, which took him to the Fitzroy Nuffield Nursing Home in Bryanston Square. On the month's final day he died of pneumonia and arteriosclerosis.

He left the bulk of his estate to Else Mayer-Lismann and appointed Hughes as his literary executor. It was nonetheless Elizabeth Grice who signed his death certificate. Shortly afterwards, she went to Bickenhall Mansions to discover that the Lowry drawing had already been removed from the wall. The piano had gone too. His suits still hung in the wardrobe, the pockets full of Bendicks chocolate wrappers. Grice found a 'surreal scene' in the bathroom. In the bath, tipped as unceremoniously as rubbish, she found a lifetime's worth of manuscripts, photographs, letters, poems, old chequebooks and even cartoons, which he had continued to draw – forever the pavement artist at heart. One of the taps was dripping on to it all, damaging paper and smudging ink. Grice took the trunklike boxes that had contained his laundry and rescued the precious archive.

Cardus had adored the *Four Last Songs* by Richard Strauss, which became intensely personal to him. The final song, 'Im Abendrot' ('At Sunset'), epitomised in music 'something of my own life, the poet journeying towards the end in the evening glow', he said. At the end, the poet 'speaks of how red the sunset is . . . he becomes tired and a nightingale sings'. In the 'last moments' of his life, he had hoped for two things: that a nightingale would sing for him and that he would hear Barbe Ede reading to him from Tennyson's *Maud*: 'Go not, happy day,/ From the shining fields'.

What he got was a private ceremony among the red brick and pantile roofs of Golders Green Crematorium, where his own 'Love Me, Love Me' and also *The Merry Widow* was played.

Only two years earlier, aged 85, Cardus had written a piece that was generally overlooked. It appeared in *The Guardian* beneath the headline 'Changed Times in the Long Room', a sentence bland enough to dissuade readers from bothering to even glance at it. The accompanying photograph showed him hunched and crabbed in a wooden seat.

He had finally been made a full member of the MCC in 1972 – though only because associate membership was abolished in a surprising gesture of egalitarianism. From April to September, he went to Lord's 'most days', searching for company even when there was no match to see. When games were played, he would stand with his back to the pavilion windows, engaged in three monologues at once. Anyone who tried to escape before the punchline would be gently prodded in the chest.

Near the end of his life, Cardus was always worried about being 'written out', having nothing left say. But in eight long paragraphs he produces something exquisite about the ground. The article is worthy of a frame. He goes to the first game of that summer. He has misplaced his MCC pass. 'Would I be admitted to the sanctuary on my face?' he wonders. He is met at the Grace Gates with 'Buckingham Palace courtesy' and the pavilion doorkeepers 'almost bow me in'.

Being there, unsure of how many more seasons are left for him, he looks back on all things lovely in the Long Room, and feels the company of ghosts. There is the eccentrics' eccentric, the Hampshire captain Lionel, Lord Tennyson, who goes into a tantrum because Donald Bradman won't give him an audience during a Test. 'Refused to see a Peer of the Realm,' he rants, promising to send Bradman 'a letter he won't forget' and then sitting down to write it with a bellowed appeal to an attendant: 'Bring me a dictionary.' There is Denis Compton, who has just run out three men in his brother Leslie's benefit match – including Leslie himself. 'Am I such a bad runner as all that?' he asks. 'I never run myself out.' There is George Gunn, sitting there for the first time and likening the sombre atmosphere and the stultifying men in it to Sutton Vane's *Outward Bound*, a play in which every character 'was dead though they all thought they were still alive'. There is S. F. Barnes discussing first Garry Sobers and then Bradman. And there is the sightless Wilfred Rhodes staring through the window, his ears telling him what his blind eyes cannot after the ball leaves the bat. 'The slips are too deep,' he says, his neighbour confirming the judgement as correct.

Every vignette is wonderfully weighted, cut and crafted. From them you appreciate how much cricket at Lord's was a comfort to him.

Knowing where Cardus's last resting place ought to be, John Arlott asked Lord's to allow his ashes to be scattered on the outfield, a rare distinction.

The MCC refused.

EPILOGUE

TIME PRESENT AND TIME PAST

Old Trafford, July 2018

Even on days that began warmly still and full of sunshine, he claimed not to entirely trust the Manchester weather. He was always 'afraid', he said, of the trick it might pull on him 'behind my back'. He had seen too often piebald cloud, double-banked and gathering lowly in the distance, carry the threat of either 'good honest rain' – a proper soaking – or the kind of 'miserable drizzle' that is 'always promising to cease' but settles for hours before the wind gets up and chases it away. He knew, too, all about the 'wintry blast' that could descend at any hour on Old Trafford – even when the 'gateway to high summer' was softly opening elsewhere. This, he argued, was integral to the 'atmosphere' and 'curious charm' of 'one of the great county grounds'.

Neville Cardus would feel perfectly at home today, a Sunday soggy and bedraggled-looking. The sun, as if in a sulk, is refusing to come out and play. It is just a pale shape casting scant shadows. The outfield is damp, which adds a velvet-like sheen to grass richly emerald. The air is cold enough to cause a little shiver, a sniff of more rain detectable in it too.

I am here because, four decades on from that bleakish day at Trent Bridge when John Arlott graciously gave me an education, Old Trafford is the only appropriate spot to pay my respects to Cardus, and also because the Roses match is the only appropriate game in which to do it. Cardus called it 'the greatest of all tussles between county rivals' and found it impossible to be impartial. 'I become as prone as anyone else in the crowd to the passions of the partisan,' he explained, thinking nonetheless that the conflict had brought him more suffering than satisfaction. Arlott believed the 'splendid best' of Cardus came out in the ancient feud; he drew out of them every 'pennyworth of character'.

Cardus said that if a psychoanalyst was to engage him in word association, his response to 'cricket' would include: 'Lord's . . . buckle missing on pad . . . next man in . . . shady pavilion with shirts on pegs all inside out . . . Nursery End . . . Mound Stand . . . dots on a scoring card . . . a new bat . . . linseed oil . . . first practice in April weather.' It's a lovely evocation, and anyone who adores the game will create their own images from it, but conspicuously absent from that list is a mention of Old Trafford. Cardus was in his most besotted 'Lord's phase' when he wrote it, slightly estranged from Lancashire through geography. In the late 1950s, he went as far as to declare: 'I am a supporter of Middlesex – an act of apostasy which the boy that I was once myself could never have dreamed could possibly happen to me.' By 1971, back in a Lancastrian embrace, he was 'proud' of being the club's president and prouder still of giving back something to a place from which he had taken so much. The honour nicely coincided with the 'full and glorious noon' of the team's renaissance.

I have spent the past seven years in an on-and-off search for Cardus, aware now of this: however much he loved Lord's, all roads lead back to Manchester, the city that made him. He proved – despite what Thomas Wolfe thought – that you can go home again.

I have reread the books and articles produced so prodigiously that, if laid end to end, the pages would stretch from here to the Grace Gates at Lord's – a road made fabulously of words. I have seen for the first time his letters, scattered in disparate archives across three continents. I have become so used to his handwriting – the long, sideways slant of his y, the steeply upward flourish of the cross on every t, the ragged stroke of a g almost curling back on itself – that it seems as familiar to me as my own. I have looked at the journal he sporadically kept and the articles he wrote in fountain pen on foolscap or on small squares of Basildon Bond. I imagined his hand passing over the paper and the scratch of the gold nib. I have turned the dark albums containing cuttings that, miraculously, have hardly yellowed with age and also black-and-white photographs tiny enough to fit into a child's palm. I have combed through his reports on Championship and Test matches for the *Manchester Guardian*, comparing them with the work of his contemporaries in those relatively peaceful summers between the wars. In trying to root out factual discrepancies between them, I discovered instead that Cardus wrote about games so differently because his talent and his taste for detail enabled him to see them so differently. He looked at them through a lens no one else then possessed. I have watched again those BBC interviews he did with Arlott, who set one memory after another in motion for him. The pair of them could have talked away a full fortnight and still found something more to say afterwards. And I have stood on the stone steps of Bickenhall Mansions and stared at the wide front door, amazed to find no blue plaque beside it to record his residency in the basement flat.

Cardus deserves such recognition but doesn't need it. In his era, when a newspaper's second career was wrapping cod and chips, the pieces in it were gone and forgotten in hours, recoverable only in bound library volumes weightier than paving slabs. That Cardus's writing survived, placed between hard covers, is testament to his poetic art. That he survives now – quoted in contemporary match reports, name-checked during commentaries, cited on social media – is confirmation of a special talent. Back in his formative days, after his breakthrough on the *Manchester Guardian*, it must surely have felt to the reader as though cricket and cricketers had been practically still before and had only begun to move because he was describing them. Every morning, breakfasts were ignored and went cold to concentrate on Cardus. Nowadays you realise that without him the game's past – and some of the names in it – would be nothing more than ghostly smoke and a murmur of voices.

The books that preserved his summers were supposed to be the pick of him, but you only have to read everything else – the unanthologised articles, for example – to know most of it more than passes muster. There are plenty of writers who have committed a million words to paper without crafting a memorable or original line. With Cardus, you'll find in almost every piece something illuminating. A compilation of his most eloquent phrases would be an inch and a half thick. 'History flies by and few of us see her thrilling colours,' he wrote. Well, he saw and heard well enough, leaving a record of it like a gift.

In his honour, I approached Old Trafford along the route he preferred – a walk down the Warwick Road. I have come in the Cardus spirit too. 'The best way to love cricket is to see it against the background of the years. To see today's heroes treading the same places where not so very long ago the great old masters stood,' he said. He was convinced Time Past and Time Present are intertwined, which means some far-off Then is always folded into the Now. I will be watching Joe Root and Jonny Bairstow, Jimmy Anderson and Jos Buttler. Each is making an especially rare appearance in the Championship, showing us for a few days only what the competition would regularly look like – if England duty didn't always come first, and also if the white-ball game wasn't so rapidly subsuming the red. But I will also be thinking of those figures Cardus knew, such as A. C. MacLaren and R. H. Spooner, Wilfred Rhodes and Len Hutton – giants in the genealogy of a 'family tree' of cricketers and a fixture dating back to the 1860s.

Of course, I will mostly be thinking about Cardus. About the way in which he would have written up this match. About the player he would have alighted on, choosing to flatter him like another Emmott Robinson. About his reaction to contemporary cricket.

I will also go and seek him out too. For Cardus is here, tucked into a corner of the ground which still belongs to him.

The rinsing of rain that Old Trafford got around dawn has delayed the start. A tractor is dragging a loop of rope around the outfield, scraping off surface water. The teams, still in tracksuits, warm up far apart from one another, like fighters shadow-boxing in opposite corners.

Less than 48 hours ago, more than 22,000 – the sort of high number Cardus saw pour through the gates for a Championship fixture – watched the Twenty20 Roses match, which Lancashire won by one run off the very last ball of the very last, pulsating over. That game, also weather-hit, saw 351 runs scored in just 28 whiz-bang overs. The temporary stand, accommodating the public demand for tickets, still looms skeletally over the midwicket boundary. The stand is as vertiginous as an Alpine ski slope. About a dozen or so workmen, wearing hard hats and fluorescent jackets, swarm over it, dismantling the huge structure bit by bit. The din of clanking metal echoes across the ground.

Today's crowd totals about 1,200 so far. Old Trafford looks cavernously empty. If Neville Cardus saw it now, I doubt he would recognise the place, particularly if he turned his back on the three-tiered Victorian pavilion. He'd see the glass and steel of the media centre and within it the press area – a rectangular, blazing red box of a building, reminiscent of the brutalist architecture of the 1950s. In his peripheral vision he would catch sight of the electric scoreboard, so efficient that it makes the old 'card of the match' unnecessary unless you are either a traditionalist or a collector. And, gazing upward, he'd register the elegantly slender line of the floodlights, no doubt a little taken aback by the sight of them.

A blare of music is being pumped from loudspeakers, which would not please the old boy either. On the opening morning of the Roses match of 1933, also at Old Trafford, Cardus chastised Lancashire for being unable to live without it. He forecast sarcastically that 'other attractions' would soon follow: 'Say a few side-shows for dancing and a bearded lady ... then, gradually, the cricket can be got rid of altogether.' The loudspeaker is useful to us. The news it brings, expressed mournfully, is that play won't begin for another hour at least. The floodlights begin to glow dimly through the gloom.

I have found an end-of-row space in The Point, where I can stare over the shoulder of whoever is fielding at long-on. Around me Thermos flasks are unscrewed, newspapers opened, conversations begun about the weather. 'Much martyrdom is necessary to watch cricket in the cold,' said Cardus. We know it today. The elderly man behind me, born I suppose when Cardus was in his zenith, is leaning on his walking stick and peering disapprovingly skyward, cursing the clouds. His hearing aid starts to whistle like an old kettle about to boil. One spectator is already unpacking lunch from a bag large enough to contain the entire contents of her fridge – and then attempting the impossible task of stuffing the bag beneath her seat. Another has curiously brought sunscreen, cold drinks and a wide straw hat, as though he believes the Met Office's forecast was meant to fool him. A third is slipping on a second sweater and soon produces a hooded windcheater.

Cardus liked to flit around Old Trafford, often watching from the 'popular' side, and insisting the notes he was seen taking there were actually 'love letters' (for Barbe Ede, I'd guess). Eventually he would head to the top of the pavilion and 'behold the stretch of fields and open land reaching towards Stretford and Chorlton', the smoky centre of Manchester seeming far off to him. He could see Seymour Grove distinctly then. On hot afternoons it spread before him in the distance 'like a white ribbon'. That greenery was long ago devoured by hulking buildings and high-rises, the outline of a modern city that he would no longer be able to navigate without a map.

If Cardus saw the current Championship table, he'd be similarly disorientated. He'd assume someone had printed it upside down. This season has been an arduous chore for Lancashire and Yorkshire, both of whom lie miserably near the bottom. Lancashire are sixth. Yorkshire are one place below them, three points in arrears and all too aware that relegation will await whoever loses this game and also the return at Headingley in September.

The elderly man, who has come alone but is looking for company, tells whoever is willing to listen that he saw his first Roses match here 'before the war' when Yorkshire had Verity and Hutton, Bowes and also Cardus's friend 'Ticker' Mitchell. 'Not a bad team,' he says, a wink implicit in that deliberately understated assessment of them. He winds down memory lane a little more, discussing Paynter and Washbrook. (His ideal neighbour would be Cardus – though the elderly man would be unlikely to get a word in edgeways between monologues.)

The match starts at almost ten to twelve, the play immediately a slow grind of sweat and struggle.

Yorkshire, who have decided to bat, are dour and ponderous, barely able to hit the ball off the square. Even with Jimmy Anderson sweeping in from the Statham End, Lancashire are no more convincing either. It's the bland against the bland. Anderson tries to simultaneously dry and polish the ball, the streaks of red dye from it soon evident on his flannels.

Cardus began one Roses report like this: 'The cricket at Old Trafford was futile and hardly worth discussion.' He could dust that line off, recycling it profitably now. We tolerate rather than relish the first hour. It comprises only 14 overs, brings Yorkshire 30 runs and Lancashire one wicket. Cardus admired what he termed the 'Manchester School' of the cricket spectator, someone so steeped in the game that any comment offered was always knowledgeable, sensible and finely weighted. He described the mood at Old Trafford as 'jannock', a dialect expression that has faded from regular use. Its dictionary definition is 'honest and straightforward'. Cardus reached for it to point out that Lancastrians would be fair-minded, but felt entitled to receive fairness in return. Since the game so far is worth neither the admission money nor the time spent to come to see it, the present 'Manchester School' is very jannock in its opinions. Dissatisfied and restless, we've begun to worry that every session could be as sterile as this one, each side simply too scared of losing.

The elderly man says aloud, as though wanting the rest of us to shout our agreement: 'This is awful.' The words have barely left his lips when everything happens all at once, the pace too giddy for the eyes to follow it.

Jordan Clark has replaced Anderson. Clark is a dark-haired Cumbrian. He's 6 ft 4 in tall and broad-shouldered. Anderson, straining for effect, hasn't significantly moved the ball off the pitch or in the air. With less physical effort, Clark gets some wobbly swing after a delivery leaves his hand and some deviation when it lands fractionally on or short of a length.

Joe Root, on 22, shuffles tentatively at him; he's like a man afraid of falling off the edge of something. The ball raps him loudly on the pads, giving the umpire a straightforward decision. Next ball Kane Williamson, barely there long enough to take a good snort of air, gets trapped on the crease. Off he goes too, staring at his bootlaces. Jonny Bairstow strolls from the dressing room and across the outfield, a process done with laborious care. He's determined to keep the bowler waiting at the top of his mark, drawing the heat out of the situation.

Clark, who knows this, impatiently digs his spikes into the grass and scuffs it up. Still Bairstow prevaricates. He asks for and takes his guard. He pats down the pitch. He looks around the field – one, twice, a third time. He tugs at the sleeves of his shirt. Finally Clark is able to set off on his muscular run, which is like a charge. Old Trafford is so quiet that you can almost hear his every hard breath and the thump of his big feet on the turf. The delivery is on the line of off stump and well up to Bairstow. He plants down a foot and pushes the bat out to meet it defensively. The ball goes thickly off the outside edge. Third slip takes the catch at knee height.

Pandemonium. The 'partisan passions' that Cardus wrote about are at last alight.

Clark has removed not only the belly of Yorkshire's batting, but also the ICC's third-, fourth- and 16th-rated Test batsmen. This trio, featuring the captain of England and the captain of New Zealand, have scored almost 30,500 first-class runs at an average of nearly 50 between them. It is the first Roses hat-trick at Old Trafford since Cardus came to Old Trafford, complained about the loudspeaker music and saw George Macaulay perform the feat with 'tremendous power of will' and 'cunning flight'.

Bairstow walks away anonymously. Everyone is looking at Clark rather than at him. The bowler is wheeling towards the covers – arms outstretched, running with a high step, screaming his achievement. His team-mates give chase, eventually smothering him in congratulations, the celebration intensified because it is so unexpected. I think about 'Ticker' Mitchell. When Mitchell's son was asked how his sternly indomitable father would have reacted to modern cricketers hugging one another after the fall of a wicket, he replied: 'I can't even remember him hugging my mother.'

Lancastrians have forgotten their early boredom, remembering only Clark's hat-trick and now Macaulay, here and alive again because he is being spoken about too. Time Past has run into Time Present. Those who are scrolling down the screen of their mobile phone, wanting to read about Clark, also find staring back at them the long face and dark sunken eyes that belong to Macaulay.

At lunch I set off from The Point on a small expedition to the opposite end of Old Trafford, where the second-hand bookstall is waiting for me. On the way I think how inappropriate it would be if none of Neville Cardus's books were here today. It would be like going to Stratford and discovering *The Complete Works* were unavailable there. I need not have worried. I come across a dozen Cardus titles. Some go back as far as the 1920s. There are also the posthumous collections, published in the second half of the 1970s, when interest in him reached such a peak that Matthew Engel christened it 'the Cardus nostalgia industry'. It 'just stopped short of selling souvenir knick-knacks and T-shirts,' he said.

I like second-hand books. You never know what might fall out of them. In the past I've found ticket stubs, receipts, library cards, photographs, scribbled messages or letters. You're in touch with someone who's been unknown to you until that moment, the book bringing together your life and theirs. I find a copy of *The Essential Neville Cardus* in green boards. It is exactly like the one I own. Inside I learn someone called Charles gave the book as a present in 1950 to someone called Angela as a thank you for 'Happy summers at Canterbury, Lord's and elsewhere'. The note, written in blue ink, ends with kisses.

I flick randomly through the book, always finding something I want to read aloud or share. The way Cardus defines Walter Hammond: 'The great batsman lifts us out of our utilitarian selves; we admire his work for its beauty, not merely for its value in runs.'

His description of a slow delivery from Cecil Parkin, which 'could well be called a very gargoyle of a ball' as it drops from the air 'with a twisting grin'. His pithy summary of umpires, likened to 'the geyser in the bathroom ... We can't do without it, yet we notice it only when it is out of order.' There are passages so unmistakably Cardus that attribution would be instant – even if you heard them read aloud by a complete stranger to cricket who did not have the foggiest clue about what the words meant. Other passages, which can be plucked and gathered like flowers from every one of his books, come to my mind.

There is a description of Maurice Tate, who Cardus thought was 'another case of human nature unaffected and unaware of its own comic implications'. He wrote of him 'arms akimbo' in the outfield, following a shot. 'He shades his eyes – like a longshoreman sweeping the horizon.' Tate was a 'great conversationalist' too. 'He sometimes goes on to bowl at the sea end at Hove in the middle of a sentence.'

There is a game at Yeovil, where a storm has left wide puddles along the lane towards the main gate. 'When the weather momentarily cleared, they reflected the blue of the sky like magic mirrors.'

There is his claim that 'a snick by Jack Hobbs is a sort of disturbance of cosmic orderliness'.

A scene at The Parks, which he first sketches and then colours in so brightly, is a personal favourite, always making me want to go there. Cardus looks into the strong light slicing across Oxford. He gives the names of the trees – chestnut, stately poplars and the 'gorgeously stained' copper beeches. He mentions the undergraduates who loll on the boundary, and the 'aged men', presumably retired dons, who clutch books and pencils and paper. He likes the dogs that shove a wet nose in his hands. Cardus considered The Parks 'an English heaven' and 'an eternal ideal image of all the cricket fields ever dreamed of by lovers of the game.' Going there gave him succour every spring because 'in such

The Parks, Oxford.

a place it is easy to get the illusion that the world's ugliness and animosities are fleeting and unreal, that only beauty and friendliness are the abiding facts of life.'

In a shallow box, beneath one of the crowded tables of books, I also discover a few dozen copies of *The Cricketer*. In one of them, dated from the late 1960s, Cardus writes about 'one of life's remembered pleasures', which for him was playing the game rather than chronicling it. 'To spin a ball from the forefinger,' he writes. 'To see the ball floating, perfect length, and then pitching on the right spot, luring the batsman from the position of second line of defence and then taking the middle or leg stump.' He described bowling as 'joy unconfined'.

Cardus is opening a door and beckoning us through it. I've read the piece before; now I read it again.

It is the 1920s. The *Manchester Guardian* XI is pitted against A. C. MacLaren's XI on 'the sacred turf' of Old Trafford. MacLaren, white-haired and past 50, opens the batting. Cardus exercises his captain's prerogative, putting himself on to bowl against him 'at once'. With his third or fourth ball – Cardus could never be sure which – he deceives him in flight. MacLaren comes forward, playing and missing. The ball spins so wickedly past him from the off that it nearly shaves leg stump. The delivery flummoxes the wicketkeeper as well. He turns and sees it scuttle away for a bye. Cardus has come within 'an inch' of claiming MacLaren's wicket. When MacLaren gets to the non-striker's end, he compliments him generously. 'Well bowled . . . I didn't know you could bring 'em back . . . But so long as we do know . . .' The last line, spoken dispassionately, is an assurance from MacLaren that Cardus will not outfox him again. Nor does he. 'To every subsequent off break from my fingers, he moved back the right foot and – woosh, bang! Four after four, imperiously pulled square,' explains Cardus. That he had come so close to dismissing MacLaren still consoled him, not only then but also decades later. So did the fact that in surprising his hero he also proved something to him. 'So long as he knew,' said Cardus of his cherished ability to 'bring 'em back'.

The end of something is supposed to bestow a sliver of meaning and perspective on it. As I lay the magazine back in the box, I settle on this: Cardus bowled to MacLaren when he was a relatively young man. He wrote about the occasion when he was a relatively old one. His account of it makes me think, more than ever, that he was forever a boy at heart, always waiting for life to astonish him and also always harking back to those days when it had. I think this too. However modest his abilities as a cricketer, the enjoyment Cardus got out of them explains why he was able to put the feelings of the ordinary cricket-watcher into words; he related to 'fans' like us better than anyone had done before.

Cardus's manifesto, explaining how he did it, is hidden in an obscure anthology, one of the last places anyone would dream of looking. In *The MCC Book for the Young Cricketer*, published in Coronation Year, you'll find a piece entitled 'How to report a cricket match'.

Cardus says the cricket reporter should be 'a trained spectator', able to express himself. He must see the 'things and happenings' that the 'ordinary watcher' misses and also look for 'certain moments, certain things done' which escape others. He should treat cricketers 'as human beings' and ought not to 'believe everything the scoreboard tells him'. Cardus distils his philosophy into two sentences: 'It takes all sorts to make a world, and there is no one and indispensable way of writing a cricket report. The reporter who looks too much at the scoreboard and at the clock and at the records is likely to miss all the fun, and end in boring his readers to death.'

To read is also to experience. The best writers make you a participant on the page, creating a landscape in which you can walk and characters to whom you can talk. Cardus did this. Every match report, profile or essay becomes in his hands a short story, packed with nuance. No wonder one Nobel prize winner, Samuel Beckett, is said to have admired *The Summer Game*. No wonder another, Harold Pinter, a life-long devotee, regarded Cardus as simply 'marvellous'. The poet Siegfried Sassoon even said he was prepared to read him 'for ever'. And P. G. Wodehouse sent a letter to a friend that quoted a lovely slab of words, including the sentence 'The quality of greatness, surely, is most evident when an artist or craftsman so sums up in his work the typical charac-teristics of his occupation that we regularly speak of him as an apogee of his art.' Wodehouse teased his friend with the writer's identity: 'Ah, you say to yourself, another of those thoughtful essays on Shakespeare or Milton.' When Wodehouse reveals Cardus as the author, he asks: 'Don't you wish you could get as worked up as that about cricket?'

Yes, I do.

The afternoon wears on. The sky begins to clear and the sun breaks through to warm us. Yorkshire toil beneath it nonetheless, run-making no easier for them. At tea, nine down for 168, I decide at last to go and see Mr Cardus formally.

He always found reassuring the 'noise of cups and saucers and spoons', recognising it as a sign of cricket's civility and sociability. In the pavilion, the queue for the tea urn snakes raggedly past his gold-framed portrait. No one is taking much notice of him apart from me. There are two reasons for this. First, the oil has hung at Old Trafford so long – given as a gift to Lancashire in the year Cardus died – that it has about as much visual impact as a roll of beige wallpaper. Second, it isn't terribly good.

You can stare at it for a few minutes without registering the likeness. For a start, it is peculiar that someone whose reputation was predominantly established during more than half a century of summers is dressed in a wide-lapelled winter coat and a polka-dot scarf. The colour tone is off too. Cardus's skin is yellowish, as if he's just contracted – or recovered from – jaundice. He's holding his favourite brown pipe in his left hand and is wearing a pair of rimless glasses, depicted so faintly that you strain to see them. The painting's biggest failing is that it doesn't tell you anything at all about Cardus. The grand masters of portraiture – think of Holbein, think of Velasquez – detected in the intimate space of the studio some buried secret in the soul of their subject. They showed character. They presented what lies beneath. You almost know what the sitter was thinking and feeling during the hours when the artist held him in benign captivity. This painter, the little-known Hungarian Denes de Holesch, conveys nothing of this. The eyes are just black dots. The mouth is rigid. The expression is so stiff and inscrutable that the face may as well be blank. The artist had been friendly with Cardus, first meeting him in Australia, but evidently hadn't really known him. Cardus escapes him. Whenever I look at the portrait, I hear John Arlott discussing those 'several Neville Carduses' and the masks he wore.

The painting, commissioned and completed in 1951, does him another grave disservice for which de Holesch cannot be held responsible. It reinforces the image we have of Cardus as perpetually aged. He lived so long that the mind's eye is conditioned to summon a

Denes de Holesch's portrait of Cardus in his winter coat and scarf. Today it hangs in the pavilion at Old Trafford.

picture of the old man who sat in front of Arlott and fished prize catches out of his memory for him. When Cardus was born, the camera was an expensive novelty. When he grew up and matured, portrait snaps weren't routinely taken. The most often reproduced pictures of Cardus are consequently post-war, showing a man anywhere between 60-odd and 80-odd years old.

That's why I prefer one black-and-white photograph of him. In it he looks so relatively young that it could have been taken on his first same. The shade and grain of the photograph contains more life than de Holesch's flat, dark brushstrokes. This is the Cardus we never met,

The young Neville Cardus, still a relatively nascent Manchester Guardian *man, as he set off to cover his first seasons as a fledgling cricket correspondent.*

striving to accomplish something wonderful. This is the obscure fellow who set off to see England with what he said was 'a passion for cricket that passeth all understanding' and returned after changing fundamentally and for ever the way the game was written about.

The photograph also reminds me of all those what-ifs, the infinite routes lives might have taken but didn't. What if C. P. Scott hadn't summoned Cardus back into his employment? What if Cardus hadn't fallen sick during the late winter of 1919? What if he had refused the unasked-for task the *Manchester Guardian* gave him? And what if, simply to conform to the staid journalistic norm, Cardus hadn't taken the risk of writing so lyrically about Cecil Parkin's rout of Yorkshire's batting? Lancashire ought to buy a blown-up copy of the photograph and place it prominently beside de Holesch's inadequate portrait. This is the Cardus we ought to remember.

I give de Holesch's Cardus a nod of farewell and retreat back to The Point, ready to watch Yorkshire being tortured again.

They limp to 192 all out.

Jordan Clark, still on the adrenalin high of his hat-trick, fittingly takes the last wicket, finishing with five for 58. He could claim half of a sixth wicket as well, responsible as he was for one of those run-outs that always seem to be a gross miscarriage of justice. Clark stuck out a hand and deflected a firm drive off his own bowling on to the stumps, catching Tim Bresnan on the turn and out of his ground.

The elderly man and his freshly made companions start talking about a first-innings lead for Lancashire of 'at least 250'.

As Joe Root comes back on to the field, taking a few days off from the duties of captaincy, I ponder about whether – or how closely – Neville Cardus would compare him to Len Hutton. For what he said of Hutton – 'good cutter . . . drives with easy power . . . moves naturally on his feet' – could be said of Root too. Cardus could also have told us how different one is from the other. At the moment, with the game going dismally against Yorkshire, Root looks a little forlorn, which is something else he and Hutton had in common. Not for long, however.

I know Cardus relished the 'imp of mischief' in cricket, the unpredictability that made it so special for him. This game becomes a classic example of that, a somersault in fortune.

Lancashire move serenely to 46 without loss, the occupants of The Point and the pavilion more comfortably optimistic than ever about the outcome of the match and also the outcome of the rest of the season. Then calamity strikes – from nowhere and out of nothing. Root takes a smart catch at short mid-off to remove Keaton Jennings, the first twisting of the plot. Soon Haseeb Hameed shoulders arms and regrets it, his off stump knocked back. This small rockfall of wickets becomes an avalanche lasting 15 overs. Lancashire's members, too numb to groan, sit in silence and give one another sullen looks. At the close their side, which have been dominant for two thirds of the day, are 109 for nine, far in arrears.

In 1923, after Lancashire were bowled out for 73 at Bradford, Cardus wrote about it as a 'bitter hour' and admitted: 'One really has no heart to discuss the latest bowing of the knee of our XI to the old enemy.' When George Macaulay took that hat-trick, Lancashire collapsing twice in a day, he couldn't bring himself to scold them because the pitch was 'deplorably worn' and 'even worse than I had expected it to be'. And, as the Second World War loomed, he asked for 'no tears' to accompany Lancashire's second-innings total of 92; superior bowling had outdone them again.

Today I wonder how he would describe and rationalise what has just happened.

The Guardian's obituary of Cardus spoke of his 'long innings', the writer unaware that it wasn't over and never will be. As I leave Old

Trafford, I am certain about this because one line above all others floats ahead of me. Cardus said:

A cricketer's art is thrown out on the summer air; it enchants us for a while, and then it is gone.

The Great Romantic is reflecting, somewhat melancholically, on the briefness of life. The mere glimpse we get of it. The ephemeral nature of almost everything around us. The way Time moves on, leaving everyone behind and turning them into history.

But Cardus got it wrong. He underestimated himself and his craftsmanship.

For all the cricketers he saw will survive because he wrote about them. And he will survive because of the way he did it – vividly, vibrantly, imperishably.

The summers in which Cardus lived are with us still; they always will be . . .

AUTHOR NOTES AND ACKNOWLEDGEMENTS

For MYRIAD REASONS – a few of them too dull-dreary to dwell on – I moved house five times between very early autumn 2003 and very early spring 2008.

You're sure to appreciate – because psychologists are quoted on the matter so frequently – the anxiety so much gadding from one place to another is supposed to inflict and where it sits in the league table of life's stresses.

I found it peculiarly liberating.

In retrospect, I think this was because I felt like Neville Cardus did when he walked into Cross Street and talked about being 'baptised' again. I was in a new city and working my way into a new job. I was also mercifully coming out of that period which Dante described as the 'dark wood'.

Yes, I got exhausted as I packed and unpacked boxes, a process which almost chafed the skin off my fingers. Yes, it was a time in which I got rid of a lot of stuff (only to replace it with other stuff). And, yes, it was frustrating to discover that a book or a newspaper, a magazine or a cutting that I urgently needed, was in storage rather than easy to hand.

The downside of such a peripatetic existence is obvious. Some things get lost. The upside is obvious too. Other things get found. Well settled at last, and sorting through a box probably untouched for a decade or more, I came across a ring-binder. It contained six loose pages of a diary/journal that I had kept at the end of my teenage years.

The pages were slightly tatty and a little tea-stained, but the contents pushed me along the path to this book.

Evelyn Waugh is partly to blame for the fact I kept a diary/journal at all. I read his diaries after their publication in the mid-1970s. Everything I did was typed out on the first typewriter I ever owned, often in a wild rush late at night or at weekends. There is the odd crossing-out (the x came in useful) and bad misspellings. Most of my thoughts and observations surely counted as embarrassing or naive gibberish, which is why so much paper surely perished – torn up or burnt, no doubt. I was less Waugh and more Adrian Mole, I suppose. I read those pages back now and barely recognise the decade, which seems so different from today, or the person I was back then; I seem *so young*.

Those days with John Arlott in the Trent Bridge press box survive because, at some stage, I must have thought them worth saving. It counts as one of my better decisions.

The diary sadly reminds me of a chance that I missed too. JA arranged a wine-tasting in the hotel he was staying in (the Albany on Maid Marian Way, then popular among visiting journalists and cricket teams). He asked me to go. I had to politely decline the invitation; I had an evening job to do for the freelance agency for which I then worked. I will always wonder: What else would I have learnt that night?

It seems a little late to say a formal thank you to JA for his enormous benevolence and kindness towards me. I'll do so anyway. I have never forgotten him or it. To mark the centenary of his birth, which fell in 2014, I contributed a long article to *Backspin* magazine about his writing. To mark the 200th anniversary of my former cricket club, Plumtree, I wrote about him again in the introduction to the club's commemorative book. As for the letter he wrote to me in 1975 . . . that hangs in the room in which I write.

I am also grateful to his son Tim for the research he undertook on my behalf after we first met and became friends. JA had said he was working on a Cardus biography in the 1980s. Tim found no evidence of it and didn't recall his father even discussing the possibility, which leaves behind an unsolvable mystery. I can't help but hope, however, that someone, somewhere may have the fragments of such a work . . .

I ought to record that Dick Streeton of *The Times* engaged JA in the conversation I describe in the Prologue. My diary reminds me of that, but I knew it anyway because I remember Dick so fondly. The biography he wrote not long afterwards of Percy Fender is one of my favourite cricket books. Dick used to wear some very bright V-necked sweaters; one of them would have outshone a Van Gogh sun. Early in his career he worked in Nottinghamshire and he would talk to me about what I assume was a fairly brief stint as a news reporter in the Mansfield office of the *Evening Post*. 'Sometimes I'd get a bowls match to cover on a Saturday,' he'd say, recalling his desperation then to get into sport.

I never tire of saying that biography is a collaboration. You rely so much on the good will of others. What follows are a few bows in words towards all those who played a part in the making of *The Great Romantic*.

I spent a privileged and treasurable morning with John Woodcock at his home in Longparish. When I rang to arrange the visit, John was concerned that travelling from Yorkshire was an 'awfully long way to come'. I explained that I had recently returned from China, Canada and America, where I'd gone to research a book on the Olympic athlete and missionary Eric Liddell. Making it to Hampshire and back would be like a stroll, I said. John laid on the hospitality and even drove me to and from the railway station.

Christopher Brookes took me to Sam's Chop House in Manchester and talked at length about writing his biography of Cardus, published in the 1980s.

David Frith, as generous and helpful as ever, shared both his thoughts on Cardus and the contents of his fantastic archive.

Peter Wynne-Thomas, indispensable in the birth of so many cricket books, was his usual, remarkable self – full of knowledge and wit, opinions and stories.

Sir Michael Parkinson and his son Mike sent copies of interviews with Jack Fingleton, some of which were broadcast only in Australia.

Fiona Hertford-Hughes spoke to me about her aunt, Margaret Hughes.

Michael Meadowcroft dug around the National Liberal Club Archives.

Sir Harold Evans sifted through his archive in New York.

Mark Pottle got permission to comb Violet Bonham Carter's diaries, which are held at the Bodleian Library and unavailable to the public. Edward Bonham Carter set this process in motion and Virginia Brand, VBC's granddaughter, arranged copyright permission for me.

I was fortunate enough to hear NC's friend Michael Kennedy speak twice – and at length – during one of the now annual lunches arranged by the Cardus Archive. On the second occasion, Michael Henderson introduced us. Over the odd pint of Landlord last winter, Michael then shared his own thoughts on Cardus and the old boy's legacy.

Sarah Lindsay did some excellent and valuable research for me in the Collins archive in Glasgow.

Julie Frear was indispensable on the keyboard.

Paul Edwards and Tanya Aldred answered queries.

Two fine and lovely people deserve special mentions in particular. The first is Bob Hilton, a Cardusian par excellence. The second is Elizabeth Grice.

Bob answered numerous questions, shared his intelligence, scanned and sent photographs. We sat together at Old Trafford and also spent time going through NC's archive in the library there. Liz shared her memories of NC and then went away to think about the follow-up questions I asked, replying to them in detail. Bob and Liz could not have been more supportive. They say no good deed goes unpunished. Well, their punishment is my friendship, now and for ever. You won't get rid of me, I'm afraid.

The gimlet-eyed, who saw the hardback of *The Great Romantic*, will notice a couple of additions to this paperback edition, plus two fresh photographs. These come courtesy of Elton and Barbe Ede's grand-daughters, Julia Donaldson and Mary Moore. I had tried to track Barbe's descendants through family history sites, each search sending me into a cul-de-sac and a plain brick wall. Fortunately, Julia and Mary found me.

I was watching the rain fall at Taunton, where Somerset and Essex were locked in a County Championship decider. On the penultimate day of the game, I returned to my hotel to find an email from Julia. She and Mary had heard Radio 4's serialisation of the book in mid-summer. They had stories to share. I thank them for their help and great kindness.

I'm grateful for those who did the behind-the-scenes work at Hodder. The legend that is Roddy Bloomfield, who commissioned and championed the book with gusto; the exceptional Tim Waller, who edited it and saved me from myself on more than a few occasions; Fiona Rose, who was always there to pick up precious pieces.

My agent, Grainne Fox, has learnt to put up with me, her voice calm and sane and analytically rational. She constantly sees what I don't when I'm immersed in the head-down graft of writing. She is, most importantly of all, a very good person and very good company.

It was once the prerequisite of a first-rate short story to end tidily and often where it began. The method has fallen out of fashion. Let me revive it, albeit fleetingly.

Did I mention that I moved house the odd time during the noughties?

You may have already guessed one of the reasons why this happened. I met Mandy, who became my wife.

I was once on a train that passed through a suburb of Leeds. As if echoing 'Adlestrop', one of my favourite poems, it stopped 'unwontedly' there. I liked the name of the place and wondered what it would be like to live in it. Only two years later, I found out. Mandy's house was a five-minute walk from the station . . .

Flash forward two more years.

We received an invitation to lunch in a village neither of us knew. It came from Derek Hodgson and his wife Doreen. Derek, a former cricket and football writer of national renown, wanted to talk about a book I had written. He didn't know we were looking to buy a new property. We didn't know he was looking to sell one. Within 48 hours we had agreed a price. I call it the most expensive lunch I ever had.

I would sometimes ring Derek with queries about books or articles. For instance, beginning research on *The Great Romantic*, I got in touch to ask about Cardus and John Arlott. Derek had arranged for JA to come to Old Trafford and unveil a plaque to his friend.

In the summer of 2017, I rang him for a different reason. More than 30 years before, Derek had co-authored David Bairstow's autobiography. Now I was co-authoring Jonny Bairstow's (what a small world . . . what big coincidences exist within it). I was about to set off for Southport to watch Lancashire against Middlesex. Derek asked me to say hello to the hotel where newspapermen, visiting the resort for matches, were known to have the occasional lemonade. On Saturday, I called in there. On Sunday morning, I sent a postcard to tell him so. On Sunday afternoon, I heard Derek had died.

The readings at Derek's funeral included 'Adlestrop', *The Wind in the Willows* (another favourite of mine) and an extract from Cardus's report of Kent v Lancashire at Dover. I thought of Derek often as I wrote *The Great Romantic*, believing him to be one of the ideal readers for the book.

*　　*　　*

Mandy and I still live where Derek and Doreen once did. All things, however, must pass.

We have talked frequently about moving again, a prospect which doesn't seem as 'liberating' as all those other moves all those other years ago.

But . . .

I was halfway through these notes and acknowledgements when I read an extract in the *New Yorker* from Robert A. Caro's book *Working*. The genius – for that's what Caro is – explained the nuts-and-bolts background to his multi-volume and still-unfinished biography of Lyndon B. Johnson.

Caro makes clear, explicitly and implicitly, how much of a debt he owes to Mrs Caro.

I thought I did a lot of research and sometimes went to crazy extremes to carry it out. My head spun when I read what Caro once did. He decided he must move to Johnson's home town to understand his subject better. The spot in question was the Texas Hill Country, which Caro described as a 'vast emptiness'. Looking at that landscape and thinking of somewhere a tad more scenic and lively, Mrs Caro responded by asking her husband: 'Why can't you do a biography of Napoleon?' The couple nonetheless spent 'much of the next three years' there. They were happy too.

That story reminded me of one thing. It doesn't really matter where you live – providing you live with the right person.

I'm not sure Mandy got it right, but I did.

I think Mr Bacharach and Mr David put it best: 'A house is not a home . . . when there's no one there to kiss goodnight'.

So, of course, I'll go anywhere with my much superior half. I'm just hoping she'll pack and unpack most of the boxes . . .

PHOTOGRAPHIC ACKNOWLEDGEMENTS

The author and publisher would like to thank the following for permission to reproduce photographs:

Geoff Elliss, Neville Cardus Archive, Hulton Archive/Getty Images, Kirby/Topical Press Agency/Getty Images, Jimmy Sime/ Central Press/Getty Images, Manchester Libraries, Information and Archives, Aylwin Sampson, Evening Standard/Getty Images, Popperfoto/Getty Images, Bob Thomas/Popperfoto/Getty Images, mooziic / Alamy Stock Photo, Topical Press Agency/Hulton Archive/ Getty Images, Punch/Topfoto, Alan Webb/Fox Photos/Getty Images, Fox Photos/Getty Images, Evening Standard/Hulton Archive/Getty Images, Central Press/Hulton Archive/Getty Images, George Beldam/Popperfoto/Getty Images, Historic Collection / Alamy Stock Photo, Central Press/Getty Images, Harry Todd/Fox Photos/Getty Images, David Savill/Topical Press Agency/Getty Images, Alan Webb/Fox Photos/Hulton Archive/Getty Images, Reg Speller/Fox Photos/Getty Images, S. C. Smith/Topical Press Agency/Getty Images,

Other photographs are from private collections.

Every reasonable effort has been made to trace the copyright holders, but if there are any errors or omissions, Hodder & Stoughton will be pleased to insert the appropriate acknowledgement in any subsequent printings or editions.

SELECTED BIBLIOGRAPHY AND SOURCE MATERIAL

Books

Ackroyd, P., *Dickens*, Sinclair-Stevenson, 1990

Arlott, J., *A Reader's Guide to Cricket*, Cambridge University Press, 1950

———, *Vintage Summer: 1947*, Eyre & Spottiswoode, 1967

———, *Basingstoke Boy*, Collins Willow, 1990

Arlott, T., *John Arlott: A Memoir*, Andre Deutsch, 1994

Arnot, C., *Britain's Lost Cricket Grounds*, Aurum, 2011

———, *Britain's Lost Cricket Festivals*, Aurum, 2014

Ayerst, D., *The Guardian Omnibus: 1821–1971*, Collins, 1973

Bailey, A., *Standing in the Sun: A Life of J. M. W. Turner*, Sinclair-Stevenson, 1997

Barrett, N. (ed.), *The Daily Telegraph Chronicle of Cricket*, Guinness, 1994

Batchelor, D., *The Game Goes On*, Eyre & Spottiswoode, 1947

Bearshaw, B., *From the Stretford End: The Official History of Lancashire CCC*, Partridge Press, 1990

Benaud, R., *Anything but . . . An Autobiography*, Hodder & Stoughton, 1998

Birkenhead, Earl, *The Hundred Best English Essays*, Cassell, 1929

Birley, D., *A Social History of English Cricket*, Aurum, 1999

———, *The Willow Wand*, Aurum, 2000

Bose, M., *Keith Miller: A Cricketing Autobiography*, 1979, Allen & Unwin

Bowes, B., *Express Deliveries*, Stanley Paul, 1949

Bradman, D., *Don Bradman's Book*, Hutchinson, 1938

——, *Farewell to Cricket*, Pavilion, 1988 (new edition)

——, *The Bradman Albums*, Queen Anne Press, 1988

Bright-Holmes, J. (ed.), *Like It Was: The Diaries of Malcolm Muggeridge*, Collins, 1981

Brooke, R., *A History of the County Cricket Championship*, Guinness, 1991

Brookes, C., *His Own Man: The Life of Neville Cardus*, Methuen, 1985

Bryant, M. (ed.), *H. M. Bateman*, Prion, 2002

Canynge Caple, S., *The Cricketer's Who's Who*, Lincoln Williams, 1934

Cardus, N., *A Cricketer's Book*, Grant Richards, 1922

——, *Days in the Sun*, Grant Richards, 1924

——, *The Summer Game*, Jonathan Cape, 1929

——, *Good Days*, Jonathan Cape, 1934

——, *Australian Summer*, Jonathan Cape, 1937

——, *Autobiography*, Collins, 1947

——, *Second Innings*, Collins, 1950

——, *Cardus on Cricket*, Jonathan Cape, 1951

——, *Close of Play*, Collins, 1956

——, *The Playfair Cardus*, The Dickens Press, 1963

——, *Full Score*, Cassell, 1970

——, *Cardus in the Covers*, Souvenir Press, 1978

——, *A Fourth Innings with Cardus*, Souvenir Press, 1981

——, *The Roses Matches 1919–1939*, Souvenir Press, 1982

Carew, D., *England Over*, Martin Secker, 1927

——, *The House is Gone*, Robert Hale, 1949

Carr, A. W., *Cricket With the Lid Off*, Hutchinson, 1935

Chapple, F. J., *Some Cover Shots: A Cricket Anthology*, Jonathan Cape, 1924

Clarke, N., *Alistair Cooke: The Biography*, Weidenfeld & Nicolson, 1999

Coldham, J. D., *Early Cricket Reporters*, Monograph No. 6, 2017

Cooke, A., *Fun & Games with Alistair Cooke: On Sport and Other Amusements*, Pavilion, 1994

Daniels, R., *Conversations with Cardus*, Gollancz, 1976

——, *Cardus: Celebrant of Beauty*, Palatine, 2009

Dodds, T. C., *Hit Hard and Enjoy It*, The Cricketer, 1976

Down, M., *Archie: A Biography of A. C. MacLaren*, Allen & Unwin, 1981

Drabble, M., *Arnold Bennett: A Biography*, Weidenfeld & Nicholson, 1974

Duckworth, L. B., *Cricket from the Hearth*, Cornish Bros, 1948

Ellis, C., *C. B.: The Life of Charles Burgess Fry*, Dent, 1984

Engel, M. (ed.), *The Guardian Book of Cricket*, Pavilion, 1986

Farnsworth, K., *Before and After Bramall Lane*, privately published, 1988

Fay, G. (ed.), *The Bedside Guardian*, 1965–66, Collins, 1966

Fingleton, J. H., *The Immortal Victor Trumper*, Collins, 1978

——, *Batting From Memory*, Collins, 1981

Foot, D., *Cricket's Unholy Trinity*, Stanley Paul, 1985

——, *Wally Hammond: The Reasons Why*, Robson, 1996

——, *Fragments of Idolatry*, Fairfield Books, 2001

Fowler, C., *The Book of Forgotten Authors*, riverrun, 2017

Frewin, L. (ed.), *The Boundary Book*, MacDonald, 1962

Frith, D., *Silence of the Heart*, Mainstream, 2001

——, *Bodyline Autopsy*, Aurum, 2002

Fry, C. B., *Life Worth Living*, Pavilion, 1986

Geddes, M., *Remembering Bradman*, Viking, 2002

Green, B. (ed.), *Wisden Book of Cricketers' Lives*, Queen Anne Press, 1986

———, *The Wisden Papers of Neville Cardus*, Hutchinson, 1989

Grimshaw, A. (ed.), *Cricket/C. L. R. James*, Allison & Busby, 1986

Growden, G., *Jack Fingleton: The Man Who Stood Up to Bradman*, Allen & Unwin, 2009

Haigh, G., *The Big Ship*, Aurum, 2001

———, *Stroke of Genius*, Simon & Schuster, 2016

Hammond J. L., *C. P. Scott of the Manchester Guardian*, G. Bell and Sons, 1934

Hennessy, P., *Having It So Good: Britain in the Fifties*, Penguin, 2006

Hetherington, A., *Guardian Years*, Chatto & Windus, 1981

Hilton, B., *My Dear Michael: Cricketing and Other Extracts from Neville Cardus's Letters to Michael Kennedy, 1959–74*, LCCC, 2007

———, *The Elusive Mr Cardus: Letters and Other Writings, 1916–1975*, LCCC and Max Books, 2009

———, *Neville Cardus Reflects: Pages from a Writer's Notebook and Correspondence*, LCCC and Max Books, 2015

———, *Cardus Undimmed: The Last Decade*, Max Books, 2017

Hilton, C., *Bradman and the Summer that Changed Cricket*, JR Books, 2009

Hodcroft, G., *My Own Red Roses*, Book Guild, 1984

Hodgson, D., *The Official History of Yorkshire County Cricket Club*, Crowood Press, 1989

Hopps, D., *A Century of Great Cricket Quotes*, Robson, 1998

Howat, G., *Learie Constantine*, Allen & Unwin, 1975

———, *Plum Warner*, Unwin Hyman, 1987

———, *Cricket All My Life*, Methuen, 2006

Hughes, M., *All on a Summer's Day*, Stanley Paul, 1953

———, *The Long Hop*, Stanley Paul, 1955

Hutton, L., *Cricket is My Life*, Hutchinson, 1949

———, *Just My Story*, Hutchinson, 1956

James, C. L. R., *Beyond a Boundary*, Stanley Paul, 1963

Johnston, J., *The Lord Chamberlain's Blue Pencil*, Hodder & Stoughton, 1990

Kay, J., *A History of County Cricket: Lancashire*, Arthur Barker, 1974

Kennedy, M., *Portrait of Manchester*, Robert Hale, 1970

Lancashire County Cricket Club: Diamond Jubilee 1864–1924, Manchester Guardian, 1924

Ledbrooke, A. W., *Lancashire County Cricket, 1864–1953*, Sportsman's Book Club, 1953

Lewis, J., *David Astor: A Life in Print*, Jonathan Cape, 2016

Lyttelton, G., and Hart-Davis, R., *The Lyttelton Hart-Davis Letters* (six volumes), John Murray, 1981–82

Mailey, A., *10 for 66 and All That*, Phoenix, 1958

Malies, J., *Great Characters from Cricket's Golden Age*, Robson, 2000

March, R., *The Cricketers of Vanity Fair*, Grange Books, 1993

Marshall, M., *Gentlemen and Players*, Grafton, 1987

Mason, P., *Learie Constantine*, Macmillan, 2008

Meredith, A., *Summers in Winter: Four England Tours of Australia*, Kingswood, 1990

Miller, K., *Keith Miller Companion*, Sportsman's Book Club, 1955

Moult, T. (ed.), *Bat and Ball: A New Book of Cricket*, Sportsman's Book Club, 1960

O'Brien, C., *Cardus Uncovered: Neville Cardus: The Truth, the Untruth and the Higher Truth*, Whitethorn Range, 2018

Oxford Dictionary of National Biography

Parkin, C., *Parkin on Cricket*, Hodder & Stoughton, 1923

——, *Parkin Again*, Hodder & Stoughton, 1925

——, *Cricket Triumphs and Troubles*, Nicholls, 1936

Peebles, I., *Batter's Castle: A Ramble Round the Realm of Cricket*, Souvenir, 1958

Plumptre, G., *Homes of Cricket*, Macdonald, 1988

Pollock, W., *The Cream of Cricket*, Methuen, 1934

———, *So This is Australia*, Arthur Barker, 1937

———, *Talking About Cricket*, Gollancz, 1941

Powell, W., *The Wisden Guide to Cricket Grounds*, Stanley Paul, 1992

Prittie, T. C. F., *Cricket North and South*, Sportsman's Book Club, 1955

Ramsden, J., *George Lyttelton's Commonplace Book*, Stone Trough, 2002

Ranjitsinhji, K. S., *The Jubilee Book of Cricket*, Blackwood, 1897

Ratcliff, A. J. J. (ed.), *Prose of Our Time*, Thomas Nelson, 1931

Ratcliffe, S. (ed.), *P. G. Wodehouse: A Life in Letters*, Hutchinson, 2011

Rayvern Allen, D., *Cricket's Silver Lining*, Collins Willow, 1987

Rendell, B., *Gubby Allen: Bad Boy of Bodyline?*, Cricket Lore, undated

———, *Gubby Under Pressure*, ACS, 2007

Renshaw, A., *Wisden on the Great War*, John Wisden, 2014

Roberts, E. L., *Cricket in England, 1894–1939*, Edward Arnold, 1946

Robertson-Glasgow, R. C., *46 Not Out*, Hollis & Carter, 1948

———, *Crusoe on Cricket*, Pavilion, 1985

Robinson, R., *On Top Down Under: Australia's Cricket Captains*, Cassell, 1975

Rose, J., *The Intellectual Life of the British Working Classes*, Yale, 2001

C. P. Scott 1846–1932: The Making of the Manchester Guardian, Frederick Muller, 1946

Sewell, E. D. H., *A Searchlight on English Cricket by A County Cricketer*, Robert Holden, 1926

———, *From a Window at Lord's*, Methuen, 1937

Sissons, R., *The Players: A Social History of the Professional Cricketer*, Kingswood, 1988

Spring, H., *The Autobiography*, Collins, 1972

St John, J. (ed.), *The MCC Book for the Young Cricketer*, Naldrett Press, 1953

Swanton, E. W., *Sort of a Cricket Person*, Collins, 1972

Synge, A., *Sins of Omission: The Story of the Test Selectors 1899–1990*, Pelham, 1990

Taylor, A. J. P., *English History, 1914–1945*, Clarendon Press, 1986 edn

Taylor, G., *Changing Faces: A History of The Guardian*, 1956–88, Fourth Estate, 1993

Tebbutt, G., *With the 1930 Australians*, Hodder & Stoughton, 1930

Thomas, P., *Yorkshire Cricketers, 1839–1939*, Derek Hodgson, 1973

Travis, A., *Bound and Gagged: A Secret History of Obscenity in Britain*, Profile, 2000

Valentine, B., *Cricket's Dawn That Died*, Breedon Books, 1991

Warner, P., *Cricket Between Two Wars*, Chatto & Windus, 1942

Waugh, A., *My Brother Evelyn and Other Profiles*, Bloomsbury, 1963

———, *A Year to Remember: A Reminiscence of 1931*, Bloomsbury, 1975

Westcott, C., *The History of Cricket at The Saffrons*, Omnipress, 2000

Whitehead, R. (ed.), *The Times on the Ashes*, History Press, 2015

Wilde, S., *Ranji: A Genius Rich and Strange*, Kingswood, 1990

Wilkinson, G. (ed.), *A Century of Bradford League Cricket, 1903–2003*, (no publisher given), 2003

Williams, J., *Cricket and England: A Cultural and Social History of the Inter-War Years*, Routledge, 1999

Wisden Cricketers' Almanac, various editions, 1919–1976

Wright, D. (ed.), *Cardus on Music: A Centenary Collection*, Hamish Hamilton, 1988

Wynne-Thomas, P., *The History of Lancashire County Cricket Club*, Christopher Helm, 1989

———, *Cricket's Historians*, ACS, 2012

Yardley, N. W. D., and Kilburn, J. M., *Homes of Sport*, Peter Garnett, 1952

Newspapers/Magazines

Adelaide Advertiser: 15 July 1937; 11 March 1940; 21 February 1940; 3 September 1940.

The Argus (Melbourne): 16 September 1922.

Athletic News: 17 July 1922; 11 September 1922; 9 June 1924.

Belfast Telegraph: 6 July 1932; 5 December 1932; 1 May 1936.

The Bookman: September 1922; February 1927; July 1930; August 1933.

Country Life: 2 August 1924; 26 July 1930; 5 September 1947; 24 February 1950; 20 May 1952; 1 June 1963.

Courier Mail (Brisbane): 5 May 1934; 10 May 1934; 18 June 1934; 29 June 1934; 11 August 1936; 15 October 1936; 17 October 1936; 28 December 1936; 31 December 1936; 27 February 1937; 28 May 1938; 22 August 1939; 9 March 1940; 12 March 1940; 30 November 1946; 2 December 1946; 8 January 1947.

The Cricketer: June 1924; May 1931; July 1947; Spring Annual 1950; March 1952; Spring Annual 1966; February 1967; Spring Annual 1967; April 1967; May 1967; June 1967; July 1967; August 1967; September 1967; October 1967; November 1967; Winter Annual 1967; February 1968; Spring Annual 1968; April 1968; May 1968; June 1968; July 1968; August 1968; September 1968; October 1968; November 1968; Winter Annual 1968; Spring Annual 1969; April 1969; January 1970; November 1970; January 1971; April 1971; January 1973; April 1974; April 1975; March 1976; April 1977; February 1988; May 1988; November 1989.

Eastbourne Gazette: 3 August 1921; 10 August 1921; 17 August 1921; 31 August 1921.

Encounter: April 1961.

English Review: September 1929.

The Field: 15 June 1922; 22 June 1922; 21 August 1922; 2 May 1929; 16 May 1929; 31 May 1929; 15 June 1929; 22 June 1929; 29 June 1929; 6 July 1929; 20 July 1929; 3 August 1929; 9 August 1930; 17 August 1929; 30 August 1930; 6 September 1930; 2 May 1931; 21 May 1931; 6 June 1931; 4 July 1931; 18 July 1931; 25 July 1931; 8

August 1931; 29 August 1931; 30 April 1932; 14 May 1932; 4 June 1932; 23 July 1932; 30 July 1932; 26 August 1932; 3 September 1932; 17 December 1932; 25 February 1933; 6 May 1933; 27 May 1933; 10 June 1933; 12 August 1933; 19 August 1933; 4 May 1934; 12 May 1934; 19 May 1934; 2 June 1934; 30 June 1934; 28 August 1934; 18 May 1935; 25 May 1935; 1 June 1935; 8 June 1935; 15 June 1935; 29 June 1936; 6 July 1935; 3 August 1935; 10 August 1935; 17 August 1935; 24 August 1935; 6 May 1936; 26 May 1936; 6 June 1936; 13 June 1936; 20 June 1936; 4 July 1936; 1 August 1936; 5 June 1937; 12 June 1937; 19 June 1937; 27 July 1937; 7 May 1938; 4 June 1938; 11 June 1938; 18 July 1938; 6 August 1938; 21 August 1938; 20 May 1939; 2 June 1939; 19 June 1939; 8 July 1939; 15 July 1939; 22 July 1939; 13 August 1939; 27 August 1939; 8 August 1942.

Fortnightly Review: May–June 1934.

Illustrated London News: 6 April 1969.

Illustrated Sporting and Dramatic News: 9 May 1925; 6 June 1925; 20 June 1925; 22 August 1925; 19 September 1925; 8 May 1926; 7 August 1926; 21 August 1926; 11 September 1926; 23 April 1927; 7 May 1927; 14 May 1927; 21 May 1927; 28 May 1927; 18 June 1927; 27 June 1927; 9 July 1927; 20 August 1927; 27 August 1927; 3 September 1927; 2 June 1928; 9 June 1928; 16 June 1928; 30 June 1928; 25 May 1929; 6 July 1929; 20 July 1939; 17 August 1929; 24 September 1929; 31 May 1930; 12 July 1930; 12 July 1930; 19 July 1930; 20 September 1930; 30 May 1931; 11 July 1931; 28 May 1932; 30 August 1932.

Irish Times: 18 April 1922; 23 August 1948; 17 April 1975.

Kent Messenger: 25 September 1937.

Lancashire Evening Post: 17 February 1926.

The Listener: 20 September 1947.

Litchfield Courier: 25 June 1898.

Liverpool Echo: 25 October 1934.

Manchester Courier: 25 June 1898; 26 April 1912.

Manchester Guardian/The Guardian: 8 July 1898; 8 August 1898; 27 January 1919; 31 March 1919; 5 May 1919; 12 May 1919; 21 May 1919; 10 June 1919; 11 June 1919; 27 April 1920; 25 September 1921; 28 June 1922; 27 June 1923; 19 July 1924; 14 February 1925; 30 July 1925; 20 July 1926; 31 August 1926; 15 September 1926; 27 April 1927; 25 May 1927; 28 May 1928; 5 September 1928; 3 January 1929; 29 April 1929; 2 August 1929; 6 August 1929; 25 April 1930; 2 June 1930; 7 July 1930; 6 August 1930; 28 August 1930; 30 May 1931; 30 September 1931; 14 May 1932; 14 July 1932; 29 July 1932; 8 May 1933; 25 May 1933; 22 June 1933; 8 May 1934; 17 April 1935; 20 June 1935; 18 April 1936; 1 May 1937; 8 August 1936; 17 April 1936; 30 May 1936; 7 April 1937; 17 April 1937; 1 May 1937; 17 May 1937; 27 May 1937; 21 July 1937; 23 July 1937; 4 August 1937; 13 September 1937; 15 September 1937; 26 March 1938; 18 April 1938; 5 May 1938; 4 June 1938; 13 June 1938; 23 June 1938; 25 June 1938; 27 June 1938; 3 August 1938; 3 September 1938; 27 December 1938; 4 May 1939; 22 May 1939; 20 July 1939; 28 July 1939; 9 August 1939; 21 August 1939; 23 August 1939; 31 August 1939; 15 March 1940; 24 March 1941; 27 July 1941; 22 August 1941; 31 May 1952; 4 April 1959; 10 January 1964; 20 October 1967; 19 June 1968; 2 April 1969; 19 November 1969; 22 November 1969; 1 March 1975.

Melbourne Age: 27 June 1947; 8 July 1947; 6 September 1947.

The Methodist: 13 March 1943.

Morning Bulletin (Rockhampton): 22 August 1935.

Musical Times: April 1988.

The Observer: 4 December 1932; 11 December 1932; 25 December 1932; 8 January 1933; 29 January 1933; 12 February 1933; 19

February 1933; 5 March 1933; 9 September 1947; 5 September 1948.

The Oldie: October 2012.

Picture Post: 6 April 1955.

Playfair Cricket Monthly: April–December 1960: January–December 1961; January–December 1962; January–December 1963; January–December 1964; January–December 1965; January–December 1966; January–December 1967; January–December 1968; January–December 1969; January–December 1970; January–December 1971; January–December 1972; January–April 1973.

The Referee: 4 July 1928.

Saturday Review: 8 June 1922; 28 October 1950; 7 April 1956; 30 November 1957.

The Spectator: 8 March 1975.

Sporting Globe (Melbourne): 13 March 1937; 16 November 1940; 23 November 1940; 30 November 1940; 7 December 1940; 14 December 1940; 21 December 1940; 28 December 1940; 1 January 1941; 4 January 1941; 11 January 1941; 18 January 1941; 25 January 1941; 1 February 1941; 5 February 1941; 8 February 1941; 12 February 1941; 19 February 1941; 26 February 1941; 5 March 1941; 12 March 1941; 19 March 1941; 27 September 1941; 4 October 1941; 11 October 1941; 19 October 1941; 26 October 1941; 1 November 1941; 8 November 1941; 15 November 1941; 22 November 1941; 29 November 1941; 6 December 1941; 13 December 1941; 20 December 1941; 27 December 1941; 3 January 1942; 10 January 1942; 17 January 1942; 24 January 1942; 31 January 1942; 7 September 1942; 14 September 1942; 21 September 1942; 28 September 1942; 7 March 1942; 14 March 1942; 21 October 1942; 12 April 1943.

Sunday Times: 2 July 1922; 28 October 1934; 17 August 1947; 7 September 1947; 14 September 1947; 8 February 1948; 15 February

1948; 4 April 1948; 18 April 1948; 25 April 1948; 2 May 1948; 16 May 1948; 23 May 1948; 6 June 1948; 13 June 1948; 20 June 1948; 27 June 1948; 4 July 1948; 11 July 1948; 18 July 1948; 1 August 1948; 8 August 1948; 15 August 1948; 22 August 1948; 29 August 1948; 17 April 1949; 1 May 1949; 15 May 1949; 22 May 1948.

Sydney Morning Herald: 17 July 1930; 17 August 1940; 24 August 1940; 31 August 1940; 26 October 1940; 30 November 1940; 7 December 1940; 14 December 1940; 11 January 1941; 18 January 1941; 11 February 1941; 15 February 1941; 14 June 1941; 12 July 1941; 26 July 1941; 12 September 1942; 22 May 1943.

The Tatler: 1 March 1950; 23 April 1952.

The Times: 25 June 1898; 19 October 1959; 21 October 1959; 26 October 1959.

Times Literary Supplement: 12 June 1924; 20 September 1947.

Times of India: 21 September 1929; 1 May 1949; 4 September 1960; 7 September 1969; 1 June 1969; 1 March 1975.

West Australian: 31 July 1926; 15 October 1936; 16 October 1936; 4 December 1936; 1 March 1937; 26 November 1938.

Western Mail: 11 March 1995.

Wisden Cricket Monthly: December 1985.

World Digest: May 1950.

World Sports: January–December 1948; January–December 1949; January–December 1950; January–December 1951; January–December 1952; January–December 1953; January–December 1954; January–December 1955; January–December 1956; January–December 1957; January–December 1958; January–December 1959.

Yorkshire Evening Post: 26 April 1952; 1 April 1959

Yorkshire Post: 22 October 1934; 11 November 1957; 3 April 1959; 3 April 1964; 12 March 1966; 22 July 1966.

Television

John Arlott in Conversation with Sir Neville Cardus, BBC, 1973 and
1974 (later programmes broadcast in 1977).

Conversations with Cardus (Carwyn James), HTV, 1975.

LWT documentaries of Neville Cardus's life (two surviving from five-
part series), 1969.

Libraries/Archives

The Neville Cardus Archive, Old Trafford. Manchester Guardian
Archive at the John Rylands Library, Manchester. The Guardian
Newspaper Archive, London. Brotherton Library, University of
Leeds: Thomas Moult Collection, the Ernest Bradbury Archive:
1948-1975, the letters to Alan Ross in the London Magazine
Collection. The British Library, London and Boston Spa. The
London Library. The BBC Written Archive, Reading. The British
Film Institute, London. The Bradman Museum of Cricket, Bowral.
MCC Library, Lord's. National Archive of Australia: Papers relat-
ing to Neville Cardus. State Library, Adelaide. The Mitchell Library,
Sydney. The University of Tulsa: Rupert Hart-Davis Collection.
University of Texas, Harry Ransom Center: The letters of J. T.
Garvin, J. B. Priestley, Hesketh Pearson, Leonard Russell. Glasgow
University Library: The Archive of William Collins Publishing.
The Bodleian Library, Oxford: The Violet Bonham Carter Archive.
Wheaton College: The Malcolm Muggeridge Archive. National
Library, Jamaica: The Learie Constantine Archive.

INDEX

'NC' in the index indicates Neville Cardus. Page numbers in *italic type* refer to illustrations.